Guarding Cultural Memory

Guarding Cultural Memory

AFRO-CUBAN WOMEN IN LITERATURE AND THE ARTS

Flora González Mandri

New World Studies

A. James Arnold, editor

University of Virginia Press

Charlottesville and London

University of Virginia Press
© 2006 by the Rector and Visitors of the University of Virginia
All rights reserved
Printed in the United States of America on acid-free paper
First published 2006

9 8 7 6 5 4 3 2 1

Library of Congress Cataloging-in-Publication Data
González Mandri, Flora María.
   Guarding cultural memory : Afro-Cuban women in literature and the arts /
Flora González Mandri.
       p.   cm. — (New World Studies)
   Includes bibliographical references and index.
   ISBN 0-8139-2525-8 (cloth : alk. paper) — ISBN 0-8139-2526-6 (pbk. : alk. paper)
   1. Cuban literature—Women authors—History and criticism. 2. Cuban
literature—Black authors—History and criticism. 3. Cuban literature—20th
century—History and criticism. 4. Arts, Black—Cuba—20th century.
5. Women artists—Cuba—History—20th century. I. Title.
PQ7372.G66 2006
860.9′92870899607291—dc22

                                                                    2005027354

Excilia Saldaña and Belkis Ayón
In Memoriam

Para Rachel y Saul

Contents

Acknowledgments

Guarding Cultural Memory foregrounds the creative accomplishments of Lydia Cabrera and five Afro-Cuban women who have guided me in the recovery of a forgotten memory, while simultaneously performing conceptions of self and nation: poets Nancy Morejón and Excilia Saldaña, artists Belkis Ayón and María Magdalena Campos-Pons, and filmmaker Gloria Rolando. I thank them and their survivors (Isabel Castellanos, Katia Ayón, and Mario Ernesto Romero Saldaña) for permission to quote and print their works. It goes without saying that I owe a great debt to all those scholars of Africana studies who have broached the subject of culture, race, and gender before me, particularly those in Afro-Hispanic studies. Rosemary Geisdorfer Feal, who has written several articles for *Afro-Hispanic Review* tracing the history of the field, broaches the subject of accountability and "demands that critics examine the shifting contexts in which they position themselves, in which they are positioned" ("Feminist Interventions" 14). From early on in my research on the subject of Afro-Cuban women, I have been conscious of my coming to it from the position of a white Cuban woman who was brought up in a racist environment. For this reason, for me, approaching issues of gender and race in Cuba, in the supportive intellectual environment of the W. E. B. Du Bois Institute at Harvard University in 1997–98, was essential. Working within intellectual communities of like mind has allowed me to pursue a kind of knowledge about the diversity of Cuban culture that has, or so I hope, chipped away at the racist assumptions with which I started. My analysis of Lydia Cabrera's *El Monte* has served me well, helping me to steer clear of the many blind spots that I encountered throughout this project. I am well aware that my struggle toward understanding has just begun. In this regard, I am grateful for the support I have received and the conversations I have held throughout these years with my friend and colleague at Emerson College, Claire Andrade-Watkins, herself a scholar and practitioner of African and African diaspora film.

This project grew out of my initial discovery of Excilia Saldaña's *Kele Kele,* a collection of *patakines* (Yoruba legends) that actualize the best of Hispanic popular poetic tradition *(romances)* and mythic stories of female deities from the Afro-Hispanic tradition so that they could become relevant to Cuban youth as they entered into the socialist arena. I received the book from the hands of the author on my first trip back to Cuba after almost two decades of absence. I had left the island as an unaccompanied child early in the 1960s as part of Operation Pedro Pan. My first return to Cuba coincided with my years as a graduate student of Hispanic literatures at Yale University, where I had begun to seriously engage the rich literary heritage of Latin American and specifically Cuban literature. The intellectual mentoring of Professors Emir Rodríguez Monegal and Roberto González Echevarría and, in addition, the informal exchanges with my fellow graduate students during those years were essential guides in my personal search for an identity that could incorporate both my Cubanness, which I thought I had lost when I left in 1962, and my newly emerging identity as a Cuban American. My years at Yale University facilitated my knowledge of Latin American male masters of our literary tradition (our studies of the works of Sor Juana Inés de la Cruz being the only exception), but on my first visit to UNEAC (the Cuban National Union of Writers and Artists) in 1980, when I met several male contemporary writers but just one female writer (Excilia Saldaña), I realized that my knowledge of a literary and cultural Latin American tradition produced by women was severely lacking. This book represents my intellectual and personal desire to compensate for that lack of knowledge.

On the personal level, meeting Excilia Saldaña, who was almost my age and who attended the same *instituto* where my uncle and aunt taught in Havana, made me raise the question of many young adults who left Cuba during the 1960s: What would have become of me had I stayed in Cuba? This question mostly reflected the increasing necessity on my part to rediscover a Cuba much transformed since my departure. The fact that González Echevarría had participated in the 1970s dialogue between the Cuban government and Cuban exiles kindled my curiosity and signaled the possibility of returning, both as the former exiled child who could return to visit family who chose to stay and the new student of Latin American literature who could intellectually return. My instant enthusiasm for Saldaña's work born during that first visit, an enthusiasm that has endured, led me to establish a friendship that lasted many years, a friendship that nurtured my growing interest in Afro-Cuban culture. When in 1997 I made a concerted effort to retrain as a Cubanist, I did it under the auspices of the W. E. B. Du Bois Institute at Harvard University, where, under the leadership of Professor Henry Louis Gates Jr., beginning and advanced students of the African diaspora congregate and work. I am also grateful to the David Rockefeller Center for Latin American Studies, also at Harvard, which has supported my work as an affiliate; and to Emerson College, which granted me funds to travel to Cuba on many occasions and a sabbatical leave to complete the writing.

I am most grateful to Priscilla Long and Richard Foerster, whose acute editorial skills helped me to clarify my thinking; to Maria Koundoura, Ruth Elizabeth Burks, and Leila de Andrade, who read parts of the manuscript; and to *Revista Iberoamericana, Cuban Studies,* and the University Press of Florida for permission to reprint my work. Thanks to Chester King of AfroCubaWeb for helping to make available the still photo from Gloria Rolando's *Las raíces de mi corazón.* Claudia Kaiser-Lenoir and Mary Berg, persistent travelers between the United States and Havana secured for me the necessary permissions to print from original sources. ¡Muchas Gracias! I thank the anonymous readers who pointed to my critical weaknesses throughout; I take all responsibility for any remaining faults. For believing in this project, my appreciation to Gustavo Pellón, who suggested I send it to the University of Virginia Press, and to Humanities Editor Cathie Brettschneider and New World Studies Editor James Arnold of the University of Virginia Press, who worked with me in this project.

This book could not have been possible without the constant support of my *compañero* Saul, who read, edited, and challenged me throughout. My daughter Rachel Werner Baldwin's reassuring conversations kept me steadfast in the years of writing and rewriting.

I invite the reader to join in the act of remembrance that the best of readings entails.

I WOULD like to acknowledge the following for allowing me to use the material reproduced in this book. From "De lo invisible a lo espectacular en la creación de la figura de la mulata en la cultura cubana: *Cecilia Valdés y María Antonia,*" ed. Aníbal González, *Revista Iberoamericana* 184–85 (Julio-Diciembre 1998): 543–557, reprinted by permission. From *In the Vortex of the Cyclone: Selected Poems by Excilia Saldaña. A Bilingual Edition,* ed. and trans. by Flora González Mandri and Rosamond Rosenmeier, Gainesville: Univ. Press of Florida, 2002, reprinted by permission of The University Press of Florida. From "Possession and Altar-Making: Reconstruction of Memory as Artistic Performance in the Multimedia Installations of María Magdalena Campos-Pons," originally from *CUBAN STUDIES 31*, Lisandro Pérez, Ed., Uva de Aragón, Assoc. Ed., © 2000 by University of Pittsburgh Press, reprinted by permission of the University of Pittsburgh Press. From Katia Ayón, *Siempre Vuelvo: Colografías de Belkis Ayón*, 2000; Collographs: *Acoso* (Harrassment) (1998); *¡¡Déjame Salir!!* (Let Me Out) (1998); *Sin Título* (Untitled: Woman in Fetal Position), 1996; reprinted by permission of Katia Ayón. From Lydia Cabrera, *La laguna sagrada de San Joaquín*, 1973; *El Monte. Igbo Finda; Ewe Orisha. Vitti Nfinda. (Notas sobre las religiones, la magia, las supersticiones y el folklore de los negros criollos y el pueblo de Cuba)*, 1992; *Páginas Sueltas*, 1994; *La sociedad secreta Abakuá: Narrada por viejos adeptos*, 1969; *Yemayá y Ochún: Kariocha, Yalorichas y Olorichas*, 1980; reprinted by permission of Isabel Castellanos. From María Magdalena Campos-Pons, *Abridor de Caminos* (1997), *History of People Who Were Not Heroes: Spoken Softly With Mama* (1998); *Meanwhile, the Girls Were Playing* (1999); *When I am Not Here/Estoy Allá* (detail) 1996; reprinted by permission of María Magdalena Campos-Pons. From Nancy Morejón, "Elogio de Manuel Mendive," *Fundación de la Imagen*, 1988; "Grounding the Race Dialogue: Diaspora and Nation," 2000; *Nación y Mestizaje en Nicolás Guillén;* "Pogolotti," *Paisaje Célebre: Poemas 1987–1992;* "Palabras por el Premio Nacional de Literatura"; "Prólogo," *Recopilación de textos sobre Nicolás Guillén*, 1974; reprinted by permission of Nancy Morejón. From Gloria Rolando, "Gloria Rolando: Speech at Black Women Writers and the Future Conference"; "Interview de Gloria Rolando, productrice et réalisatrice cubaine"; *The Eyes of the Rainbow*, 1997; *Las raíces de mi corazón*, 2001; "'Women' Interview; "Gloria Rolando: 'Searching in My Dreams'—The 1912 Genocide'"; reprinted by permission of Gloria Rolando. From Excilia Saldaña, "Autobiografía"; *In the Vortex of the Cyclone: Selected Poems by Excilia Saldaña;* "Las tres suspirantes"; "Vieja Trova sobre soporte CD ROM"; reprinted by permission of Mario Ernesto Romero.

Guarding Cultural Memory

Introduction

MEMORY, an exercise of the living, and especially of those who remember so that cultures may not die, imposes both a responsibility and a curse on those who choose to remember. In *The Black Atlantic: Modernity and Double Consciousness*, Paul Gilroy poses a series of questions regarding the act of remembering the terror and pain of slavery on the part of the African diaspora so as to create a "chain of 'ethnic' tradition" (212). This act of remembrance refuses to portray blacks as the victims of modernity's mercantile practices across the Atlantic. Rather, black writers who revive the subject of slavery in their works do so "to restage confrontations between rational, scientific, and enlightened Euro-American thought and the supposedly primitive outlook of prehistorical, cultureless, and bestial African slaves" (220).

In *Guarding Cultural Memory* I explore how black writers and intellectuals in Cuba, particularly women, restage these confrontations. I appropriate Gilroy's first question, "How do black expressive cultures practice remembrance?" (212) as I approach the works of Afro-Cuban women writers, artists, and filmmakers. These works engage the confrontation between Hispanic "modern" discursive practices regarding the issues of slavery (and consequently race) and Afro-Cuban "traditional" cultural practices of remembrance. To answer Gilroy's question, this book relies heavily on the multiple works of Lydia Cabrera, who recorded the interpretive systems of Afro-Cuban cultures. According to her texts, cultural self-preservation is accomplished through multiple strategies, including, but not limited to, the presentation of multiple versions to validate collective memory; the theatrical representations of origins; and arriving at the truth through inaccuracies, apparent omissions, the propensity to digress, simulation, and constant questioning. Throughout the history of the Middle Passage, slavery, and discrimination against subjects of the

African diaspora, these contradictory strategies of preserving memory through disclosure and obfuscation have ensured the preservation of what Gilroy terms an "'ethnic' tradition." In her study of the sources that influence twentieth-century Cuban literature, Julia Cuervo Hewitt points to the multiplicity of myths and narrative strategies found in the Cuban Ifá sacred literature (the Yoruba-Lucumí oral/written compendium of narratives used by *babalaos,* priests, for divination purposes). In the conclusion of her *Aché, presencia africana* [Ache, an African Presence], Cuervo Hewitt highlights the importance of memory in the narratives of Ifá literature, including its complex strategies later adopted by such Cuban writers as Alejo Carpentier, José Lezama Lima, Severo Sarduy, Lydia Cabrera, Miguel Barnet, and others: "[A]n attitude, a reading, the constant writing of codes that are forgotten, that are revealed and hidden, between-folds that articulate the subjectivity of being Cuban, the importance of the word that, like Ifá, becomes a continuous journey back in time, anchored in the past, re-writing the past in the present and articulating it from that present" (286; my translation). Following Julia Cuervo Hewitt's example of tracing Cubanness through the prism of African cultural manifestations as they intersect with European artistic modes, I highlight the creative efforts of Cuban women in the second half of the twentieth century to discover both a history of Afro-Cuban experience and its more contemporary cultural accomplishments. These accomplishments have survived through strategies of disclosure and obfuscation encoded in the act of remembrance in a Caribbean country purported to have integrated its Hispanic and African peoples and heritages into the project of Cubanness.

Cuban cultural concern with the role that blacks and their culture have played in defining Cuban national identity centers first on the production of a series of antislavery novels on the *idea* of emancipation of slaves in the first half of the nineteenth century. These novels were written mostly by the white Cuban intelligentsia, many of them participants in the Domingo del Monte circle. Adriana Méndez Rodenas emphasizes the importance of the literary circle in nation building: "Antislavery narrative . . . performed its ethical function by raising awareness of the many contradictions and injustices prevalent in Cuban slave society. Hence, the positivistic, pedagogical thrust of the *tertulia* is evident not only in the realist aesthetic promoted by del Monte, but also in the types of literature the circle produced. For both *costumbrismo* and the antislavery novel are narrative genres fundamentally geared toward an extraliterary goal, the imagining of a country" ("A Nation Invented," *Gender and Nationalism,* 77). Moreover, as William Luis has stated, "This narrative represents the first cohesive movement to describe blacks and slaves as a dominant element in Cuban and Latin American literatures and broadens the margins of literary discourse" (*Literary Bondage*, 2). Carlos Alonso points to the antislavery enterprise on the part of the del Monte circle as expressing the desire for modernity by conceiving of a nation that would no longer depend on the increasingly outmoded and nonprofitable plantation economy. Furthermore, rather than oppose the institution of slavery on moral or humanitarian grounds, the circle sought to incorporate blacks into the prospective nation through the practice of *blanqueamiento* ("diluting the race out of existence," in *The Burden of Modernity*, 75) on the one hand, and by erasing the memory of slavery on the other (75–76). Being modern necessitated the obliteration of any trace of the African presence in the Cuban nation, including its people and the collective memory of their experience. I highlight Alonso's quotation of Francisco Arango y Parreño because it marks the desire to dissociate Afro-Cuban experience from the Cuban national project: "I want, simultaneously, to start thinking prudently about the destruction of slavery (to which end much has been done already), to discuss something that has not been entertained, that is, the erasure of its memory" (quoted and translated by Alonso, 75–76).

Alonso holds that the erasure of the memory of slavery in the discourse of the members of the del Monte circle was counteracted by the discourse of the Cuban antislavery novel described as "a surreptitious and persistent claim of radical difference vis-à-vis modernity" (82). Alonso cites one example—Juan Francisco Manzano's autobiography—of how blacks themselves have participated in the creation of radical difference in Cuban cultural expression.[1] Alonso emphasizes a most important interplay between an intellectual antislavery national discourse that wishes to erase Afro-Cuban cultural memory and its responding fictional treatment of the subject that surreptitiously restores that memory and points to the limitations of modernity. Manzano's autobiography undermines del Monte's views on modernity and asserts his individual experience as a slave (Alonso, 71).

Another significant moment of engagement with black Cuban culture by mostly male musicians, artists, writers, ethnographers, and intellectuals occurs in the early twentieth century (1920s–1940s) when they conceive of a Cuban modernity informed by Afro-Cuban culture, a movement called Afro-Cubanism. The largely Cuban white intelligentsia involved in Afro-Cubanism was "fascinated with the creative potentiality of black culture through their association with the avant-garde" (Mullen, *Afro-Cuban Literature*, 155). Both Edward J. Mullen and Vera Kutzinski (*Sugar's Secrets*, 142) coincide in stating that Afro-Cubanism emerges "as an aesthetic response to U.S. economic imperialism" (Mullen, *Afro-Cuban Literature,* 161). In this respect, Afro-Cubanism reflects the concerns of the antislavery narratives in defining Cubanness as both an aesthetic and nationalist movement. The best-known figures during this period are ethnographers Fernando Ortiz and Lydia Cabrera, composers Amadeo Roldán and Alejandro García Caturla, writers Alejo Carpentier and Nicolás Guillén, and artist Wifredo Lam. Parallel to the work of these thinkers and artists stands the work of such anthologists and poets as Ramón Guirao and Emilio Ballagas who anthologized the work of Afro-Cuban and Afro-Antillean poets (Mullen, 155). The cultural supplement "Ideales de una raza" [Ideals of a Race] edited by Gustavo Urrutia in the Havana newspaper *El Diario de la Marina* (starting in 1926) and the *Revista de Avance,* among others, contributed greatly to the dissemination of Afro-Cubanism (Mullen, *Afro-Cuban Literature,* 131–32; and Kutzinski, *Sugar's Secrets,* 148–49).

In my view, despite these two significant moments when Afro-Cuban culture helped define a nationalist agenda, the cultural erasures of black self-representations were and continue to be considerable in the official, Eurocentric conception of Cuban national culture even at the end of the twentieth century. Contemporary novelist and cultural critic Eliseo Altunaga, in "*The Dead Come at Midnight:* Scripting the White Aesthetic/ Black Ethic," emphasizes the acceptance of some forms of black cultural expression at the expense of others: "I think that the negation of any of the components of Cuban culture and the obstinate desire to marginalize a component that has been forged, wishing only to select four or five features—music, poetry, Santería, rhythm—as what is black in Cuban culture, weakens that culture terribly. . . . I think that the Cuban white is black and that the Cuban black is white, and the idea of a mestizo society is the only one that can save the nation" (96). In *Guarding Cultural Memory,* I indicate how Afro-Cuban women producing culture in the second half of the twentieth century still must correct the overwhelming cultural erasures regarding black (race) female (gender) subjectivity and creativity, all the while asserting themselves as black women through either veiled or expressed autobiographical incursions.

For the purposes of my study, which emphasizes the contributions of Afro-Cuban women in their definition of the Cuban nation and its culture in the second half of the twentieth century, artist Wifredo Lam and poet Nicolás Guillén become key predecessors. Guillén in particular, with his emphasis on *mestizaje* (hybridity) as a form of Cuban cultural expression, becomes central to the work of poets Nancy Morejón and Excilia Saldaña.

Guillén's poetry can certainly be considered the most transcendent expression of Afro-Cubanism with its centrality in the poetic form. Vera Kutzinski describes Afro-Cubanism as "an attempt at making poetry a stage for nationalist discourse, not by turning it into a platform for political slogans but by tapping specific cultural institutions with a long history of resilience: the syncretic forms of Afro-Cuban popular music and dance became new signifiers of a desire for cultural and political independence" (*Sugar's Secrets*, 154). I also agree with Edward Mullen, who presents Wifredo Lam's work as a "paradigm of the Afro-Cuban experience": "For some readers (viewers) of his work it is not a question so much of racial admixture but of absorption and transformation of his African heritage into something uniquely and distinctively American" (*Afro-Cuban Literature*, 27).

In his presentation of Lam as modernist and surrealist, the Cuban art critic Gerardo Mosquera states: "As a modern artist, he stopped working with African geometrical forms to attempt, for the first time in modern art, to work with the African sense, reinventing it in the propitious terrain offered by modernism" ("Eleggúa at the Post-Modern Crossroads," 230). Mosquera emphasizes Lam's inventing, rather than merely representing, "a modern mythology of the Caribbean" (230). Contemporary artists Belkis Ayón and María Magdalena Campos-Pons emulate Lam's invention through working with "the African sense." Upon his return to Cuba from Paris in 1941, Lam rediscovered the world of Afro-Cuban religions familiar to him through the experiences of his childhood, particularly through the relationship with his godmother, who was a *santera* in Sagua La Grande. His work after 1941 processes in conceptual ways the knowledge about Santería (the integration of African religious beliefs and practices into Catholic ritual) that Cuban ethnographer Lydia Cabrera had been gathering from Afro-Cuban informants for years. Cabrera and Lam, both recent arrivals from Paris, engaged "modernism as [a] space to communicate Afro-American cultural meanings" (Mosquera, "Eleggúa at the Post-Modern Crossroads," 228). Particularly in the case of Lam's art, the hierarchical evaluation of Western and non-Western cultural sensibilities disappears, and they appear as an integrative tension rather than as a confrontation.

Afro-Cuban women working in a postmodern world at the end of the twentieth century learn the lessons of Lam's and Guillén's invention well, yet they work from within a historical space that discourages the communication of "Afro-American cultural meanings" (Mosquera, 228). In an interview with Pedro Pérez Sarduy regarding the issue of race, the poet

Nancy Morejón reflects on the perseverance of racist stereotypes in current Cuban society that affect black artists and intellectuals alike. Like Altunaga, Morejón feels that race is both a cultural and national issue that must be confronted by the entire nation: "I think that all Cubans, all those of us who live here and belong to different races, have an obligation to confront this problem, whatever color we are, because it's a problem of nationhood" ("Grounding the Race Dialogue," 167). My book, accordingly, focuses on the ways in which issues of gender and race have been slighted by national definitions of Cubanness, even during specific times when the incorporation of a dialogue on race has coincided with critical moments of national conception and revisionism (as in the case of the abolitionist/antislavery and the anti-imperialist/Afro-Cubanism movements). The bulk of this study concentrates on the artistic production on the part of Cuban women working after the onset of the Castro revolution, a time when the socialist enterprise purports to reformulate Cubanness to include all its citizens irrespective of race and gender.

The theoretical and critical apparatus that I employ throughout draws from Lydia Cabrera's ethnographic work and from other anthropological and literary critical interpretations of the role of Afro-Cuban hermeneutic practices as they inform Cuban culture. At the core of these practices stands the necessity to reveal "the unknown in silence" (Cuervo Hewitt, 108). Cuervo Hewitt expresses it this way: "To verbalize is synonymous with revealing the unknown in silence, to discover the unheard-of, to *signify,* and therefore to order chaos, the void of silence" (108; my translation). These critical approaches that engage the interpretive practices of the African diaspora come from both Afro-Hispanists and Afro-Americanists, as well as from various theorists and critics of the African diaspora in general. I have chosen to consider these approaches to a Cuban question because the works of the women that I analyze not only fit within the scope of a national culture but also are excellent examples of intellectual and creative representations that engage conceptual definitions of the African diaspora. In fact, these women simultaneously engage the concept of nation and African diaspora in their works. María Magdalena Campos-Pons states: "I sometimes feel torn apart because for me Africa is not a continent—Africa is my backyard in Cuba. Of course as an adult, as an intellectual, as an artist I have been looking at what constitutes Africa" (quoted in Bell, 35). Nancy Morejón expresses it in this manner: "While I respect the concept of diaspora, I believe that diaspora cannot in any way be divorced from the phenomenon of nation" ("Grounding the Race Dialogue," 163).

In chapter 1, I introduce the conception of Cuban national identity as expressed in the nineteenth-century antislavery novel *Cecilia Valdés* by Cirilo Villaverde and, later, in the depiction of pre-Castro Cuba in Sergio Giral's film *María Antonia*. In these two works, the figure of the Cuban mulatta is represented as the licentious "woman of color" whose life is dictated by national economic necessity, whether it be slavery during the Spanish colonial period or the economic manipulation of Cuban industries by the United States during the Fulgencio Batista dictatorship. These two works differ fundamentally in each creator's valorization, or lack thereof, of Afro-Cuban culture. In chapter 2, to situate the second engagement of Afro-Cuban culture in the definition of Cubanness, I focus on *El Monte,* Lydia Cabrera's monumental compilation of testimonies by Afro-Cuban informants of varying ethnic backgrounds, to illustrate how this indispensable work, when it comes to Afro-Cuban cultures, stages an encounter between the autobiographical incursions of a white privileged woman and the multiple narrative practices of her informants that ensure the survival of their black cultural memory.

My analysis of Lydia Cabrera's *El Monte* is central to my project because it marks the transition into my presentation of the creative accomplishments of Afro-Cuban women who stayed in Cuba and did not, as Cabrera did, leave after the Castro revolution. In the next chapters I analyze the essays of poet Nancy Morejón, the autobiographical poetry of Excilia Saldaña, the canvases of Belkis Ayón, the multimedia installations of María Magdalena Campos-Pons, and the documentaries of Gloria Rolando, all working since the 1960s. These creators participated in the social integration of blacks into the new revolutionary process of Castro's revolution. Most importantly, they, like Cabrera, create hybrid texts that negotiate between telling their individual stories and the history of black communities and cultures in Cuba, specifically, and more generally, of women of the African diaspora. Their incursions into the autobiographical mode mark a note of resistance to the cultural mandates of the Castro revolution, which, in cultural expression, discouraged individualism in favor of the welfare of the entire community. In the case of Afro-Cuban women's cultural discourse, individual concerns must necessarily include issues of gender and race, which have been censored for more than thirty years (Navarro, 194) and which ultimately define the work of the women I analyze in this book. Because race and gender must take secondary importance to the recovery of a national history in which blacks participated fully, Afro-Cuban women forge an autobiographical subject in a "position of damage, one in which 'the cultural formation,' languages, the diverse modes of identity of the 'minoritized peoples' are irreversibly affected, if not eradicated, by the effects of their material deracination from the historically developed social and economic structures in terms of which alone they 'made sense'" (Smith and Watson, xvi). The creative efforts of the women whose works are analyzed in this study must necessarily redefine their position as they reinstate the Afro-Cuban female subject into the historically and culturally determined spaces of Cubanness.

In their book about the politics of gender in women's autobiography, Sidonie Smith and Julia Watson state that, for the colonial subject, "the process of coming to writing is an articulation *through* interrogation, a charting of the conditions that have historically placed her identity under erasure" (Smith and Watson, xx). For Afro-Cuban women, representing their sense of self necessarily entails charting the experience of slavery, the contributions of blacks to the project of independence and revolution, the complexities of Afro-Cuban cultural practices, the definition of family and community, and the multiple manifestations of racism and sexism that have existed and continue to exist in Cuban society. When charting the conditions that have erased their identities, Afro-Cuban women writers, artists, and filmmakers position themselves as subjects of the African diaspora living in the largest Caribbean island during a time of socialist revolution. As such, they belong to an intellectual elite that in the early 1960s and for the next four decades had to redefine itself constantly, because of the political exigencies of Fidel Castro's revolution.[2]

With the 1968 film *Memorias del subdesarrollo* [Memories of Underdevelopment], Tomás Gutiérrez Alea presents one of the most sophisticated renditions of the changing role of the Cuban intellectual at the outset of the revolution. By engaging documentary and fictional cinematographic techniques, Gutiérrez Alea juxtaposes the role of his protagonist Sergio, who represents the role of the bourgeois intellectual, and that of the filmmaker himself, "creating a complex and uncompromising work of art from a perspective of political commitment" (Burton, 242). Because of the highly ironic nature of the film, the lines drawn between bourgeois and committed intellectuals fluctuate with the intent of forging an artistic consciousness deeply aware of historical contingencies. In Alea's film, the immediate past of intellectual practice must be examined at the service of the present. Further retrospective evaluations of how, in the last half of the twentieth century, Cuban intellectuals have contended with the historical, political, and social realities of a nation under a socialist regime and world economic blockade have appeared in *boundary 2* (Fall 2002), a special issue edited by John Beverly. In particular, the essay by Desiderio Navarro considers manifestations of critical expression on the part of the

Cuban intelligentsia and maps out the vicissitudes of cultural workers during forty years of Castro's revolution. He summarizes the role of the intellectual thus:

> Within the framework of such anticritical ideology and practices, the role of the revolutionary intellectual as a critic of the Revolution's social reality is seldom openly denied, but it is also seldom forthrightly affirmed or reaffirmed. Most of the time it is passed over in silence or mentioned only in passing as something secondary or optional. Even when the intellectual's critical role is explicitly recognized in a theoretical way, it is immediately neutralized through diverse restrictions and reservations, and carrying it out in concrete social practice becomes the target of all kinds of political and ethical accusations. (193)

If, as in Navarro's assertion, alternating crises in official cultural practices in Cuba have tended to erase the memory of intellectual work and action (198), how do Afro-Cuban women inhabiting those critical spaces and times rescue the memory of their selves, their cultures, and their position in Cuban intellectual history?

Starting with chapter 3, devoted to the works of poet and essayist Nancy Morejón, the films of Gloria Rolando, and the canvases of Belkis Ayón, I concentrate on how these creators envision Cubanness as they address the erasures, misconceptions, and stereotypes of Afro-Cuban women. Nancy Morejón, whose poetry was censored for a decade (1970s) as too hermetic, gains a place in Cuba's intellectual arena through her analysis of Nicolás Guillén's *mestizaje*. She prescribes for herself the role of mediator between tracing the importance of her Afro-Cuban heritage (including issues of race and gender) and abiding by Cuba's political exigencies regarding criticism by intellectuals. In the context of the intellectual environment of the 1960s and 1970s, particularly for blacks, I choose to consider her ambiguous presentation of race and gender as indispensable in opening critical intellectual paths for such women as Gloria Rolando and Belkis Ayón, who rescue the historical memory of Afro-Cubans in their films and visual art produced in the 1990s. Rolando's documentary work rescues from oblivion the diversity of African diaspora practices including those of song and dance to preserve myths of origin and of Yoruba deities, and those of religious and social practices by peoples of the Anglophone Caribbean, practices that endure in present-day Cuba. Her film *Las raíces de mi corazón* [The Roots of My Heart] uses a fictional search for self-identity to record the military-led massacre of Cuban blacks in 1912, an event forgotten in Cuba's historical record until recently. In this film, Rolando interweaves the personal with the mythical and historic. Emphasizing the mythical over the historic, the work of

artist Belkis Ayón highlights the formative aspects of Abakuá myth production to address issues of racism and sexism in Cuba's European and
African heritages. Ayón's large-scale engravings address the victimization
of women in male-centered societies and counter with new renditions of
the black female body that engage the centrality of her artistic agency,
simultaneously rescuing the Abakuá maligned Afro-Cuban culture and
empowering the black female subject in Cuba's present.

Morejón, Rolando, and Ayón present Afro-Cuban revisions of national
identity, often in conjunction with emphasis on their own artistic agency
as black women. Somewhat differently, poet Excilia Saldaña and multimedia
artist María Magdalena Campos-Pons engage the genre of autobiography
to revisit figurations of national concepts of race and gender within the
larger historical context of the African diaspora. In her autobiographical
poetry, which I analyze at length in chapter 4, Excilia Saldaña locates the
act of self-figuration in her multiple conceptions of both personal and
collective memory. The opening verses of "Monólogo de la esposa" [The
Wife's Monologue], *"I am a watery child, as well, / braiding and unbraiding / the tresses of my memory"* (*In the Vortex of the Cyclone,* 13), serve
to pinpoint Saldaña's role as a poet—in her task of rescuing lost memories as well as in her task of self-invention. She represents herself as a poet
who heals her injured self through the process of poetic knowledge of self
and of national history. After analyzing three lengthy autobiographical
poems that restore the injured body of the black woman to a position of
poetic integrity and civic action, I close with my study of Saldaña's lengthy
erotic poem, "Mi fiel" [My Faithful One]. In this long poetic letter, the
black woman poet exorcises the shared sexual violation of women of the
African diaspora through ownership of the sexual experience as Saldaña
enters into her own fabrication of personal and collective memory.

In chapter 5, I analyze the multimedia installations that María Magdalena Campos-Pons has named *History of People Who Were Not Heroes.*
In this sequence of three major installations, Campos-Pons restores the
history of Afro-Cuban women, their families, and their cultures, to their
rightful place within a transnational conception of African diaspora art.
As Campos-Pons engages Western and African versions of conceptual art,
she, like Wifredo Lam before her, privileges African sensibility and lays
bare the limitations inherent in Western art with regard to the African
diaspora subject. In her large-scale photographs as well as in her installations, Campos-Pons positions her own body as the site wherein she
problematizes the black female body as both an object of victimization
and a subject capable of perpetuating collective memory.

By way of example, I proceed by analyzing here the large-scale Polaroid photograph titled *When I Am Not Here/Estoy Allá,* 1996 (color reproduction available in *Authentic/Ex-Centric;* see Berger, "María Magdalena Campos-Pons," 128). The large Polaroid includes the artist's body from just below the neck to just below the waist. Her entire body is painted in a bright blue with white waves drawn throughout, so as to signify the sea

María Magdalena Campos-Pons, *When I Am Not Here/Estoy Allá* (detail), 1996. Polaroid photograph, 50.8 x 61 cm.

and by extension Yemayá, the Yoruba deity of the sea associated with the Middle Passage and motherhood. The artist is holding a small wooden canoe that covers her waist. From her neck are hanging two feeding bottles half filled with milk and ending with two orange nipples that hang at the same level as the artist's nipples, which are covered. The photograph is striking in its beauty because of the bright indigo-blue paint that covers the body superimposed with the small white wavelike lines. The pose of the truncated body is quite self-possessed, particularly in its symbolic meaning of a body as vessel (of milk), itself holding a vessel (of the sea).

The painted body symbolizes not only the Atlantic Ocean and the Atlantic Passage but also the Caribbean Sea and Pre-Columbian cultures (the boat is a canoe). This Polaroid reinforces the survival of African women living in the Caribbean despite their historic function as the bearers of future slaves and as the nurturers of children not their own. In Cuban vocabulary, a *criollera* (one who takes care of children) is a black woman who nurses white children as well as her own (Luis, *Literary Bondage;* and Méndez Rodenas, "Identity"). In this respect, black women become "mothers" of the Cuban nation. In most instances, because these women were separated from their offspring, they were seldom able to nurse their own. Slave women's bodies, because they were sold and raped by their masters, became vessels for public consumption rather than private bodies who could choose to reproduce and nurture children. With the Polaroid rendition of the *criollera,* Campos-Pons transcends the violence perpetrated on women of the African diaspora by painting her body with blue and white, the colors of Yemayá.

According to Lydia Cabrera, "Yemayá is the Universal Queen because she is Water, salt and river water, the Sea, the Mother of all that is created. She feeds everyone, since the World is earth and water, the earth and whatever lives in it, is sustained thanks to Her. Without water, animals, humans and plants would die" (*Yemayá y Ochún,* 20–21; my translation). By assuming the color of the Atlantic, Campos-Pons problematizes the relationship between skin pigmentation and definitions of race, and foregrounds the mythical figure of Yemayá as Mother of all created beings and as absolute nurturer of culture. The bottles hanging from her neck become props that serve to represent a tragic epoch in the history of African diaspora women, an epoch that was endured thanks to the cultural manifestation of strength and nurturance personified by the Santería deity Yemayá. With this extraordinary projection of her own body as mythological figure, Campos-Pons embodies the entire context of the black Atlantic with all its tragic and enduring connotations.

1 Constructions of the Cuban Mulatta

Cecilia Valdés and María Antonia

CUBAN NINETEENTH-CENTURY novelist Cirilo Villaverde and Afro-Cuban twentieth-century filmmaker Sergio Giral create female characters who are determined by a nationalist, domineering, patriarchal gaze. They define the mulatta not only as a child of a black parent and a white parent, but also as exceptionally beautiful and sensual, and often doomed.[1] This study of male novelist and male filmmaker is meant to stand as a backdrop against which Afro-Cuban women writers, filmmakers, and artists, who, in contrast, represent black women as independent subjects who challenge the patriarchal gaze, are presented. First, I outline the production of the figure of the mulatta and the mulatto as colonial subjects in Cirilo Villaverde's *Cecilia Valdés* (1882). In this novel, the mulatta and mulatto characters appear at radically divergent moments in their respective processes of developing a revolutionary consciousness. Considered to be Cuba's most widely known antislavery novel, *Cecilia Valdés* was published in 1882 in the United States, two decades before Cuban independence. Its story unfolds during the first decades of the nineteenth century, when Cuba's ideology regarding a national project inclusive of all races was being forged.

Foremost in Villaverde's project stands his desire to expose the abuses of the system of slavery, with its tragic consequences to the African populations brought to the Americas (particularly through the characters of María de Regla and Cecilia Valdés), as well as his need to record the valiant but futile response of black slaves and a growing free black intellectual and artistic elite, culminating in "The Ladder Conspiracy" of 1844, which destroyed that elite (165; see César Leante's seminal article). In this regard, Villaverde's novel, like Campos-Pons's image of Yemayá, attempts to portray both the victimized and heroic nature of those who were enslaved. Given its use of historical and journalistic records of the time, *Cecilia Valdés* documents the capitalistic nature of the slavery "business" ("What business provides more profit than slavery?" 99). The novel also portrays the businessman's (Cándido Gamboa's) ability to subvert the 1817 Spanish treaty with England against slavery (107), the inhumane conditions of the transfer of African slaves across the Atlantic (109), the violent treatment of slaves (211), and their sale and resale, with the consequent dispersion and separation of families (114, 133, 232; page numbers refer to the Porrúa edition).

Ironically opposed to the dispersion of slave and mulatto families, as exemplified through the lives of such central characters as María de Regla (wet nurse to both white and black children and then separated from both children and husband) and Cecilia Valdés (separated from her mother and bereft of the relationship with the white man who engendered her), Villaverde's novel revolves around the vicissitudes of the Gamboa family and its desire to perpetuate its elitist position through marriages of convenience and the bearing of offspring who carry the stigma of neither African nor Jewish ancestry.

In her comprehensive article "Identity and Incest in *Cecilia Valdés*," Adriana Méndez Rodenas describes the institution of marriage and union of slaves as generated by the system of slavery: "At the top, marriage among whites enjoys the privilege of the law, yet is often not blessed by natural desire; at the bottom, and inversely, union among slaves is founded on natural impulse, but is not legally sanctioned unless approved by the masters. The father, Cándido Gamboa, sires two families—a white family legitimized before society, though void of desire; and a mulatta family concealed from society but itself the product of passion and desire" (87).

Time and time again, Villaverde accentuates the slave nature of Cuban society that produces contradictions, particularly at the social level of family formation. Slave and mulatto families are doomed to fail so that the unity of the white family may perpetuate the abuses of slavery. The irony is not lost on the reader when, at the end of the novel, enslaver Cándido Gamboa, pleads with Mayor D. Fernando O'Reilly to arrange the detention of Cecilia, so that his son Leonardo, obsessed by his love and jealousy of the beautiful mulatta, may safely finish his law studies and marry Isabel Ilincheta, the daughter of a coffee plantation owner. Behind Cándido's interdiction against the doomed relationship between Leonardo and Cecilia lies the safely kept secret of incest, given that Gamboa has fathered both. This secret is, of course, veiled throughout the novel, until María de Regla reveals it toward the end (296). Méndez Rodenas states: "Then, toward the end of the novel, María de Regla detects not only the incestuous union between the protagonists, but more important, she is the first to recognize Cecilia's pregnancy (297). Because the slave characters fulfill the narrative function of uncovering the incestuous plot, they serve as the reader's accomplice" (96).

On the other hand, also at the end of the novel, the character Gamboa resorts to a number of unconvincing arguments that attempt to silence that incest. He insists that O'Reilly dispose of the threat Cecilia poses to his son and his way of life. A whole discussion ensues regarding the nature of fatherhood, as well as of the double standard of morality in a country of slaves, where white men often keep mulattas and their families hidden from their official wives and children ("In all slave countries, morality is neither whole nor elevated" [279; my translation]). What finally convinces O'Reilly to arrest and detain Cecilia is the following argument, presented by Villaverde in all its irony: "Don Cándido, you must understand that I do not do this out of consideration for you . . . , I do it out of respect for the phrases concluding your speech 'for the peace and happiness of family', things that are sacred for me" (282; my translation).

With this highly ironic statement toward the end of the novel, Villaverde exposes the double standard of Cuban society, a double standard that preserves white families and their corrupted values, at the expense of slave and mulatto families and their desire to remain whole. At the center of this contradiction stands the character of Cecilia Valdés, a mulatta nursed by the wet nurse María de Regla, who comes to represent both the Virgin Mary and Yemayá (Williams, *Representation of Slavery,* 166–69; Luis, *Literary Bondage,* 116; and Méndez Rodenas, "Identity and Incest," 92). Cecilia Valdés is raised by her grandmother Josefa and financially supported by her father, Gamboa. Cecilia, who grew up on the streets of Havana, nonetheless harbors high aspirations of marrying a white man, given that she can pass as a white woman, and is often confused with her white half sister Adela. Her will to succeed in society through marrying a white man is reflected in the following statement: "I am very independent and will never consent to anyone ruling over me" (93; my translation). The rest of the novel alternates between fulfilling and dashing Cecilia's wishes. The tragic and contradictory nature of her life has become emblematic of nineteenth-century Cuban nationalism, torn as it was between its ideals of independence rooted in the emancipation of slaves and the capitalist interests of the slave trade. Caught in the spaces between slavery and freedom, Cecilia Valdés represents the figure of the tragic mulatta (Sollors, 223–45), a figure who will capture the Cuban imagination for a century to come. As important as *Cecilia Valdés* is as an antislavery novel, for the purposes of my study, Cecilia Valdés as a character is studied as a mulatta whose life was crippled by the interests of the Cuban sugar industry and the institution of slavery. Mindful of the cultural heritage inherent in the nineteenth-century character, black Cuban women active in the cultural arena of the late twentieth century project artistic renditions of themselves and their equals that reject the image of the tragic mulatta.

Given its historical importance in the antislavery movement and as a foundational narrative, *Cecilia Valdés* has been studied at length as "an allegation, an accusatory document" against the abuses of the Spanish colony, particularly in respect to the perpetuation of the slave trade (Castellanos and Castellanos, *Cultura Afrocubana,* vol. 2, 209; and Leante, 31), as a novel that "calls into question the concept of family and motherhood in nineteenth-century white Cuban society" (Luis, *Literary Bondage,* 117), and as "our most representative literary myth" (Elías Entralgo as quoted by Luis, 100). Castellanos and Castellanos describe Cecilia Valdés as "a being in transition: her existence is a non-existence, her being is a non-being" (218; my translation). Nancy Morejón classifies her as the weakest link in Cuban society because "Cecilia doesn't want to be Cecilia" ("Mito y realidad en Cecilia Valdés" in *Fundación de la imagen,* 17; my translation), meaning Cecilia doesn't want to be a "colored" woman. This chapter acknowledges a good part of the existing scholarship on Villaverde's novel by way of footnotes and concentrates on the now mythical character of Celicia Valdés as a cipher of the mulatta in the nineteenth-century Cuban literary imagination, a character caught between the hypervisibility of her body as a signifier of racial and class difference and a signifier of the impossibility of the mulatta attaining real class prominence in Cuban society (Kutzinski, *Sugar's Secrets,* 7). Following Nancy Morejón's suggestion that Franz Fanon's analysis of colonialism and race may be useful in looking at issues of race in Cuba ("Grounding the Race Dialogue," 169), I study the character of Cecilia Valdés through the lens of *Black Skin, White Masks.*

In the second part of this essay, I show the transformation of the images of the mulatta and mulatto in Sergio Giral's 1990 film *María Antonia.* Just as the novel appeared during a prerevolutionary period at the turn of the nineteenth century, Sergio Giral's film depicts the 1950s in Havana prior to Fidel Castro's revolution of 1959. My analysis focuses on the image of the mulatta as the product of an Afro-Cuban patriarchal gaze even though the mulatta in the film has acquired a consciousness that Cecilia Valdés never possessed. In the novel *Cecilia Valdés* and in the film *María*

Antonia, both novelist and director project a female image that reflects the values of Cuba's dominant culture at the end of the nineteenth and twentieth centuries, respectively.

In his introduction to *Black Skin, White Masks,* Fanon affirms that "what is often called the black soul is a white man's artifact" (14). I employ Fanon's description of the black colonial subject, a subject whose identity is shaped by the colonizer's gaze, in order to read images of the mulatto and mulatta in Cuban literature and film. By assuming the image projected by the colonizing look, the colonial subject becomes split, fragmented (Bhabha, *Location of Culture,* 40–65). What has been denied to the colonial subject is his desire for "a world of reciprocal recognitions" (Fanon, 218), a world in which the black man is seen, not because he has donned a white mask, but because he is capable of creating his own consciousness through questioning. Thus Fanon's concluding remark: "Oh my body, make of me always a man who questions!" (232). As I employ Fanon's formulations on the colonial subject, I am aware of feminist criticism of Fanon's analysis of the black female subject based on his reading of Mayotte Capécia's memoir, which purportedly depicts a black woman's self-hatred.[2] I tend to agree with T. Denean Sharpley-Whiting, who concludes: "To dismiss Fanon as anti-feminist because he does not fit poststructural feminist paradigms undermines intellectual and pragmatic integrity" (161). Intellectually and pragmatically, I find his proposals regarding the hypervisibility of the female black colonial subject, on the one hand, and her invisibility in social power structures, on the other, useful in the present work. The poet Nancy Morejón establishes a link between racism and nationhood in the context of Fanon's work: "Fanon said that a society is or isn't racist. I think that all Cubans, all those of us who live here and belong to different races, have an obligation to confront this problem, whatever color we are, because it's a problem of nationhood" ("Grounding the Race Dialogue," 167).

In applying Fanon's ideas to the development of a Cuban national identity, I propose that Villaverde's discourse positions itself against the Spanish colonizers by identifying itself as abolitionist at a time in Cuban history when such sentiments often, if not always, aligned themselves with the struggle for independence from Spain. Although Villaverde favored annexation to the United States when he began writing in the 1830s, he eventually advocated for a national agenda free from either Spanish or U.S. domination. Villaverde addresses an audience of Creole elites identified with a Spanish ancestry who, by the end of the century, when the United States was no longer a country favoring slavery, advocated an independent, white-ruled Cuba. In this respect, Villaverde's discourse represents a white elite (in the characters of the Gamboa family) that positions itself against the interests of an Afro-Cuban majority. In the 1860s that majority envisioned an Afro-Cuban civil leadership by black generals from the liberating army (Antonio and José Maceo, Guillermón Moncada, Flor Crombet, and Quintín Bandera).[3] In my reading of *Cecilia Valdés,* then, I posit Villaverde's novelistic discourse as not only allowing abolitionist sentiments that will eventually constitute the origin of the nascent nation but also exposing the ambivalence of his class toward equal racial empowerment in Cuba.[4]

I highlight Villaverde's ambivalence through his representation of the nonwhite colonial subject, as defined by Fanon and as depicted in the characters of José Dolores Pimienta and Cecilia Valdés. They represent the tension between Villaverde's imperative, on the one hand, to fashion a rebellious mulatto subject who acts against the illicit slave trade in Cuba by killing the son of a slave trader and his imperative, on the other hand, to fashion a female character reflective of the ambivalence of the white elites toward the rise of a mulatto middle class that may attain power in political circles.[5] This ambivalent attitude is manifested in a female character who desires to "pass" racially and consequently hopes to rise in class status by marrying the son of a slave trader.[6] The mulatto poses no threat to the social construction of the white family, but the mulatta clearly does when she aspires to create a family with a white man.

The fact that Villaverde creates a mulatta who falls in love with a man whose father is a slave trader points to a deep contradiction inherent in his novel. The text itself is consciously aware of its antislavery message through Pimienta, a mulatto clearly conscious of the social contradictions in Cuba's hybrid society. Yet Cecilia lacks social consciousness regarding her position. Her blind perspective leads fatefully to betrayal and isolation. As we anticipate from the beginning of the novel, Cecilia does not marry Leonardo, the love of her life; instead, she bears his child and goes mad. In the character of Cecilia, then, Villaverde both describes the colonial social arrangement between white men and women of color prevalent in nineteenth-century Cuba and betrays his class's ambivalence about a true mixing of the races at the social level. This ambivalence appears prominently in the fact that even though the novel bears the name of the female protagonist, it relegates the figure of the mulatta to a sense of split identity and a place of invisibility. Cecilia's identity becomes Villaverde's tabula rasa onto which he projects his class's ambivalent sentiments. Villaverde's mulatta is Fanon's "white man's artifact."

Conversely, Villaverde creates the image of the mulatto José Dolores Pimienta as an accomplished musician, thus emphasizing his role as a producer of Cuban culture. As an apprentice at tailor Uribe's shop, Pimienta is positioned within a social milieu in which influential whites such as Leonardo Gamboa come to be fitted and to discuss national issues and men of color congregate to criticize the white establishment they serve. Ultimately, Pimienta grows capable of killing Leonardo, the slave owner's son and object of Cecilia's desire. Yet, while Pimienta symbolically emerges as a subject against slavery representing an entire nineteenth-century Cuban abolitionist movement, Cecilia, with her light skin and her internalized racism, emerges as a national popular figure defined by the gaze of the white Cuban upper class. She does not create her own consciousness through questioning, as Fanon would put it, but represents the projection of those who look down on her as a woman who is neither white nor black (Sollors). This ambivalence regarding the female protagonist may also be found in Leante's 1975 interpretation. When dealing with male characters such as the tailor Uribe and the musician Pimienta, Leante points to the realist nature of Villaverde's novel and sees such characters as representative of a black middle class in Cuba's social development (36–37). Yet when dealing with Cecilia, Leante deals with her simply as a symbol of racial and cultural mixture that determines the Cuban being (40). In Leante's analysis, Cecilia appears to have no "real" historical equivalent. Only more recent analyses of Cecilia as character view her as a Cuban woman, even though in Villaverde's novel she "is still being depicted within the confines of a male imaginary" (Méndez Rodenas, 104).

In a novel in which social boundaries based on race and class are starkly delineated, Villaverde's depiction of class ambivalence manifests itself in the relationship between Leonardo and Cecilia. Leonardo desires Cecilia passionately yet only relates to her as his concubine; in his eyes, the place of a landowner's wife is clearly reserved for Isabel Ilincheta, his equal in social and racial terms. In the following quotation, he speaks about himself in the third person to his friend Diego: "Whoever marries Isabel will have nothing to worry about, not even if he be as jealous as a Turkish sultan. With a woman like C . . . there is a constant danger and one has to be all eyes" (183, 239).[7] For Leonardo, then, passion for a mulatta leads to recklessness, while love and marriage ensure financial stability and personal comfort. His desire to experience passion with a woman whose name may not be spoken aloud need not preclude founding a family with a class equal as well.[8] Leonardo renders Cecilia nameless and therefore invisible in terms of the role she will play in his life. Because the initials of author and protagonist coincide, Cecilia's name is meant to be erased in order to bring the author's to the fore. Regarding socially sanctioned marriages among whites from the same class, Verena Stolcke states: "I thus interpreted nineteenth-century Cuba as a class society whose mechanisms of socio-political reproduction were informed by an ideological conflation of heredity and inheritance, that is, of the genetic transmission of racial purity and the legal and economic perpetuation of social privilege and rank" (xiii). Regarding interracial unions, Stolcke claims: "By contrast, black or, as they were also called, coloured, women were the prey of white men in sexual liaisons that were very rarely legitimated through marriage. Legal marriage was the appropriate form of union among social-racial equals, while interracial unions, that is unions among partners who were regarded as social-racial unequals, usually resulted in more or less stable concubinage and/or matrifocal domestic units" (xiv). While Leonardo attributes the relationships he has established with both women to emotional exigencies, they clearly answer to socioeconomic concerns. Leonardo envisions one woman in one place and the other in another: "The one in Havana [Cecilia] will be my Cytherean Venus, the one in Alquízar [Isabel], my guardian angel, my Ursuline nun, my sister of charity" (183; my translation). For the white male from the landed elite, women are to be either placed on a pedestal or considered as the objects of man's sexuality. His relationship to each can be kept separate.

Cecilia loves Leonardo, and because her grandmother has encouraged her to "better" herself she aspires to marry him: "You are almost white and you may aspire to marry a white man" (14, 24). For Leonardo the limits of their relationship are very clear, whereas for her their relationship is based on a fantasy she has created for herself. Because she is almost white and quite beautiful, she hopes for an exception to the social rule that a white man of the landed elite does not marry a hybrid lower-class woman. In this erotic relationship, then, Villaverde exposes the desires of two people who are each oblivious to the expectations of the other. Moreover, he represents the colonial practice of *blanqueamiento*, by which, through arrangements such as that between Leonardo and Cecilia, the nonwhite majority of the 1830s (56 percent) would diminish and eventually disappear. This whitening of the Cuban population was accomplished by the end of the century with the infusion of Spanish immigrants. By 1887, "black people and mulattos represented only thirty-two per cent of the population" (McGarrity and Cárdenas, 83). With this novel

Villaverde defines himself as an abolitionist, but he nevertheless betrays the ambivalence of his class regarding race by drawing the line at the mixing of races in legitimate social terms.

Villaverde depicts Cecilia's identity and proper place in society in the novel in discretely spatial terms.[9] Barreda Tomás presents an incisive analysis of the function of space in the novel, asserting that Villaverde uses space as an interpretative tool to create an atmosphere, to situate a social class, and in my view to signify the practice and theorization of specific political beliefs in the nineteenth century. Barreda Tomás concludes that ultimately space in the novel identifies the internal wars that split Cuban society at the time. Thus, Leonardo meets Cecilia in places that reflect their mismatched relationship. These include Mercedes Ayala's home, where people of color congregate for popular dances, and Cecilia's own small house, owned by her natural father, Cándido Gamboa. Unbeknownst to Cecilia and Leonardo, Cándido is Cecilia's father. Cecilia and Leonardo's relationship flourishes in spaces set aside for both colored and white males who cross class and racial lines. Conversely, the mulatta's relationship with Leonardo becomes ambiguous in those sites that are appropriate only for members of the landed class. When Cecilia crosses over to Leonardo's privileged spaces, she essentially disappears.

Two key scenes illustrate how Cecilia is caught between Villaverde's abolitionist imperatives and the ambivalence of his class regarding social integration of the races. The first scene in which Villaverde effectively erases Cecilia's character occurs in the middle of the novel, in chapter 12, part 2 (140–41). Nemesia, Cecilia's friend and confidant, who is herself in love with Leonardo, leads Cecilia to the street where Leonardo and his friends are sending his future wife Isabel and her father off to their coffee plantation. Nemesia does this to convince Cecilia that Leonardo has been deceiving her. Cecilia, angered by jealousy at seeing Leonardo with another woman, pushes him off his horse as she passes by. He lands at Isabel's feet. Isabel, surprised and almost laughing, confuses Cecilia with Adela, Leonardo's younger sister. From early in the novel, the reader has been aware of the resemblance between the two, which points to the incestuous relationship between Cecilia and Leonardo, a fact kept secret from both characters. Because Cecilia's physical gesture of pushing Leonardo is silent, she is easily confused with her half sister. Cecilia's angry response to her lover elicits laughter rather than anger because Isabel has interpreted it as a prank. Her laughter annuls Cecilia's anger. Her physical and expressive selves disappear behind her white mask, Adela.

Cecilia's invisibility conjures the mulatta as the shadow of Adela, her "better" white self. Ironically, Cecilia, who would rather be recognized as white by Leonardo and his friends, is perceived as white only insofar as she resembles another. Soon after, however, Cecilia becomes visible when her black features are seen in connection with her class behavior.

When Cecilia turns her anger toward Isabel and utters an insult against her, Cecilia's identity is revealed as lower class. Her look-alike, Adela, having been reared in the upper-class, slave-owning Gamboa household, would never have uttered such profanity.[10] Moreover, the text itself, intended for the Cuban intellectual elite, refuses to print the unspeakable (". . . Pu . . ."; 141), recording only half the insult, "You harlot" (181). Cecilia's daring but unguarded outburst ironically effects an inversion of characters, and the name "harlot" flashes back upon her, fixing Cecilia in a class stereotype. The inversion occurs the instant Isabel hears the insult and disappears into her carriage, a private space. Isabel no longer deigns to look at her. Cecilia disappears as a white upper-class young woman and reappears as a whore not worthy of a white woman's gaze. As soon as the upper classes identify Cecilia as capable of exhibiting anger and insulting a lady in public, she is described by the narrator as having harsher features than her half sister: "Cecilia, with flushed cheeks and eyes sparkling with anger, was a copy of Leonardo Gamboa's younger sister, although with more harsh and pronounced features" (141; my translation). Thus, character and moral traits are neatly tied to physical characteristics,[11] and lower-class status and race become indistinguishable. Again, it is the gaze of the upper-class woman that defines Cecilia and causes her to disappear as a subject.

Even though the scene transpires in a public space, the street, the fact that it happens in front of a private home, and that all members of the upper class involved are either on horseback or in a carriage reconstitutes the space as private.[12] The identification of Cecilia as an intruder in the private family circle prompts the Gamboas and the Ilinchetas to exit quickly to protect themselves from the perceived dangers represented by difference in race and class.[13] What is most remarkable in this scene is not so much Cecilia's invisibility based on her resemblance to Adela, but rather Isabel's inability to conceive of sharing the same space with a mulatta who insults her.

Since Cecilia Valdés is an almost-white mulatta fathered by a landowner who continues to provide for her, she theoretically inhabits a space in between races and classes. Her failed attempts at identification outside the prescribed norms for someone of mixed race leave her as a fragmented female subject who may pass as white only as long as she is confused with someone else. The anger and language she displays in confronting Leonardo and Isabel identify her definitively as a member of the lower classes and make her visible as an insulting whore. Hence, her behavior unwittingly fulfills the upper classes' expectations of persons of mixed race. Villaverde uses the Gamboa family circle as a mouthpiece for a racist image of the mulatta: at first invisible, then visible but only as a class and racial category. She becomes visible as an object of their gaze, but not as an individual with her own consciousness. Ultimately, she becomes invisible again when the landed class flees from her presence.

During the course of the novel, with the play of gazes determined by class exigencies, Villaverde transforms Cecilia's identity from that of a beautiful, proud young woman admired in mulatto social circles (20, 24) to that of an angry, emotionally unstable stereotype created by the upper classes (141, 299; see Fanon, 41–62). In the concluding pages, Villaverde characterizes Cecilia's transformation (defined by the upper classes' racist attitudes and reinforced by her black grandmother's internalized racism) as that of a lamb becoming a lioness, thus robbing her of any humanity: "It must be stated that the lamb in fact became a lioness" (299; my translation). This transformation, marked by beginning and ending descriptions of Cecilia, remains an illusory one because, from the outset, as many critics have already pointed out, Cecilia the child is already doomed to her fate by virtue of having grown up unsupervised in the streets. Ultimately, the novelist defines the mulatta as a colonized subject, as someone incapable of inhabiting multiple spaces in society or of creating her own consciousness through questioning.

The second and most important scene in which Villaverde's ambivalence toward the Cuban mulatta emerges is found at the end of the novel. In this closing scene, Villaverde constructs the mulatta as sexually deranged. Here Cecilia, having been betrayed by Leonardo (who by now has consented to marry Isabel), asks her friend Pimienta to prevent their marriage. Cecilia means for Pimienta to kill Isabel, but he ultimately kills Leonardo instead (299).

Driven by her desire to be seen as white by Leonardo so that she may become his legitimate wife, Cecilia is blind to the love of Pimienta, her most socially acceptable companion. An accomplished musician and apprentice at Uribe's tailor shop, Pimienta's social position is indicative of a rising lower and middle class of freed slaves. Cecilia fails to recognize him as a suitable companion because he is mulatto. In a conversation at the tailor shop between Pimienta and Uribe, Villaverde describes the untenable situation for the mulatto:

> "And it is mighty hard," added Pimienta, his hands trembling and his eyes clouded with tears, "it is mighty hard that they should take away our colored girls and that we can't look at a white woman."
>
> "And who is to blame for that?" asked Uribe arching his brows. "Not the white man, my boy, but our girls themselves. . . . If the colored girls didn't care for the white men, the white men wouldn't have anything to do with the colored girls."
>
> "That may be so, Mr. Uribe, but what I ask is this: Don't the white men have enough with the white girls? . . . Don't fool yourself, Mr. Uribe, if the white men were satisfied with the white women, they wouldn't look at our colored girls." (74, 96–97)

This brief dramatic scene illustrates the power structure prevalent in Cuban society, an extension of slavery in which the white landed elite continues to own the intimate lives of the supposedly now-freed mulattos. The colonial situation permeates the personal so that neither José Dolores Pimienta nor Cecilia may freely choose a romantic partner. The clear difference between man and woman resides in the fact that the mulatto comprehends the situation clearly and has a conscious analysis of it, while the mulatta remains completely blinded to the social power structures and truly believes that she has chosen a proper partner in Leonardo.

Oblivious to Pimienta as an object of desire, Cecilia considers him her greatest ally in trying to regain Leonardo's love. Pimienta's love for Cecilia and his desire to have Leonardo dead for his own emotional reasons deafens him to Cecilia's utterance at the precise moment when she clarifies that it is Isabel that she wishes dead. His misinterpretation also allows him to advance the agenda of black abolitionists against slave traders, and he thus symbolically becomes an actor in an ongoing historical movement toward a racially mixed national identity.

Pimienta represents the rebel who severs the bloodline of Spanish slave traders, while Cecilia is left as the deeply emotional subject who emerges as a malevolent stereotype based on the landed elite's fears that the sexually overdetermined mulatta will pose a threat to the racial purity of the Cuban family. Cecilia's actions in pushing Leonardo off the horse and insulting Isabel become neutralized by her class and race designations. Because she is a mulatta her actions cannot have a social and political import. At the textual level, her push merely foreshadows Pimienta's subsequent murder of Leonardo.[14] In the scene with Isabel, Cecilia is not seen *until* she is heard. In the scene of the conversation between Cecilia and Pimienta, which focuses on the failed romantic relationship between two equals, Cecilia is seen but not heard.[15] Pimienta cannot hear what Cecilia has to say precisely because he prefers to interpret her request as an opportunity to eliminate the person who stands between him and Cecilia. In both scenes, Villaverde fashions Cecilia's identity as invisible based on issues of class and race (in relation to Leonardo) and gender (in relation to Pimienta).[16]

William Luis interprets Villaverde's ending in a positive way: "Only in *Cecilia Valdés* do we have a daring killing of a white by a mulatto. Villaverde's political activism, his freedom from persecution while in the United States, and the emancipation of slaves in the northern country were important factors which contributed to his description of Leonardo's death" (*Literary Bondage,* 118). But even Pimienta's rebellious act, which symbolically curtails the power of the white landed class, rises out of his personal, emotional reaction and, therefore, lacks a conscious revolutionary import. Had Villaverde wanted to create a radical text, he might have had Pimienta flee to become involved in the Afro-Cuban political power struggle culminating in the Ladder Conspiracy of 1844 that eliminated black intellectuals. The novelist implied such anachronistic events (the action of the novel ends before 1844) earlier with regard to the character Uribe and the black intelligentsia who gathered in his tailor shop, all characters representing real people who suffered death or imprisonment as the result of their insurrection (see Leante, 36–37). By concentrating on Cecilia's failed romance with Leonardo, the abrupt ending does not permit a satisfying resolution; the reader is left with no sense of any social consciousness gained by Cecilia when she meets her mother in the hospital for the insane. Thus, hidden away from the larger society, Cecilia and her mother are no longer a threat to white morality, and they, in fact, inhabit a place where they pay for the consequences of their aspirations to marry into the Gamboa family. Rather than look toward a progressive political and social resolution, the novel splits, favoring political activism, but not social transformation.

In her study of a cigarette lithograph by Eduardo Guilló entitled "Las consecuencias" (The Consequences), Vera Kutzinski makes the connection between the lithograph depicting the prison-like hospital wherein Cuban society controls mulattas who transgress against the sanctity of the white Cuban family and the end of *Cecilia Valdés:* "'Las consecuencias' . . . shifts to the claustrophobic, institutional space of a prisonlike shelter or hospital, which is as reminiscent of both Rosario's and Cecilia's intern-ment in Villaverde's novel as it is evocative of Foucault's remarks on the prison as a locus of thought control" (*Sugar's Secrets,* 77). Although I agree with Luis that Villaverde has expressed his political radicalism by having Pimienta kill Leonardo, I contend, with Kutzinski, that the novel also makes a clear statement regarding the perceived social threat that mulattas represented to Cuban white society at the end of the nineteenth century. While Pimienta escapes, Cecilia does not, and she is made to pay for the consequences of Cuba's racism and sexism. In that respect, Villaverde exposes that racism but shows no hope regarding its transcen-dence on the part of the elite classes.

This confusion regarding her gender and class status on the one hand and her feminine desires on the other presents Cecilia Valdés as a tabula rasa onto which a multiplicity of meanings can be inscribed, ranging from that of the Little Bronze Virgin (la Virgen de la Caridad del Cobre) at the beginning of the novel (20, 35) to that of the loose woman at the end who steps out on the street half-dressed and emotionally distraught (299, 398).[17] Villaverde's cyclical narrative begins with Cecilia's mother confined to an insane asylum and ends by assigning Cecilia a similar fate.[18] For both, as for many female slaves before them, the prerogative of motherhood is denied.[19] The child, like the mother as slave or concu-bine, becomes the property of the white father. Because Leonardo dies after having fathered Cecilia's child, the novel is silent as to the fate of the newborn. In all likelihood, the baby girl would be deposited in an orphanage and become another Valdés, this time truly fatherless. Al-though the critic William Luis sees the lack of paternal intervention in the fate of Leonardo's illegitimate daughter as a break from the exploita-tion of mulattas and black women within the paternalistic family sphere, Méndez Rodenas sees the bastard daughter as "doubly marked by her condition as the last of a genealogical line resulting from slavery and incest" ("Identity and Incest," 100). Cuba's social reality points to the continued enslavement of mulattas through lower-class status and pros-titution to the present day.[20]

Although both Cecilia and her mother conceive and bear children, the nursing and rearing of those increasingly "white" children pass on to the hands of other "darker" women. In the novel, the slave María de Regla has nursed Adela, Cecilia, and her own children. In *Literary Bondage,* William Luis states: "María de Regla, whose name suggests both the Vir-gen María (Virgin Mary) and the Cuban black Virgen de Regla, known in Afro-Cuban culture as Yemayá, is not only the mother of Adela, Cecilia, and Dolores but the mother of the white, mulatto, and black races her daughters represent. Symbolically, María de Regla is the mother of the Cuban people" (116). In not nursing her child, Cecilia's mother, Rosario, occupies the same place as upper-class women, who like Doña Rosa (Leonardo's mother) never actually care for their offspring. But like the slave María de Regla, who nurses and rears most of the children in the novel, Cecilia and her mother are emotionally attached to their children as infants and see that separation as tragic. It is of interest that although María de Regla is punished for opposing the strictures of the Gamboa family regarding the nursing and care of her own children, she does not become insane because she is a slave and therefore cannot pose a real threat to white society's family structure.[21]

Moreover, her attachment to her children is clearly dictated by the color of their skin; she prefers those who bear lighter skin color. Because she is a slave and gets transported from the household to the plantation at the Gamboas' whim, she has many sexual partners during her lifetime, both black and white. This pattern of polyandry practiced by María de Regla reflects an enforced practice by both sexes in the slave population throughout the Caribbean.[22] For Rosario and Cecilia, however, who aspire to ascend in class status through marriage, being denied access to their children and to the father of their daughters ultimately signifies the death of their expectations to join the upper classes. Those expectations are not unlike those of middle-class women who desire economic stability in order to care for their children. Because Rosario and Cecilia fail in their attempt to erase through marriage their difference as lower-class mulattas, they lapse into madness.

According to Felman in *What Does a Woman Want?* a woman's madness may be interpreted as a passive contestation of assigned roles for the feminine gender (see Felman, 20–40). In the case of Villaverde's novel, however, in which the careful delineation of spaces carries racial and social connotations, the emphasis is not so much on a particular woman's madness as on the place where the insane reside. In *Cecilia Valdés* the insane asylum becomes a space of nonexistence where mulattas who contest the boundaries of race, class, and gender are forced to retire, never to be heard from again. Even though for Cecilia the asylum becomes the site where her mother, prior to death, recognizes her, there is no consciousness on the part of Cecilia as to the social determinism of their shared fates. Villaverde does not grant such agency to his female protagonist. By emphasizing the cyclical nature of the plot as it relates to Cecilia, a plot that silences her, Villaverde reveals his society's inability to come to terms with the consequences of continued racial mixing. Françoise Vergès, reading Fanon, defines colonial madness thus: "To Fanon . . . madness is not a disease but a *story,* the story of a situation, of a wandering, of the impossibility to be heard, of a filiation whose history is one of betrayal, murder, enslavement. It is the story of a black man" (see Vergès, 582). In Villaverde's novel, madness is the story of the Cuban mulatta.

Given that the novel represents a period of Cuban history (1812–30) when the Haitian Revolution was still fresh in the landed elite's minds, and when slaves and freed Afro-Cubans outnumbered Euro-Cubans, Villaverde chooses to emphasize issues of class by criticizing the social values of the landed elite, including the Caribbean-wide double standard of forced racial mixing coupled with the prohibition of socially sanctioned mixed marriages.[23] This double standard is projected onto the figure of the mulatta who has internalized Cuban society's predominant social values but is prohibited from practicing them. Furthermore, white female characters in the novel follow a similar trajectory. Isabel, herself a strong woman who runs her coffee plantation and questions the sincerity of Leonardo's love toward her, retires to a convent after Leonardo's death.[24]

In *Cecilia Valdés,* then, race and class considerations predetermine the gendering of female characters and, specifically, that of the mulatta who must bear the burden of the failure of the national project to create a racially mixed society in an independent Cuba.[25] In his study of *Cecilia Valdés* Juan Gelpí concludes: "This study about Cecilia Valdés has led us to question a rather disseminated interpretation that sees in Villaverde's novel a celebration of *mestizaje* and national unity. In fact, unlike other nineteenth-century novels that Doris Sommer has studied well, in Villaverde's novel there is no love story that may represent in an allegorical manner national unification. There is, on the other hand, a love story that ends in a sort of national dissolution" (56; my translation). Most studies of *Cecilia Valdés* that emphasize issues of national definition, or abolition through close scrutiny of class and race, are blind to gender issues. Criticism is split between readings that look to the novel as a compendium of nineteenth-century national concerns and feminist approaches that often point to the symbolic nature of the novel's female characters. In either case, Cecilia Valdés as character comes to represent a nation in its embryonic stages in which racist and sexist concerns predominate.

Villaverde created characters that embodied his opposition to slavery (Pimienta) and his class's ambivalence regarding issues of gender, class, and race (Cecilia). In so doing, the novelist represented Pimienta as the rebellious historical subject and Cecilia as the ambiguous object of desire. In his film *María Antonia*, Sergio Giral inverts these literary roles.[26] For the Afro-Cuban director, *María Antonia* represents a much-awaited opportunity to return to the mulatta the agency that Cirilo Villaverde had denied Cecilia Valdés in his novel. Giral founds this artistic enterprise on a dialectical tension between past and present, between *Cecilia Valdés* and Cuba of the 1950s, on the one hand, and María Antonia and post-Castro Cuba, on the other. Whether or not Giral is consciously revising Villaverde's novel, with this film he dismantles the racist values inherent in the novel and stubbornly present in today's Cuba.[27] Produced a century after the publication of Villaverde's novel, *María Antonia* is a critical evaluation in terms of gender, class, and race of the aftermath of Cuba's first and subsequent revolutionary movements.

In Giral's film, the male character, Julián, a prizefighter, assumes the image projected onto him by the powerful white establishment of Havana in the early 1950s, and thus becomes an object to be enslaved by those in power. The female character, María Antonia, rejects all demands placed on her, whether by her elders or by the males who pursue her. Eventually she becomes a liberated subject.

If Villaverde constructs the mulatta by a play of invisibility and visibility, Giral's film places her at the center of the spectacle. As María Antonia walks down the streets of old Havana in the 1950s, every male turns to get her attention. She stands tall on high heels, and she wears tight pants and a revealing top as she walks with certainty and in full possession of her sensual demeanor. The emphasis on the character's sensuality through dress and physical movement underlines the construction of pleasure from the perspective of the male gaze in the cinematic situation. The question arises, then, as to whether the male gaze that predominates throughout the film undermines female subjectivity or whether Giral subverts it through the contextualization of that subjectivity within Afro-Cuban culture.[28]

At all times during the film, María Antonia wears yellow, the color of Our Lady of Charity, the patroness of Cuba, and the color of Ochún, the Yoruba orisha of sensual love. Miguel Barnet, Cuban ethnographer, poet, and novelist, describes Ochún's polysemic nature:

> She is one of those divinities whose paternity is claimed by many. She is mistress of the river, fresh water, gold, and honey. . . . *Yeyé Cari*, as she is also called, is a symbol of the colonial mulatta, sensual and merry. . . . [S]he is

proud and uncivil, but in the avatar of *Iyammu* she is tranquil, profound, and grave. . . . In the avatar of *Panchágara,* however, she is irrepressible; a consummate prostitute, her mission is to wrest men away from all women, and with that in mind she does not spare any honey or gold, any erotic dance or swing of the hips. (94–95)

The latter part of this definition reflects the mulatta as perceived through a sexist gaze. Villaverde reduces her image to a dialectical tension between the figures of Cuba's bronze virgin and that of a prostitute. Villaverde creates an either/or Eurocentric image, far from the complexity of that of the Yoruba goddess. Giral's María Antonia displays all the attributes of Ochún, allowing the character to symbolize Cuba at a particular time in its social and political history when the vast majority of nonwhites in Havana lived under substandard conditions. Most key nonwhite characters in the film are involved in the sports and entertainment business predominantly run by United States interests. The less fortunate deal in drugs and offer themselves up for prostitution. In my view, Giral has attempted to give his female protagonist a social and political consciousness, but the dismal conditions under which María Antonia lives during the Cuban dictator Fulgencio Batista's regime make it impossible for her to rise above the straitjacket that the American economy imposes on the island. One of the leitmotifs of the film reiterates the need of many of its characters to get out of the slums of Havana.

A summary of the film's structure and plot will facilitate the analysis that follows. The action opens with a shot of a woman rummaging through the streets of Havana at night and then quickly turns to the flames engulfing the room where María Antonia resides, a scene that takes place much later. One of the first frames shows yellow flames around the figure of Our Lady of Charity. Our Lady of Charity is Cuba's black virgin who hovers over three fishermen—one black, one white, one indigenous. By burning the image of the virgin at the outset of the film, Giral breaks with Villaverde's construction of the mulatta so closely identified with Our Lady of Charity. After the film's title, the viewer hears Yoruba prayers and sees María Antonia and her godmother crossing the bay of Havana to the town of Regla, known as a major center of Santería (the integration of West African and Catholic religious beliefs). As the two women walk down the street toward the Yoruba priest's home, they cross a small Catholic procession. Yoruba and Catholic prayers in Latin are superimposed in the sound track to signify the syncretic nature of Cuba's culture and that of the female protagonist. The narrative is interrupted and punctuated by a series of flashbacks that show María Antonia in front of the *babalao* (Yoruba/Lucumí priest) who interprets her fate. Ifá divination, an orally delivered prophecy, then, coincides with narrative plot, with the *babalao* symbolically assuming the role of the director. Within the frame of the engulfing flames and the flashbacks to the Ifá divination, the characters' lives unfold in chronological order.

The fact that cinematic narrative and Ifá divination alternate emphasizes the director's commitment to present a story grounded in Afro-Cuban culture. Matibag's definition of Ifá will help establish Giral's narrative: "In Ifá, one performs a discursive, intertextual act in which myth and personal history are meant to interact through the medium of language" ("Ifá and Interpretation," 151). The act of mediation, usually performed by the *babalao,* and in the film performed by the director, "mediates between individual desire and the social context." The Yoruba priest possesses the Ifá system through the memorization of thousands of narratives that he then applies to the life of a specific individual. Through his prophesies, the multiple stories stored in the *babalao*'s memory take the form of divination as applied to personal life. Through prayer and sacrifice, an individual such as María Antonia could avoid danger and ultimately alter her fate. At the hands of the director, Ifá divination performs the act of looking into Cuba's political past (the Batista regime) and projects a better fate for Afro-Cubans in a revolutionary future. Giral's enterprise, then, may be seen as a performance "in which myth and personal history are meant to interact through the medium of [cinematic] language" (151). The myth of Ochún is interwoven into María Antonia's personal history in a pattern that predetermines the protagonist's fate while allowing for interpretation within the limits of the oracle's prophecy. The female character's desires clash with the economic and religious determinism of Havana's society in the 1950s. Giral's film resorts to Ifá as a vast source for his creativity.[29]

By placing Ifá divination at the crux of his cinematographic project, Sergio Giral not only discovers the possible destinies of his female protagonist but also unveils the secrets of the revolutionary moment in which the author himself lives. By making the roles of director and *babalao* (as diviner of the relationship between past and future) coincide, Giral elucidates the history of Afro-Cubans. In her thorough study of the development of Cuban literature as inextricably linked to Afro-Cuban divination practices, Julia Cuervo Hewitt explains the process by which literary texts and the history of a people become indistinguishable: "These texts, in their entirety and in their relationship to the discourse from which they are engendered, like the multiple letters of Ifá, also relate the history of a people" (*Aché, presencia africana,* 285; my translation). Cuervo Hewitt establishes an important link between Cuban literary texts that reject the current institutionalized culture and are often silenced, and Ifá. Both serve as repositories of a culture by encoding the wisdom of a people. By blending the roles of director and *babalao* into one, as well as those of message (word) and cinematographic image (artistic voice), Giral rescues Afro-Cuban culture, its divination practices, and its deities from silence and oblivion and relates the history of the Afro-Cuban people prior to and after the 1959 Cuban Revolution.

Giral places María Antonia at the heart of Havana's drug and prostitu-tion rings prior to the revolution without allowing her to be swallowed up by despair. Like Ochún, she is proud yet uncivil, given that to survive she must rebel against her surroundings. She rebels against her lover Julián when she realizes that he is unfaithful. Even though she prefers Julián to other men, she does not limit her sexual activity to one man. Julián rep-resents the macho in society, and her other lover typifies the sensitive, shy individual. They both seek to possess her and to limit her every action. She confronts and rejects both, emerging as a highly independent indi-vidual who exerts control over her sexual life by refusing to allow men to own or restrict her.[30] At the spiritual level, she rebels against the *babalao*'s prophesy that announces that "the grave is open." María Antonia fights vigorously against the diviner's "truth." There are admonitions through-out the film that predict her defeat: one of her lovers finds a dead bird as they walk down the railroad tracks; a goat is sacrificed in her honor at her godmother's altar, and María Antonia flees in horror; the figure of an old prostitute who roams the streets of Havana drunk portends María Antonia's future. Her story is thus defined as a series of personal struggles to stave off her fate. As the plot develops, María Antonia's will to transcend her social and mythical milieu crumbles under the pressures of predetermination. The narrative ends with María Antonia stabbed to death at her godmother's altar by a neighborhood admirer and lover who would rather entrap her as a good, faithful wife than accept her as the free spirit she is.

If, in social terms, the film were to follow the same program for the female protagonist as does Villaverde's novel, María Antonia would depend solely on Julián's ability to extricate her from the circle of poverty that surrounds them. However, María Antonia sees Julián's strategy for what it is: an escape. She detects and exposes his agent's extortion and manipulation. Julián hopes to find freedom through fame and chooses to remain blind to the fact that by signing a $200 (pesos) per fight contract, he has effectively sold himself to the control of those who will exploit him.[31] When María Antonia points to his virtual enslavement under his new contract, Julián rejects her outright.

Upon first viewing, the film reproduces the image of the highly sensual mulatta caught in a lower-class environment. María Antonia dresses and moves in a sexually provocative manner and acts out her rebelliousness in relation to the men in her life. Her naked body is the focus of attention in the two love scenes depicted. Moreover, there are two other female characters whose presence serves to map out María Antonia's life trajectory. A young dancer from Santiago attracts Julián's attention, and soon after he sees her dance, they retreat to private quarters. The owner of the cabaret complains that Julián took this dancer away as he had done earlier with María Antonia. At the opposite end of the spectrum, the old prostitute whose image opens the film predicts María Antonia's future. Even though María Antonia dominates the screen in visually sensual terms, her individuality disappears as her image is spectacularly repeated by the other two female characters. The only strong female character firmly rooted in Afro-Cuban culture is María Antonia's godmother, a black woman who nurtures and supports her, but María Antonia rejects her. There is no attempt in the film to create a community of women who work together to better their fate.

Despite the sexual determinism of the female image, throughout the film Giral exploits the symbolic power of the visual to reiterate María Antonia's refusal to be enslaved either by the constraints of her class or by male demands that she conform to their notions of a woman's role. When she makes love to Julián, African drums play in the background, and there are shots of her altar to Our Lady of Charity. When she is with her more tender lover, a bolero plays softly, and the camera alternates between the naked bodies and an image of Christ. Sexuality becomes linked to Christian religious martyrdom through visual images and to cultural vitality through Afro-Cuban music. Christian images lose their power when María Antonia sets fire to her room.

But Afro-Cuban influences prove to be much more powerful. Like Cecilia Valdés, María Antonia is closely associated with a national religious icon. But whereas Cecilia's nickname Little Bronze Virgin signals her race, María Antonia's consistently yellow attire refers more directly to the Afro-Cuban face of the virgin as Ochún, the Yoruba goddess of love. María Antonia's coquetry, her unfailing sexual power, and her procreative gifts linked to the flowing waters of the river point to her association with Ochún. As such, she need not bow to anyone. If Cecilia as bronze virgin stands as a mere vessel to carry the white man's child, María Antonia embodies the power of sexuality without ever succumbing to the male's reproductive power. Even though she is in her late twenties or thirties, she has no children. Although the Catholic Virgin stands as a national icon that symbolically unites the white, black, and indigenous races, Ochún "is a goddess of powerful magnetism" (Barnet, 95) capable of engineering powerful, historical changes.

The scene in which María Antonia kills Julián and burns her apartment symbolically represents a definitive break with prerevolutionary Cuba. Giral places María Antonia in control of both her own fate and that of Julián. Not quite as independent and spirited, Julián hopes to escape the environment that surrounds him by becoming a prizefighter who will eventually star at New York's Madison Square Garden. But to do so, he depends on his agent, who forces him to sign a contract that exploits him financially. As a reward from his boss for having signed the contract, Julián wins the company of a Marilyn Monroe look-alike. Having consulted a *santera* to keep control over her man, María Antonia arrives to reclaim Julián's attention, ultimately drawing him away from the American woman. Because María Antonia refuses to share his "American dream," Julián informs her that he cannot take her away with him. At this point she leads Julián up to her room, where she poisons him and sets fire to the place. By killing him, she rejects the American values he desires. The scene acquires high symbolic value because María Antonia wears a yellow dress, because there are repeated shots of her altar to the Virgen de la Caridad del Cobre, and because the yellow flames engulf both Julián and the altar. Giral uses yellow flames at the beginning and near the end of the film to signal his rebellion against the enslavement of Afro-Cubans both by breaking with religious symbols that predetermine the role of women in society and with a capitalist society that enslaved through economic means.

By having María Antonia kill Julián, Giral gives the female subject her own agency. In this sense, the image of María Antonia is diametrically opposed to that of Cecilia Valdés, who must ask Pimienta to act on her behalf. Because Giral's protagonist can only symbolically kill the American Dream, she ends up offering herself, and the despair she represents, at the altar of Ochún. María Antonia's death signals the close of one era and the beginning of another. The film adds an epilogue symbolizing María Antonia in the streets of postrevolutionary Cuba, presumably still independent yet now capable of transcending the ghetto walls that contained her in the past (through the image of the gold shoes and purse). After the penultimate frames that focus on a yellow backdrop behind an altar honoring Ochún, the camera shows a windy field, and the action shifts to Cuba after 1959. A renewed María Antonia jumps out of a red car as young children walk in school uniforms and several teenagers dance to rap music. The last frame zeros in on the protagonist's gold shoes and purse. When she reappears in postrevolutionary Cuba, the red car she steps out of may well represent Castro's revolution. The new emerging María Antonia has broken with the colonial stereotypes of the mulatta, with her saintly and perverse faces. She rises from the flames of revolution as a triumphant phoenix, still identifying with Ochún through the visual image of gold-colored shoes and purse, both objects of physical and economic upward mobility.

With *María Antonia,* Sergio Giral transforms the image of the Cuban mulatta from that of a passive subject, limited by the constraints of gender, class, and race in nineteenth-century Cuba, to an individual who actively rejects the racial, social, and sexist values of a postcolonial nation. By highlighting the multiplicity of interpretations inherent in Ifá divination, Giral reinterprets the death of his female protagonist as a willful act of refusal to succumb to the dismal fate of an old prostitute. The mulatta of the 1950s dies to rise again in a society where her culture is valued and her economic prospects are much better. There is no question that in *María Antonia* Sergio Giral charges his female character with a social and political consciousness truer to an individual living in Cuba in the 1990s than to one living there in the 1950s. Yet, he still creates a character whose rebelliousness is disappointingly couched in purely sexual terms and viewed cinematographically from a predominantly male gaze. Even at the end of the film where María Antonia jumps out of the car triumphantly, she does so wearing very sensual attire, denoting prostitution, rather than, say, the garb of an artist, poet, or filmmaker. Integration of the mulatta into the multiple roles of revolutionary society is still to be accomplished, according to the film. Moreover, one wonders why Giral does not question the exclusionary values of the male-centered Abakuá society throughout the film, a society to which Julián belongs, and which the Afro-Cuban filmmaker Sara Gómez criticized in her 1974 documentary *De cierta manera* [One Way or Another].[32] Giral seems not to have profited from Gómez's valiant effort to both value and criticize the Afro-Cuban culture that nurtured her creativity. Ultimately, in his highly successful film, Giral prefers to focus on issues of social, political, and cultural import over those of gender.

María Antonia's refusal to be enslaved found an echo in a revolutionary movement that promised to eradicate all determinisms during the 1960s and 1970s when the social and economic fate of Afro-Cubans improved substantially. Whether that promise has continued to be fulfilled since the fall of the Soviet Bloc in 1989 and its curtailment of economic subsidies to Cuba is another question. Because of the enigmatic quality of the film's short epilogue, a more current interpretation arises. Beginning in the 1990s, tourism has dominated the economy with dreadful consequences for educated young men and women who, often unable to find appropriately compensated jobs, turn to prostitution, especially in Havana. Tourism pamphlets privilege images of the sensual mulatta. Unfortunately, whiter Cubans do work in prominent jobs in the tourist industry that caters mainly to Canadians, Europeans, and South Americans, while darker Cubans have entered the underground economy in large numbers. Even though the Cuban government has targeted prostitution to eradicate it, the practice persists openly.

In this context, Giral's enigmatic epilogue may be read to mean that the María Antonia of the 1990s is to be sexually exploited and that her gold-colored attire merely updates her situation. Giral may have placed his film in the context of the 1950s purely to avoid censorship. If viewed as a criticism of today's Cuba in relation to its Afro-Cuban population and culture, *María Antonia* represents a strong indictment of the failures of Castro's revolution in terms of race. Its female character walks between the *pioneros,* the uniformed children who will presumably fulfill the promise of the revolution, and the youth who dance to the American-influenced Cuban rap (see Olavarria). At the end of the film, Giral appears to turn to African American musical expression to single out the presence of Cuban-style racism. The figure of the mulatta, interposed between Cuba's socialist future represented by the children and Cuba's present by a second generation that looks to the Afro-American north for its rebellion, sends a highly ambivalent message regarding Cuba's ability to tackle issues of race. Unfortunately, Giral's emphasis on social and racial issues as viewed through the sensual image of the mulatta again displaces the gender issue. Presently, there is a rich debate among Afro-Cuban intellectuals inside and outside the island as to the success of the revolutionary program, especially in relation to the problem of racism. Whatever the outcome, Giral's images have sent a clear signal that there must not be a return to the enslavement of Afro-Cubans.[33]

The novel of Cirilo Villaverde and the film of Sergio Giral both raise issues of national concern by focusing on the figure of the mulatta as symbolic of the nation in moments of political identity formation. The works engage the issue of Cuba's relationship to Spanish and U.S. imperialism in implicit and explicit ways and foreground the fragility of nationhood in the context of colonialism and postcolonialism. In this respect, *Cecilia Valdés* and *María Antonia* exploit the female protagonist in her invisibility and spectacularity by effectively divorcing issues of gender from issues of class and race. In so doing, Villaverde exposes the white intelligentsia's ambivalence toward granting women of color a place in the Cuban social and political arena. Castellanos and Castellanos express it this way: "Villaverde could not withdraw himself from the judgment and prejudices of his class and his time, although one must say to his favor that he never gave them free reign" (*Cultura Afrocubana,* vol. 2, 221). Giral's cinematic enterprise restores visibility to the mulatta but does so by focusing exclusively on her sexual agency. A new paternalism emerges, this time rooted in an Afro-Cuban context. Giral's reliance on the intertextuality of Ifá divination as the structuring model for the film could have yielded an interpretation of Cuba's contemporary society that included gender. He fails in this respect because he defines María Antonia too narrowly.[34] At least for this viewer, the image of director as *babalao* points to patriarchal determinism rather than to the diviner's ability to open new roads.

Like Cirilo Villaverde before him, Sergio Giral creates a mythic character that highlights the general issue of race and consequently forsakes the individual female subject. In his *Neither Black nor White Yet Both,* Werner Sollors defines the word *mulatto* thus: "The word "Mulatto," of sixteenth-century Spanish origin, documented in English since 1595, and designating a child of a black and a white parent, was long considered etymologically derived from "mule"; yet it may also come from the Arabic word *muwallad* (meaning 'Mestizo' or mixed)" (127–28). The image of the Cuban mulatta, prominently featured in these two works produced roughly a hundred years apart, positions the Afro-Cuban female subject at two diametrically opposed poles of the racial divide. Villaverde creates a sexist image of the mulatta: "Female sexuality, as it is externalized and encoded in specific details of *both* skin and dress, can then be valorized, on the basis of visual evidence, as moral degeneracy—Villaverde's equation of voluptuousness with presumed lack of moral fortitude is a case in point" (Kutzinski, *Sugar's Secrets,* 65). Giral foregrounds that image by contextualizing it within a valorized Afro-Cuban context. In artistic terms, both creators continue to present the image of the mulatta in its most derogatory sense, meaning that the mulatta is made to carry the burden of being a national icon as defined by paternalistic interests.[35]

Only when Afro-Cuban women represent themselves as subjects of the Cuban nation does their objectification cease. As with Giral, the artistic enterprise of such women as Morejón, Rolando, Ayón, Saldaña, and Campos-Pons is deeply rooted in Afro-Cuban signification. But before embarking on a presentation of their works, I find it necessary to present Lydia Cabrera's *El Monte* as a work in which Afro-Cuban modes of remembrance find expression.

2   *El Monte*

A Matrix for Cultural Encounters

LYDIA CABRERA'S 1954 work *El Monte* [The Sacred Wilderness], with its subtitle, Notes on Religions, Music, Superstitions and Folklore of the Creole Negroes and the People of Cuba, presents, according to Cabrera in her introduction, what "I have heard and seen with absolute objectivity and without prejudices" (10).[1] The ethnographer inserts clear autobiographical interventions to establish her own authority while also representing her informants as subjects by identifying them with their names. Her introduction raises issues inherent in ethnographies, such as that of fidelity of representation and of recording the actual voices of the informants without the "dangerous filter" of interpretation. Cabrera declares that in order to gain the trust of the elders, she had to begin to think like them. In this she separates herself from established ethnographic practices. For example, Bronislaw Malinowski purports to observe closely, but to write from a distance. Cabrera, more akin to women ethnographers in the United States, such as Ruth Benedict, ultimately became transformed by the experience she recorded. She states that the voices she records may at times seem contradictory or repetitious. She refuses to edit these contradictions and, in leaving them intact, claims she supports her informants' insistence on imposing their own methodology. Finally, Lydia Cabrera declares that her work intends to transform the image of blacks in Cuba. She begins by making clear that her use of the word *negro* (the Spanish word) is meant to dispossess it of its derogatory connotations and give the black informant the authority to record the influence of African diaspora cultures at the heart of Cubanness.

El Monte, which I consider here as a paradigm for Cabrera's entire ethnographic work, consists of ten chapters that define Afro-Cuban beliefs, rituals, songs, and language. Throughout, it concentrates on multiple definitions of cultural practices that originated in the Yoruba and Bantu cultures in West Africa and were transformed by the Cuban experience of slavery (see Isabel Castellanos). Early in the first chapter, dedicated to the definition of the word *monte* (Afro-Cuban forest/temple), Cabrera addresses the issue of a European hegemony that doubts the contributions of blacks in Cuban culture and that relegates African diaspora beliefs to the realm of atavistic superstitions. In so doing, because she is part of that European milieu, she exposes her own prejudices and alerts the reader to do the same.

Most chapters begin with an introduction to the subject, including the definition of Afro-Cuban terms. Her intent is to prepare the reader for the testimony of the elders who are named and introduced as subjects to be respected as living exponents of a culture. She differentiates the practices of the Yoruba from those of the Bantu regarding the uses in Havana and Matanzas provinces of herbs to heal and to counteract magical forces. She introduces the *orishas,* the deities of the Lucumí (Yoruba in Cuba) pantheon; describes sacred ceremonies, the practices of initiation and possession; the preparation of *ñgangas,* receptacles that hold the spirits; and the importance of the palm tree and the silk cotton tree *(ceiba)* as receptacles of the sacred. The second half of the book collects the names of more than 450 plants used by practitioners for medicinal and spiritual purposes. It also includes photographs of sacred objects and practices, as well as an index.

The ethnographer Morton Marks asserts that "The remarkable achievement of Lydia Cabrera is that her works can be read as literature, folklore, ethnography, ethnohistory, ethnobotany and ethnopharmacology" (244).[2] Marks's assertion regarding the multiplicity of discourses that Cabrera utilizes in her writing of *El Monte* points to a late-twentieth-century consciousness in the field of anthropology of the ethnographer as writer. This consciousness has been recorded by James Clifford and George E. Marcus in their critical anthology *Writing Culture: The Poetics and Politics of Ethonography,* by Clifford Geertz in *Works and Lives: The Anthropologist as Author,* and by Ruth Behar and Deborah A. Gordon in *Women Writing Culture.* These writers concentrate on the second moment of what Clifford Geertz describes in a deadpan manner as "the archetypal moments in ethnographical experience, soaking it up and writing it down" (83).

In writing it down, anthropologists from Bronislaw Malinowski to Ruth Benedict vacillate between the description of "the Other" gleaned from field notes and the description of the ethnographer's own experience in his or her desire to establish authority. Writers like Malinowski catalog the ethnographic experience at the beginning of the text in an effort to assert the authority of having "been there." The autobiographical moment disappears to give way to the more "objective" description of what was observed and interpreted.

Clifford Geertz, however, questions the ethnographer's ability to separate one voice from the other: "Though it is, of course, part of my argument (the heart of it in fact) that the relation between *ars intelligendi*, the art of understanding, and the *ars explicandi*, the art of presentation, is so intimate in anthropology as to render them at base inseparable" (46 n. 18). Thus, Geertz emphasizes ethnographic writing as paramount to the anthropological enterprise. But lest anthropology be reduced to the mere creation of texts, whether they purport to be literary, ethnographic, ethnohistoric, and so forth (to return to Morton Marks), Clifford Geertz suggests that the future of anthropology lies in the possibility of "enabling conversations across societal lines—of ethnicity, religion, class, gender, language, race" (147). In his concluding chapter to *Works and Lives*, "Being There," Geertz sees "the next necessary thing" in anthropology in the following statement: "It is to enlarge the possibility of intelligible discourse between people quite different from one another in interest, outlook, wealth, and power, and yet contained in a world where, tumbled as they are into endless connection, it is increasingly difficult to get out of each other's way" (147).

It is within this context of an almost utopian enterprise of cultural encounters that I approach Lydia Cabrera's writing of *El Monte*. Her methodology, carefully laid out in her introduction, of allowing her informants to speak and to determine the way she writes about their experience and her own, promises to produce a multivocal text that Geertz, writing in the 1980s, anticipates for the future of anthropology. Cabrera, who wrote her introduction in 1954, reveals a consciousness regarding the polyvocality of her ethnographical writing that was later to be made self-evident by anthropological debates in the 1980s and 1990s in the United States. In response to James Clifford and George E. Marcus's *Writing Culture: The Poetics and Politics of Ethnography* (1986), in which multiple writers address the issue of ethnography as "hybrid textual activity" (26), Ruth Behar, in her introduction to the collection *Women Writing Culture* (1995), asserts that women anthropologists throughout the first half of the twentieth century had already tackled and achieved goals that the male canon places in the future: "In an act of sanctioned ignorance, the category of the new ethnography failed to take into account that throughout the twentieth century women had crossed the border between anthropology and literature—but usually "illegally," as aliens who produced works that tended to be viewed in the profession as "confessional" and "popular" or, in the words of Virginia Woolf, as "little notes" (quoted in Behar, 4). In regard to what has come to be classified as literary interventions in anthropology and women's consequent professional status within the field, Behar goes on to say: "Abu-Lughod suggested that the alternative 'women's tradition' of ethnographic writing, which is both literary and popular, is associated with the 'untrained' wives of anthropologists, from whom feminist anthropologists need to detach themselves in order to assert their professional status" (14). I use these two quotations to place Lydia Cabrera, not as a consciously feminist anthropologist like Behar, but as a woman who was an "untrained" ethnographer and who "had crossed the border between anthropology and literature."

Cabrera (1900–1991), who grew up in Havana as the youngest in the intellectually rich household of Raimundo Cabrera y Bosch and Elisa Bilbao Marcaida y Casanova, was home-schooled and self-taught as an ethnographer. Starting at the age of fourteen, Cabrera wrote a social column, "Nena en Sociedad" [A Child in Society], in her father's prestigious magazine *Cuba y América*. From early on, her main interest was in the arts. She attended the Havana art school, Academia de San Alejandro, between 1915 and 1916, and prepared herself for her baccalaureate diploma in 1917. After her father's death in 1923, she attended L'École du Louvre in Paris (1927–30) with funds she raised from her own interior decorating firm, Alyds. The 1922 Salón de Bellas Artes showed her artistic works, and that same year, with other associates, she founded the Cuban Association of Retrospective Art [Asociación Cubana de Arte Retrospectivo].

Between 1927 and 1938 Cabrera lived in France, Spain, and Italy with sporadic visits back to Havana. The Cuban writer Alejo Carpentier remembers her attendance at an Abakuá procession in 1927 in the company of her brother-in-law, renowned ethnographer Fernando Ortiz.[3] During her stay in Europe, under the influence of modernism, with its interest in African and Asian arts, Cabrera, at the insistence of Venezuelan writer and friend Teresa de la Parra, began writing her folktales based on Afro-Cuban legends she had heard from the black servants in her household. Her first book of short fiction was published in translation in Paris in 1936 and later in Spanish in 1940, *Cuentos negros de Cuba* [Black Stories from Cuba].

According to the critic of Afro-Cuban culture Isabel Castellanos, Cabrera's interest in Afro-Cuban cultures can be attributed to three factors: her studies of Asian art while in Paris, her contact with European arts and their "discovery" of Africa between the world wars, and Teresa de la Parra's influence (introduction to Cabrera, *Páginas sueltas*, 37–38). During those years spent in Europe, where she read H. Frobenius and other Africanists (see her essay "La influencia africana en el pueblo de Cuba" [African Influence on the Cuban People] published in *Páginas sueltas*, 541–50), Cabrera returned to Cuba on several occasions to see her mother, and in 1930 she began to establish her first contacts with her informants and started collecting her field notes (*Páginas sueltas*, 37). According to Castellanos in her introduction to *Páginas sueltas:* "From the start, ethnography and narrative are intimately linked" (39; my translation). Upon her return to Havana in 1938, with her mother dead and her inheritance dwindled, Cabrera and her life companion, María Teresa de Rojas, embarked on the restoration of the Rojas property, the Quinta San José. The Quinta, located in the vicinity of Pogolotti, Marianao, where Cabrera did her fieldwork, housed a collection and restoration of colonial arts and artifacts that would become a museum.

Between 1942 and 1946, Cabrera established a close relationship with Wifredo Lam, who, like her, had returned to Cuba from Paris during the war. In 1943, Cabrera and Lam collaborated on the translation of Aimé Césaire's 1939 work *Cahier d'un retour au pays natal* ("Retorno al País Natal"). She also promoted Lam's works, which were not readily accepted in high Cuban society because of their subject matter. In her reviews in *Diario de la Marina* [Daily from the Marina], she pointedly asks: "Why does Wifredo Lam, Cuban, the only Cuban painter of this generation truly renowned and admired outside of Cuba, the most unrecognized of painters in Cuba, why does he not show his works in his country? Why is he silenced?" (*Páginas sueltas*, 265). Through her statements about Lam, Cabrera also expressed the rejection she experienced from her family and friends when it was evident that her work with Afro-Cubans in the Pogolotti neighborhood went beyond a passing interest. During these years, Lam and Cabrera explored together the meaning of *el monte* in the practices of the African diaspora in Cuba. Lam would, of course, produce *La jungla* [The Jungle] in 1943.[4] With a dedication to the Cuban ethnographer Fernando Ortiz, Cabrera published *El Monte* in 1954.

Following Fidel Castro's rise to power in 1959, Cabrera and Rojas left the island in 1960, never to return. During her exile in Miami, after almost a decade of silence that she later recorded in her 1977 memoir *Itinerario del insomnio: Trinidad de Cuba* [Itinerary of Insomnia: Trinidad, Cuba], Cabrera re-edited *El Monte* and published more than twenty works of ethnography and fiction. Upon leaving Cuba, almost as if anticipating that she would never return, she collected all her field notes and carried them out of the country in her French trunk. Before her death in 1991, she received several honorary degrees from U.S. universities, and in 1976 the Congress of Afro-American Literature was held in her honor.

Cabrera's works in many respects fall within what Behar has termed the "'women's tradition' of ethnographic writing" (14). The essays in *Women Writing Culture,* with a section devoted to the analysis of works by women anthropologists mentored by Franz Boas at Columbia University in New York, point to ethnographers who at times in their professional careers were dismissed because of their writing polyphonic anthropology: incorporating the ethnographer's experience as well as the informants' with a narrative voice too literary compared to the more sanctioned texts (Malinowski's, for example). In describing Elsie Clews Parsons's early work, Louise Lamphere refers to her style as "ethnographic detail that was written up in this polyphonic Boasian mode," which "recognizes the position of the ethnographer and gives voice to her informants" (93). Cabrera's narrative methodology is not unlike that of the mostly older women who worked under Boas, who practiced textual innovations such as "first person narration, multivocality, transcription of dialogue, reflection on the impact of the ethnographer's feeling with subjects and interlocutors" (Cole, writing about Ruth Landes, 181). Cole also points to the importance of considering other written materials such as "letters, diaries, memoirs, biographies, autobiographies, novels, poems and prefaces as ethnographic writing" (181). In this respect, I take Cole's lead and analyze Cabrera's *El Monte* in the context of her entire body of work, including her letters, interviews, and successive versions of *El Monte.* Moreover, I contend that while Cabrera includes her own autobiographical experience in the text, she does so not to follow a purely autobiographical impulse but to record what Graciela Hernández calls "the asymmetrical relationships that exist between researchers and the communities they study" (Hernández on Zora Neale Hurston, 151).

The clearest difference between Cabrera and the women writing from the Boasian school of anthropology lies in their conscious and ironic rendering of what Nancy C. Lutkehaus describes as Margaret Mead's "authorial subjectivity" (201). It is I, writing about Cabrera, who interprets

Cabrera's implicit construction of her own authorial subjectivity. It is I, profiting from the analytic contribution of the critics anthologized in *Women Writing Culture*, who can now make explicit what I consider to have been left implicit in Cabrera's writing: "the polyphonic Boasian mode" (Lamphere, 93). Cabrera developed her methodology from a fusion between her informant's own methodology and her own apprenticeship in the arts alongside such other outstanding figures interested in Afro-Cuban culture as Wifredo Lam, Nicolás Guillén, Fernando Ortiz, and Alejo Carpentier.[5]

Outstanding figures such as Ruth Benedict, reevaluated in Behar and Gordon's critical anthology, include Elsie Clews Parsons, Ruth Landes, Margaret Mead, and Zora Neale Hurston. Unlike Cabrera, these American anthropologists had received formal training with Boas, a thinker who was consciously transforming the conception of race within the field of anthropology. Without having been trained at Columbia University, Cabrera's writing on the issue of race reflects Boas's desire "to separate man's culturally acquired characteristics from his innate endowment" (Bunzel, 7).

In a lecture presented in the United States, "La influencia africana en el pueblo de Cuba" [African Influence on the Cuban People], Cabrera counteracts "the ethnocentrism of our 'superior race'" (*Páginas sueltas*, 541), to rectify widely held misconceptions about religious African diaspora practices in Cuba and to make evident the large extent of African diaspora contributions to Cuban culture. In her introduction to *El Monte*, she clarifies the fact that she does not employ the word *negro* (black) within a pejorative context; rather, she wishes to endow it with new meaning (10). Her writing addresses the two most disseminated stereotypes of Afro-Cubans in the early part of the twentieth century: the "*ñáñigos*," members of the secret Abakuá society organized by former slaves imported from the Calabar region of Nigeria, connoted in the minds of secular sectors of Cuban society a high incidence of criminality; and the "black witches," largely associated with human sacrifices, implied the sacrifice of infants in black magic. These stereotypes essentialize diversity of religious ethnic groups among Afro-Cubans (Yoruba and Bantu) into the homogeneity of cultural practices that are considered atavistic *ñáñiguismo*. She speaks directly to the fact that "the idea of the uncivilized black was a European invention" (*Páginas sueltas*, 544).

In order to dispel essentialist notions of Afro-Cubans, Cabrera purports to disappear from the text and let the informants represent themselves.[6] In her introduction to *El Monte*, Cabrera addresses issues of methodology and authority that may be traced throughout the entire text. She offers herself as a mouthpiece through which the voices of the "real" authors of Afro-Cuban culture may speak. Her concern is that the informants "may be heard without intermediaries" (7). She refers to them as "living documents" (8), direct descendants of those who made the Atlantic passage, whose testimonies she must preserve without "the dangerous filter of interpretation" (8). By referring to them as living documents, she appeals to the "objectivity" of representation that the social sciences, and in particular anthropology and ethnography, wish to maintain. Cabrera also implies an urgency in her task of recording the voices of informants whose living memory of things African will be lost with the coming generations as they transform African culture into Cuban culture. Even though she posits herself as a non-essentializing intermediary, being faithful to the words of the informants, she confesses that she "must clarify only those points which appear unintelligible to the secular observer" (8). With this statement, she crosses the line between objective observer and active authority in a nonself-reflexive manner and exposes the contradiction inherent in representing herself and the voice of the other.

Even though in her introduction Cabrera warns against her own and the reader's propensity to blur understanding based on preconceived notions about Afro-Cuban culture, her own voice betrays the tinted glass through which she perceives the highly valued information she disseminates. For example, Cabrera takes great pains to present Afro-Cuban practices as grounded in a diversity of cultures, mainly Yoruba and Bantu, yet there are enough instances of the use of the possessive adjective attached to her informants to illustrate ethnographic paternalism. A simple example opens a paragraph: "One of my old men" (176). When describing the act of possession, in which a person's body is inhabited by a deity, she speaks of the ease with which practitioners, black and white, fall into a trance; of their autosuggestive predisposition, which she believes to be congenital; of their puerile psychology; of their impressionable dispositions (30). In this particular instance, which is the exception rather than the rule in *El Monte,* Cabrera adopts the attitude of the European outsider who tends to point to certain psychological propensities on the part of Afro-Cubans.

Lydia Cabrera, member of the Cuban upper classes, recorded the voices of the Lucumí and the Bantu across class, gender, and racial lines. In order to minimize such differences, Cabrera takes pains to describe how it is that a white woman from the upper classes was able to gain the trust of her informants. To do so, she resorts to an inversion of roles. She posits herself as an apprentice and the informants as the teachers: "it's necessary to learn to understand them, that is, to learn to think like them" (8). Cabrera thus attempts to reverse the ethnographer/informant relationship by inverting the hegemonic hierarchies in the outsider/insider equation. In fact, Cabrera goes so far as to dissociate herself from the interpretative practices of the social sciences in order to present her work as "merely what I have heard and seen" (10). By presenting herself as a direct witness, she appears to place herself in the position of the native informant who is able to speak from first-person experience. In an intervention in which she speaks directly to the reader, Cabrera allows the reader to openly question any of the narratives that her informants put forth, stating that she is ready to believe them because she herself has witnessed events that verify their testimonies: "For my own part, I'm inclined to accept it as true, since I'm a witness to other events that may seem equally or much more unbelievable" (66). With this statement, Cabrera resorts to the often-used anthropological narrative that establishes "being there."

While attesting to the veracity of their voices through her personal experience, Cabrera claims that any methodology present in *El Monte* was set by the informants themselves (7). Editorial intervention for the sake of clarity would only serve the essentializing forces among white Cuban intellectuals that she wishes to counteract. Again, in her lecture "The African Influence on the People of Cuba," in her characteristically ironic tone, mainly reserved for her fiction and academic presentations, Cabrera states: "By pointing to the interest that things African provoked in the most illustrious circles of the world, I only pretend that, when I refer to Cuba, no compatriot who, perhaps unconsciously, still suffers from certain intellectual and racist prejudices upon hearing that our Island is strongly saturated with African influences, feels wounded in his pride" (*Páginas sueltas*, 545).

With these words, Cabrera emphasizes the fact that her presentation of authoritative voices attests to her task of rectifying the racist erasure of Afro-Cuban contributions to Cuban culture. Because in *El Monte* she includes both blacks and whites as equal contributors to national culture, she places her informants on the same authoritative plane as herself. In her particularly emotive ending to the same lecture delivered in the United States after her exile to Miami (1960), she exclaims: "Aché! [Power!] and long live free Cuba, white and black!" (*Páginas sueltas*, 550).

The entire text of *El Monte* is permeated by interventions sometimes explicit, other times unconscious, which displace the voice of the informant and engage in autobiographical strategies that emphasize Cabrera's role as an apprentice. In the second chapter, Cabrera narrates how she came to know Teresa M., Omí-Tomí, the informant who opened for her the doors to the world of Afro-Cuban culture (26–27). In this brief narration, Cabrera follows an intellectual coming-of-age format. She begins by paying homage to her father, under whose tutelage the young Cabrera became an intellectual and out of whose liberal practices she began to differentiate family behavior toward blacks from that of other whites. It is noticeable how in the text Cabrera speaks of white people's behavior toward blacks in those days as if she were not white as well. She also shows awareness that, in the first decades of the twentieth century, it would take a "miracle" for the black woman who sought legal assistance from Cabrera's father to win a case in the courts. Her father, unable to help her in legal terms, welcomed Omí-Tomí, as the family seamstress. The young Cabrera insistently questions Omí-Tomí on Afro-Cuban religions. Cabrera's inquisitive behavior as she asks questions regarding Lucumí practices, though defined as impertinent and indiscreet, differs from that of her father, who "took pity on the black client" and gave her a subservient position as seamstress in the household. The narrator acknowledges that Omí-Tomí was justified in assuming that Cabrera's questions could lead to a confirmation of racist assumptions, yet the informant ultimately realized that the inquiries were sincere and respectful. Cabrera's obvious respect for the subject is reflected in divulging the woman's two names, one used among whites, the other, truer name, among blacks. This initial scene of trust takes place within the Cabrera family home, a safe place for the white woman before she ventures into unknown territories. Once a trusting relationship was established, Cabrera was ushered into the inner circle of an initiation ceremony where she could observe and be guided toward understanding.

This entire scene first describes the unusual family surroundings in the Cabrera household that tolerated a questioning of prevailing racist attitudes, encouraged inquisitive behavior on the part of Cabrera, and fostered an intellectual environment from which Cabrera could venture out to explore and understand the then highly undermined Afro-Cuban cultural contributions. This passage is clearly meant to distance Cabrera from common racist assumptions held by whites in the first decades of the twentieth century and to establish her credibility as a willing student of African diaspora practices. It is also exemplary of her having gained a consciousness inherent in an intellectual coming-of-age story.

Cabrera's development of an open mind and her willingness to become an apprentice may be traced through the transformations of her text from a much shorter, first version of *El Monte* published in the *Revista Bimestre Cubana* in 1947 under the name "Eggüe o Vichichi Nfinda," and then reprinted by Isabel Castellanos in her edited *Páginas sueltas* (273–356). The earlier version is obviously less developed, but it already contains many of the sections that later appeared in the 1954 publication of the work. What is distinctly different in the two versions is the abundant number of footnotes in the 1947 version, some of which are incorporated into the main text of the 1954 version, but some of which are omitted. These are of an academic character, defining terms, providing historical context, and so on.

Of particular interest is footnote 21 (344–45). Toward the end of this footnote, Cabrera incorporates a highly autobiographical narration that divulges her own lack of sensitivity in one of her conversations with an informant. Here she exposes herself as having asked whether certain ceremonies require human sacrifices. Just as she asks the question, she is aware of her error. The consequences of such questioning lead to the loss of communication with the old informant, with Cabrera justifying his anger (344). In this 1947 passage, deleted in subsequent versions of the text, Cabrera confesses to having committed the unpardonable error that would betray her ambivalence regarding the belief that Congo (Bantu) practitioners engage in human sacrifice. Yet immediately after she affirms that "Of course, I do not believe it," Cabrera goes on to justify her curiosity by relating the criminal incident of the death of the child Zoila linked to the supposed black witch Bocú. Such incidents, Cabrera posits, could be responsible for the belief in a relationship between criminal activity and purported human sacrifices. She states that according to Bocú's black contemporaries, he was considered to be innocent. Yet she goes on to rely on the authority of Fernando Ortiz, who, "in his fundamental study of criminality in Cuba" (*Páginas sueltas*, 344, referring to the 1906 title *Los negros brujos* [Black Witches], considered sorcery as the breeding ground for criminality. Cabrera then postulates the possibility that criminals, and only criminals, could engage in such unspeakable sacrifices. After citing Ortiz, Cabrera relates the testimony of her informant Baró, who admitted that even if an African deity asked for human sacrifice, it could be convinced of accepting other offerings, such as a rooster. She finishes with an unequivocal denial that human sacrifices are an integral part of Afro-Cuban rituals (345).

Even though Cabrera begins and ends this section of the footnote with her denial of the existence of human sacrifice, the fact that she uses Ortiz's

Los negros brujos as an authority linking Afro-Cuban rituals to criminality forces the reader to analyze her denials further. Moreover, just after resorting to Ortiz's authority, Cabrera introduces her informant Baró's testimony, which entertains the possibility that African deities could request human sacrifice. The fact that a rooster's blood could substitute for the requested human blood may not have appeased the doubts on the part of her contemporary unenlightened white readers that Cabrera was trying to allay (345). Could Cabrera's implicit purpose in writing this passage be to counteract the fears that ran rampant after the death of the child Zoila? If so, why run the risk of confirming people's fears by presenting such ambivalent evidence? After all, Ortiz's *Los Negros Brujos* provides police records that imply the existence of human sacrifices on the part of *ñáñigos:* "In possession of certain privy information, the police captain undertook a search in a house of General Escario Street, close to the corner of San Miguel Street, household of A. R. Rl., and there they seized the skull of a child and a fragment of another skull" (209).

Ultimately, it is clear that the ambivalent 1947 passage, meant to rectify stereotypes, troubled the writer enough to edit it out of the later version of the text. This dissatisfaction, I believe, reflects an acknowledgment that her intellectual curiosity and interest at the time were still tainted with her own ambivalence. Her revision of the text could also have to do with her increased questioning of the value of Ortiz's assertions in *Los negros brujos*. Ortiz's positivist vision acknowledges the necessity to become acquainted with Afro-Cubans and their religions with the purpose of acculturating them. He even goes as far as "talking about their social redemption" (6; my translation). In his prologue to the 1917 edition of the work, he concludes, "And the author esteems the opportunity, as well, to diffuse more and more the knowledge of religious atavism that may delay the progress of the black population of Cuba, worthy of all efforts that one may make toward their true liberation: that of the mind" (7; my translation). His main task in *Los negros brujos*, then, entails the psychological transformation of an entire sector of the Cuban population so that they may be capable of joining Cuban society in its forward progress.

Even though Cabrera acknowledges Ortiz's authority, does she not contradict his study by her final denial of the existence of human sacrifice in Afro-Cuban practices? Perhaps the ambivalence apparent in this passage has more to do with dissociating herself from her relationship to Ortiz as an authority (he was also her brother-in-law), than with her own ambivalence as to whether to pursue a question that she knew to be laden with insensitivity. Perhaps her need to include Ortiz as an authority in the 1947 version had to do with the fact that her initial publication of *El Monte* bore an introduction by Ortiz that concluded, "The book that just appeared, is without a doubt one of the most informative and well documented that has been published in our fatherland about these dark and popular subjects and is very affectionately Cuban" (*Páginas sueltas,* 320; my translation). Is Cabrera perhaps attempting to clarify and rectify Ortiz's use of the words "dark subjects" as well as distancing herself from his positivism?

Moreover, after publishing *Los negros brujos,* Ortiz had to contend with severe criticism from Afro-Cubans. He stated: "Blacks felt it to be a work expressly against them, since it uncovered secrets thus far very hidden, as well as things sacred and revered, including customs which, taken out of context, could be embarrassing, and could lead to their collective contempt. I felt their hostility very close by, but it did not frighten me" (*Los negros brujos,* xviii; my translation). Clearly, Cabrera's intentions are to secure rather than alienate the trust of her informants. Furthermore, contrary to Ortiz's desire to acculturate Afro-Cubans, Cabrera's intent is to preserve the Afro-Cuban legacy as is, as integral to Cubanness. It is for this reason that, in her 1954 version, she must distance her work from that of Ortiz in *Los negros brujos.*

Most importantly, when Cabrera reedited her book, Ortiz had abandoned the positivism of his 1906 work and ultimately published his *Contrapunteo cubano: Tabaco y azúcar* [Cuban Counterpoint: Tobacco and Sugar] (1940, 1963) with an introduction by Bronislaw Malinowski. In "Towards a Reading of Fernando Ortiz's *Cuban Counterpoint,*" Enrico Mario Santí states, "Fernando Ortiz articulated in Cuba a 'critique of sugar.' It was not simply a reformist plea, but rather a full-blown critique of everything sugar meant; the industry's central power and its deleterious effects upon the entire breadth of Cuban society" (12). In his introduction to the 1995 English translation of the work, the Venezuelan anthropologist Fernando Coronil concludes by "remembering *Cuban Counterpoint* as a text in which 'cultural treasures,' as Walter Benjamin and Angel Rama recognized, cease to owe their existence exclusively to the works of elites and become, as products of a common history, the achievement of popular collectivities as well" (xlvii). In this respect, Cabrera and Ortiz share the ethnographic impulse of describing Cuban culture as the integral project of both blacks and whites as they come into contact with each other (transculturation). As Coronil rightly asserts, unlike Malinowski, who in his *Argonauts of the Western Pacific* (1922) writes about a culture in transformation from the Westerner's point of view (xxxiii), Ortiz in *Cuban Counterpoint* and, I contend, Cabrera, by extension, "view cultural transformations from a nonimperial perspective and support the claims of subject peoples" (xlvvii). So why does Cabrera in the 1970s still wish to dissociate herself from Ortiz's historical mode of anthropology? After all, she dedicated *El Monte* to Fernando Ortiz. In the 1970s, in an interview with Rosario Hiriart, Cabrera responded to the question whether it was Ortiz who led Cabrera to pursue her interests in African culture in Cuba, by saying, "No, Fernando did not lead me to those studies. . . . I repeat, it was in Paris where I began to be interested in Africa" (73).

In his essay on the "queer" space that Cabrera occupies in Cuban letters, José Quiroga addresses the fact that, particularly in his introduction to Cabrera's *Cuentos negros de Cuba,* Ortiz implicitly opposes his own "science" in his anthropological works to her "curiosity" about Afro-Cuban folklore in her short fiction: "Ortiz explains that the book is the first written by a woman 'whom we initiated in the taste for Afro-Cuban folklore.' For Ortiz, the distance marked by gender defines the author's work as a 'taste,' that is, a kind of 'hobby' rather than science or even creative endeavor" (96). What is curious is the fact that Ortiz should feel that he had initiated Cabrera into the field when it was Teresa de la Parra who encouraged the Cuban ethnographer to write the tales she related to Parra while the latter was dying of tuberculosis. *Cuentos negros de Cuba* was dedicated to Parra. Cabrera's reference to Paris in her answer to Hiriart aligns her work with the interest in Africa on the part of "enlightened circles of the world" and against the "intellectual and racist prejudices" of her compatriots ("La influencia africana," *Páginas sueltas,* 545). In view of Quiroga's interpretation, Cabrera's words regarding the "intellectual and racist prejudices" of her compatriots unmask Ortiz's sexism and homophobia, given Cabrera's unspoken lesbian relationship with Parra (for this relationship see Molloy, 238–48). Moreover, with these words, Cabrera demonstrates her ability to defend her performance of ethnography and autobiography with one phrase.

While in Paris, Cabrera participated in the avant-garde movements with their search for the exotic and the primitive in Asian and African arts. In her short stories, *Cuentos negros de Cuba,* Cabrera rescues countless Lucumí songs and legends in a matter-of-fact, humorous narrative style that came to be recognized much later as magic realism by Rosario Hiriart. According to the critic Isabel Castellanos, "Cabrera's short stories surprise the reader by the overflowing nature of a fabulous imagination"

(*Páginas sueltas,* 64). In his introduction to the Spanish edition of her stories, Fernando Ortiz characterizes them as a collaboration between black folklore and its Spanish translator. Alejo Carpentier, in his commentary for *Carteles,* asserts that her stories place "Caribbean mythology in the category of universal values" and describes her book as "an exceptional work in our literature" (quoted in Hiriart, *Vida hecha arte,* 38; my translation). The publication of *Cuentos negros de Cuba* established Lydia Cabrera as a leading exponent of the autochthonous in Latin America. The prestigious Paris publisher Gallimard brought out her short fiction along with Miguel Angel Asturias's *Leyendas de Guatemala* in 1936. Rosario Hiriart comments on the value of these two works for European audiences as capturing a Latin American vitality (humor for blacks and fatalism for the indigenous) through the authors' accomplished use of local lexicons that emphasize a particular language's rhythmic qualities rather than specific meanings: "They hold correspondences in their authors' accomplished use of vocabulary, in the creation of words emptied of meaning to achieve pure rhythm," and "Black ethos smiles in *Black Stories,* the indigenous is clothed in a vital fatalism in *Legends of Guatemala*" (Hiriart, 39, 40; my translation).

Even though Cabrera is well known for her ethnographic work, particularly for *El Monte,* it is for the literary impulse of her Paris years that she wants to be recognized, particularly when associated with Fernando Ortiz. Furthermore, her statement that she came to recognize the value of Afro-Cuban culture while in Paris refers any reader of Cuban literature to Alejo Carpentier's introduction to *El reino de este mundo* [The Kingdom of This World] in which the Cuban novelist discovers the "marvelous real" in Latin America after having traveled far and encountered many cultures: "And it is because of the virginity of its landscapes, of its makeup, of its ontology, of the splendid presence of the Indian and the black, of the revelations of its recent discovery, of the fruitful creolizations that it propitiated, that America is very far from having exhausted its wealth of mythologies. What else could the history of all of America be but a chronicle or the marvelous real?" (Carpentier, *Tientos y diferencias,* 119–20; my translation).[7] If, in Carpentier's oeuvre, narrative strategies of history and fiction contaminate and enrich each other, in Lydia Cabrera's work, ethnographic writing avails itself of narrative strategies prevalent in literature, particularly as it concerns itself with autobiography.[8]

Placing Cabrera's writing within a larger Cuban historical and cultural context highlights, as I see it, the transformation that she accomplished in revising the concept of race as it had been culturally constructed to justify racism. In *El Monte,* in a Boasian move, she proposes to observe the cultural practices of Afro-Cubans in their complexity, valorizing them and placing them in the context that Cuban European society has defined for itself. In the anthropological work of *El Monte,* the European is represented by the ethnographer herself, who posits her experience as that of an apprentice to her informant's knowledge.

In placing Cabrera's work within a larger societal context, I follow the lead of George E. Marcus, who suggests in "Contemporary Problems of Ethnography in the Modern World System" that ethnographers are "more interested in problems of cultural meaning than in social action" and therefore "have not generally presented the ways in which closely observed cultural worlds are embedded in larger, more impersonal systems" (165–66). Although it is true that Cabrera creates cultural meanings for herself and for Cubans, I suggest that, in implicit ways, Cabrera is responding to and addressing historical and sociopolitical events in her writing as well.

The most critical event that Cabrera as ethnographer must respond to, moreover, is not imprinted in *El Monte.* It is Fidel Castro's 1959 assumption of power in Cuba. In a revealing interview with Rosario Hiriart, Cabrera relates the incident that, on an unreasoned impulse, since she planned to return to Cuba after a short visit in Miami, she packed all her field notes in a French trunk:

> Packing my bags I saw one of those great French trunks with which we traveled before, and allowing myself to be swept by an inexplicable impulse, I filled it with all my field notes that I had compiled in my long years of conversations with the children and grandchildren of the Africans. I used to collect antique gold jewelry from the time I was very young, and, I put in the collection with the field notes. It seemed absurd . . . but that, the field notes, have allowed me to continue to write, and the collection of chains, bracelets, crosses, pins, etc., helped us to subsist for a while. (Hiriart, 167–68; my translation).

With this dramatic scene, she leaves us with a metaphor for her ethnographic enterprise after leaving the island. Cabrera's ethnographic observations for *El Monte* and many of her other works later published in Miami started in the 1930s. Presumably, her fieldwork stopped completely in 1960 when she left for Miami. Her ethnographic work was done primarily in the neighborhood of Pogolotti, close to her residence with Rojas in the Quinta, and in the province of Matanzas, near Havana. Her field of study is therefore circumscribed very close to home and for a period of about thirty years. Her research, unlike that of many ethnographers, did not take her far and wide to a pristine location where a culture could be said to be observed just as it is about to disappear because of Western influence, but rather in the context of a cosmopolitan milieu in the ethnographer's present. When Cabrera privileges the gesture of placing all her field notes in a trunk on the verge of her own political escape from communism, and away from her own reconstruction of a colonial past in the Quinta San José, she in fact creates a sort of metaphorical, spatial, and temporal capsule. She will not return to Cuba to witness any transformations that her informants or their culture may undergo as a result of the radical changes brought about by Castro's revolution. In *La laguna sagrada de San Joaquín* [The Sacred Pond of San Joaquín], Cabrera records her symbolic good-bye as one her most beloved informants waves to her: "—Olodumare ogbeo! the old Brígida yelled to us forever, upon turning on her ranch wagon, herself a "horse" of Yemayá Mayeleo, waving her blue handkerchief, blue like the sea that was about to separate us . . . forever, forever!" (105). This heartfelt good-bye records for Cabrera her ultimate departure from those who enriched her life with their culture and their trust. It also records the fact that Cabrera would not share in the fervor of a changing society with Wifredo Lam, Alejo Carpentier, and Fernando Ortiz, all of whom stayed and supported the revolution. In her essay on Teresa de la Parra, Sylvia Molloy also considers the issue of exile for prominent Latin American lesbians as an opportunity to write their difference:

> I would argue that Parra's lesbianism allows her to see clearly, and critically, into a Latin American modernity whose regimentation of sexualities *and* sensualities radically excludes her. In this light, Teresa de la Parra's exile—like that of Lydia Cabrera, of Gabriela Mistral, not to mention their North American counterparts—should be read as a political gesture, signifying much more than a circumstantial decision to live abroad. Geographic displacement offered what Venezuela for Parra, Cuba for Cabrera, and Chile for Mistral could not (cannot even now) give, that is, both a place to be (sexually) different and a place to write. Or perhaps, to put it more accurately, geographic displacement provided a place to write (however obliquely) one's difference. (248)

In Cabrera's case, writing about the Afro-Cuban experience allows her to write about her own marginality away from the increasingly male revolutionary zeal of the new man. The metaphor of the French trunk containing her life's work will provide Cabera the ethnographer with all the material that she will "unpack" in her ethnographic writings until close to her death in 1991. In that sense her field notes capture a time and a place that for Cabrera as an exile will never be recovered other than in her writing. In this respect Cabrera personifies what George Marcus has termed "the salvage mode," a mode of ethnographic study in which "the ethnographer portrays himself as 'before the deluge' so to speak. Signs of fundamental change are apparent, but the ethnographer is able to salvage a cultural stage on the verge of transformation" (Marcus, 165 n. 1).

In the 1970s, Afro-Cuban filmmaker Sara Gómez, in a docudrama called *De cierta manera* [One Way or Another] documents the social and economic transformation of a black neighborhood on the outskirts of Havana that was "saved" from its poverty and "backwardness" by the positive forces of the Cuban revolution. This neighborhood may easily have been Pogolotti. Despite the transformations brought about by the revolution, whether the culture recorded by Cabrera in her field notes in fact continued to survive is another matter.[9] What concerns me here is the context that Cabrera establishes for her ethnographic work vis-à-vis her decision to leave Cuba in 1960. My analysis of Cabrera's literary contribution to the field of ethnography, then, assumes Cabrera's salvage of Afro-Cuban cultures to be a progressive attitude regarding culture and race in Cuba. In 1960, however, she felt her views and her ethnographic work to be in peril.

I now wish to return to the methodology Cabrera presents in the introduction to *El Monte,* particularly in relation to the author's desire to establish the authority of her informants' narratives in relationship to her own. Numerous critics who concentrate on the study of *testimonios* and testimonial literature in Latin America have already pointed out the presence of literariness in the language of the social sciences. The critic Alicia Andreu, for example, analyzes the contradiction inherent in the anthropologist David Stoll's critique of Nobel Peace Prize–winner Rigoberta Menchú's testimony as laden with fictional assertions. Andreu describes Stoll's *Rigoberta Menchú and the Story of All Poor Guatemalans* thus: "Just like Menchú's testimony, Stoll's study consists of a multiplicity of texts where two or more dissonant and sometimes incompatible sociocultural universes crisscross in a combative manner" (41; my translation). Exemplifying this multiplicity of texts present in Stoll's book, Andreu cites those representative of the Maya Quiché culture, permeated with their mythological language; the narratives of the Guatemalans that Stoll interviews; historical and political texts; as well as narratives recollected by informants laden with literary figures such as hyperbole, synecdoche, and repetition. Finally, Andreu points to Stoll's autobiographical voice and its use of possessive adjectives to establish his own intellectual authority above that of Menchú.

As a counterpoint to her analysis of Stoll's book, Andreu turns to Ruth Behar's anthropological study *Translated Woman: Crossing the Border with Esperanza's Story*. Behar establishes a new relationship between the informant, Esperanza, who constructs oral narratives, and the anthropologist Behar, who recollects those narratives through writing. Behar posits herself as a translator of the Mexican panhandler Esperanza, who tells her life story. Behar's *Translated Woman* thus constitutes a hybrid genre, characterized by a duality of voices. Behar emphasizes that Esperanza's oral narrative, as located in the book, moves between two forms of expression, the oral and the written, between two discourses, the popular and the scientific, between two cultures, Mexico and the United States, between two languages, Spanish and English, and is bereft of the anthropological authority that sees itself as promoting an informant's life story (Andreu, 51). Finally, Behar concludes that her function as an anthropologist was dictated by Esperanza herself: "my comadre left me the task of putting the words down in this book" (Behar as quoted in Andreu, 53).

Behar's contribution to anthropology is that, in her ethnographic writing, she interjects her own life story and how she came to gain the authority to translate Esperanza's story. My analysis of Lydia Cabrera's construction of her own authority is thus indebted to Alicia Andreu's readings of two styles of anthropological research and writing at the end of the twentieth century, one that seeks to undermine the authority of the informant in order to establish that of the anthropologist (Stoll) and one that presents its own authority as working in tandem with that of the informant (Behar). Andreu's presentation of these two paradigms allowed me to gain insight into Ortiz's desire to place himself morally above the voices of black criminals in *Los negros brujos* in parallel to Stoll's enterprise. Likewise, Andreu's analysis of Behar's methodology helped me to illuminate Cabrera's tendency to wish to disappear so that the voices of the informants could speak for themselves, while at the same time interjecting her own autobiographical account as to how she gained the authority to tell the "life story" of Afro-Cuban cultures.

In her introduction to *El Monte*, Cabrera insists that the informants themselves have imposed their methodology, with their narratives full of explanations and digressions (7). At the end of chapter 7, dedicated to the silk cotton tree, Cabrera concludes: "Whoever has had the patience to follow the *explanations and digressions* of our guides will hold the name of the silk cotton tree as the perfect type of the sacred tree" (194; my emphasis). A clear example of this ability to digress on the part of Cabrera's informants becomes explicit in chapter 8, where most of the chapter, rather than being about the Abakuás and the sacred tree, is about describing the Abakuá and dealing with the stereotype of the *ñáñigo*.

Right away, Cabrera, appropriating her informants' propensity to digress, resorts to an Anglo-Saxon authority from the nineteenth century to present a view of the *ñáñigos* that is contrary to that held by most Cubans early in the twentieth century: "very industrious and avaricious; also choleric and hasty in temper. Most of the free Negroes in the island who are rich belong to this tribe" (195). Here, Cabrera seems to address Ortiz's depiction of the *ñáñigo* as criminal and emphasizes their industrious nature. Cabrera is also careful to point out that contemporary Afro-Cubans have the same concept of *ñáñigos* as did the outsider: "The *ñáñigos* are the Masons of Africa, and we the Cubans, their descendants" (199). The informant goes on to imply that Spaniards cannot be trusted because they profited from the associations that the secret society afforded them, then denied them in their ascent to power. Finally, Cabrera's informant concludes: "In true conscience, no one who knows it in depth can say that *ñañiguismo* is bad because its rules are bad. It is humanity that is bad, if you would excuse my saying so" (200).

By compiling a series of authorial statements, beginning with a European statement and following with an Afro-Cuban one, Cabrera abolishes hierarchies between the European and the Afro-Cuban authorities. Even though the chapter begins with a clear digression from the subject of the *ceiba* (silk cotton tree), the core of the chapter has a very clear focus, that of denying *ñáñigo* stereotypes and of clarifying for the outsider the true nature of the Abakuá society, its myth of origin, and practices. In her aim to clarify, Cabrera resorts to at least two forms of authority, one European, to satisfy any doubts on the part of the European reader, and one indigenous, to establish Cabrera's desire for veracity and full understanding.

The narrative sequence may be classified as digressive because of its reliance on oral narrative conventions that may appear at first not to follow the logic of a written text, but that nonetheless repeat a truth from various points of view. Cabrera's text is full of multiple versions of the lives of the deities *(patakines)*, of myths of origins, and so forth. She introduces each myth in such a way as to emphasize the fact that veracity lies in the multiplicity of versions. Here are but two examples of her approach: "according to another version" (79); "it would not occur to us to disprove the informant who assures us" (276); and so on.

At the root of this multiplicity of versions stands the validity of a collective memory that preserves cultural traditions and myths as practiced and remembered from ancient times: "nothing is done that is not established in the knowledge that was created at the beginning. That is, in the *illo tempore* of all myths" (286). By classifying the informant's methodology in the context of mythological narratives, Cabrera points to the creative impulse that drives her informants to narrate. Moreover, she describes for the reader the narrative structures utilized by the Abakuá that privilege a polyvocal rather than a univocal authority. In making explicit the Abakuá's strategies as authoritative (because they have persisted throughout the ages), Cabrera establishes their authority as a priori in her text.

At the crux of the narrative strategy found in *El Monte* stands the necessity to establish a relationship of trust between the informant and the listener: "whites want the mystery" (137). To begin with, Cabrera acknowledges that all information she has received may not be accurate. In her introduction to *El Monte* she thanks those informants who agreed to collaborate with her, "opening the doors to a world so different from [hers]" (10), but she also appreciates "those who tried to trick [her]" (11), because their contributions were no less charged with charm and verve. Cabrera explains that each informant sets up a methodology meant ultimately to arrive at the truth, a truth that may even be found in lies. The white person who wishes to inquire about Afro-Cuban practices must be aware that informants often omit and alter details when providing information. Such a recognition implies a certain amount of knowledge already gained on the part of the listener. The listener must then insist and continue to ask questions, ask for clarification in the answers, and consult with several authorities (137). The informant explains the road to understanding by resorting to a popular saying: "walk along a long road to go on amassing the truth, piece by piece, which is scattered everywhere" (137). The procedure follows a dialogical narrative, based on a back-and-forth that is meant to establish the listener's real interest despite the fact that she may not be willing to become a member of the religion. With this passage, then, Cabrera gives the reader another clue as to how she arrived at her own understanding of informants' narratives and how the reader may also become adept at understanding a text that may appear to be full of lies, digressions, and inaccuracies. Through the words of one of her informants, Cabrera thus provides a hermeneutics for the reading of *El Monte*.

Understanding in *El Monte* must be gleaned in its multiplicity of versions, some of which are clearly not meant to be reliable. An example of Cabrera's ability to discern between true and false practices concerns possession. This refers to the practice in which a particular deity takes possession, or mounts, the body of a practitioner in order to reveal himself to those present at a spiritual session where drums are played and offerings are made (a *bembé*). Cabrera, again in an autobiographical mode, speaks of her first witnessing such a possession, which filled her with fear because the person fell to the ground and appeared dead (37). Those around Cabrera assured her that any violence done to the possessed would not be felt by the person mounted because the force of the deity does not harm the person's body: "It's nothing, child. It's a real deity" (38). Just as there are "real" deities that take possession, Afro-Cuban people recognize that there are individuals who fake an act of possession, and they are referred to as *"Santicos de mentiritas"* (little fake or simulated lying deities) (38). Those that do not signify a true possession by a real deity are characterized "as the worst of actors" (38). Those faked possessions grow out of the necessity of practitioners to participate in the ceremonies, particularly in those where a real deity does not choose to possess any of those present. Such simulations are then accepted as a substitute for the real thing, yet are recognized as mere substitutions: "When the truth is missing one has to conform with lies, as one may say, in the absence of bread, cassava bread" (39). Such simulations are done, not in the spirit of deception, but in the spirit of propitiating the coming of a real deity to the gathering. This act of simulation to arrive at a true possession points to the theatrical nature of Afro-Cuban cultural narratives and practices.

Even though in *El Monte* the vast majority of myths, legends, and ceremonies are presented in oral narrative form, these are sometimes illustrated through scenes with multiple "actors" dramatizing an event in the life of the deity *(orisha)*. Cabrera presents this performative impulse with a dramatic exchange taking place between Elegguá, the keeper of the doors and all roads, and several other *orishas*. They would enter his house and abuse his hospitality by eating all the offerings left by those who came to consult with him regarding the direction of their lives. Elegguá, tired of eating the leftover bones, decides to shut his door to the ungrateful *orishas,* but then the offerings cease to come as well. Ochún, the deity of love and sensuality, intercedes, urging Elegguá to open the door again for consultations, and the offerings would continue to come. Elegguá opens his door, and enough offerings showered his house for all to be fed. When telling of this incident in the life of Elegguá, practitioners play with the repetition of scenes with different variants, one in which Elegguá opens the door, another in which he does not (82).

> "Good morning Elegguá. Is Ochún in?"
> "Yes, come in. And he would open the door for them."
> "Good morning Elegguá. Is Yemayá in?"
> "Yes, come on in." (81)
>
> "Good morning Elegguá. Is Regla in?"
> "She's not in."
> "Good morning Elegguá. Is Caridad in?"
> "She no longer lives here."
> "Good morning Elegguá. Is Merced in?"
> "She's off on a trip". (82)

This form of repetition points to the formulaic and dramatic nature of oral narratives with the purpose of facilitating the memory of a dramatic mode of representation (other such dramatic scenes may be found on pages 155 and 224 of *El Monte*).

Acts of possession themselves can be construed as dramatic scenes in which an *orisha* represents his own powers. For example, Cabrera describes a scene of possession in which Changó, the deity of fire, lightning, and war, reveals himself as he mounts a large woman: "Seized by convulsions, the large woman snorted and hit her head. . . . She got up, and that raging bulk, moved by an extraordinary amount of energy, inconceivably agile, performed several forward rolls" (38). This performance acts out the power of a specific deity; dances may also reenact myths of origin, as with the Abakuá *(ñáñigos),* who are particularly known for their performances involving dance and elaborate costumes during the celebration of the Feast of the Three Kings or even just before the time of an election.[10]

Cabrera describes the impression these dances leave on the European observer: that of a performance worthy of García Lorca's poetic imagination or Diaghilev's dance productions (217). With Lorca and Diaghilev, Cabrera stands back and sees the performance as an aesthetic experience, not as a dance representing mythical and religious meanings. Here, like a poet and an artist, and not as an observer who wishes to understand a culture, Cabrera reverts to her experience of modernism in Paris, which through the appropriation of "primitive" cultural artifacts hoped to endow the arts with an authenticity and a spirituality missing in the modern world. Even while standing next to a Lorca who responds through poetic means to the experience, Cabrera aims to counteract the classification of these performances as primitive and obscure by pointing to their value as spectacle: "It is an incredible spectacle, disconcerting and lamentable for many who feel that *ñañiguismo* represents a national shame" (216). Unlike most other times when Cabrera's voice enters the text, here she cannot help but make an aesthetic value judgment in order to dispel stereotypes. In this telling instance Cabrera's *El Monte* engages in ethnographic as well as artistic ways of narrating. Most importantly, however, she points to the value of performativity inherent in Afro-Cuban culture, a value that did not go unnoticed by Cabrera's contemporary Alejo Carpentier, who choreographed African diaspora dances.[11]

Even though Cabrera insists that it is her informants who impose whatever methodology dominates the narrative, her presence is felt as the ethnographer who clarifies, indulges in autobiographical narrations to define her subservient authority, points to narrative strategies in her informant's testimonies, guides the reader in ways of understanding the truth under apparent contradictions, and confronts "European" ethnocentric misconceptions and racist assumptions. To counterbalance her interventions as literary narrator, there are hundreds of pages in which her multiple informants are indeed allowed to speak. For the reader, her interventions regarding narrative strategies are invaluable because they lay bare a hermeneutics developed over centuries in Cuba to preserve the memory of a time when African diasporic cultures flourished in the absence of constant racist attacks. These narrative strategies, rooted in polyphony, self-preservation through simulation of inauthenticity, and the performative rituals, gain authoritative status in *El Monte* because they coexist with Cabrera's autobiographical interventions in a nonhierarchical manner. Ultimately, Cabrera has created a narrative persona that functions as an apprentice and transcriber of Afro-Cuban culture.

I have concentrated thus far on how *El Monte* may be read as a narrative that, to paraphrase the critic Alicia Andreu's words when describing Ruth Behar's text, moves between two forms of expression, the oral and the written; between two discourses, the ethnographic and the literary; between two cultures, Euro-Cuban and Afro-Cuban; between two languages, Spanish and Afro-Cuban; with the intent of allowing the other to speak in a written text. Ultimately, Lydia Cabrera's greatest legacy in *El*

Monte, a text paradigmatic of her extensive ethnographic oeuvre, lies in her having produced an "open-ended dialogic work" (Marcus, 166 n. 2) in which the single voice of a Cuban self-taught ethnographer enters into dialogue with and gives voice to the polyphonic voices of her informants. In an extensive footnote regarding experimental work in ethnography, George Marcus could be giving us an insightful description of Cabrera's writing strategies: "Dialogic interchanges between ethnographer and other, the sharing of textual authority with subjects themselves, auto-biographical recounting as the only appropriate form of merging other cultural experience with the ethnographer's own—these are all attempts to change radically the way the conventional subject matter of ethnography has been constituted in order to convey authentically other cultural experience" (168 n. 5).

Cabrera has constructed a highly authored text, particularly in those moments when she merges the voice of her informants with her own. Such autobiographical interventions allow her to bare her own preconceived ideas regarding her subjects as she approaches an unknown culture. As I have shown, her consciousness of the cultural complexity in the narrations and in the ritual performances of her informants creates a transparency in her text that divulges the Afro-Cuban self-reflexive culture. The cultural critic Mary Louise Pratt could be describing Cabrera as she speaks of Firth and Malinowski: "What Firth and Malinowski (his teacher) seem to be after is a kind of *summa,* a highly textured, total-izing picture anchored in themselves, where "self" is understood not as a monolithic scientist-observer, but as a multifaceted entity who partici-pates, observes, and writes from multiple, constantly shifting positions" (39). Thus, Cabrera shifts from using such now objectionable phrases as "my old blacks" to the gesture of the ethnographer who allows those same informants to confront her preconceptions in ways that will prompt her to "edit" out her own insensitivities regarding purported human sacrifices. Such "insensitivities" are later published in *Páginas sueltas,* allowing the reader to see the ethnographer in her vulnerable moments.

Lydia Cabrera's legacy presents for the reader the interpretative systems of Afro-Cuban cultures. Her analytical presentation of her informants' narratives, rather than foreground the passage from the oral to the writ-ten, as most early anthropology purports to do, points to her informants' practice of self-reflexivity inherent in their cultural narrations. Thus, Cabrera implicitly records what James Clifford, after Derrida, describes as the fact that "cultures studied by anthropologists are already writing themselves" (118). Clifford explains:

There is no need here to pursue in detail a disorienting project that is by now well known. What matters for ethnography is the claim that *all* human groups write—if they articulate, classify, possess an 'oral literature,' or inscribe their world in ritual acts. They repeatedly "textualize" meanings. Thus in Derrida's epistemology, the writing of ethnography cannot be seen as a drastically new form of cultural inscription, as an exterior imposition of a "pure," unwritten oral/aural universe. The logos is not primary and the *gramme* its mere secondary representation. (117–18)

In *El Monte* Cabrera inscribes Afro-Cuban cultures' ability to textualize meanings in their narratives and in their highly performative rituals. *El Monte* records in ethnographic fashion what literary critics such as Henry Louis Gates Jr., Julia Cuervo Hewitt, José Piedra, and Eugenio Matibag have termed as the highly sophisticated art of signifying in the Ifá interpretative system. The Ifá system was used and transformed by Afro-Cuban writers and artists throughout the twentieth century in Cuba.[12] In her groundbreaking work on the influence of *Yoruba-Lucumí* interpretive systems on Cuban literature, Cuervo Hewitt states: "As it occurs with Ifá, in which the recitations of the oracle (word) and the mythological character of the great Babalao Orula (narrator and voice) are confused, so too, in Cuban narrative, there arises a complex relationship between text and author" (285; my translation). Matibag expresses the same in this manner: "In Ifá, one performs a discursive, intertextual act in which myth and personal history are meant to interact through the medium of language" (151). In the pages to come, I record a few examples of this revisionary impulse in African diaspora practices as they intersect with autobiographical explorations by Cuban women during the second half of the twentieth century.

3   Cuban National Identity in Morejón, Rolando, and Ayón

THIS CHAPTER explores the critical work and essays of the eminent Afro-Cuban poet Nancy Morejón (born in Havana in 1944) as a gesture of mediation between the Afro-Cuban heritage that she fervently upholds and a Castro revolutionary mandate that constricts the space available for discussions and considerations of race. Castro's much quoted words are "Within the Revolution everything, against the Revolution nothing" (quoted by Luis, "Politics of Aesthetics," 35). Because in the new socialist revolution racism could not exist, discussion of race could not be tolerated. I argue that Morejón, within her fervent support of the revolution and need to gain status in its context, finds numerous if subtle ways to "discuss race" and to celebrate her African and female heritage. She opens the way for younger Afro-Cuban artists to consider issues of gender and race in a more open manner. I conclude the chapter with a consideration of two of these artists—the filmmaker Gloria Rolando and the visual artist Belkis Ayón.

Edward Mullen compares Morejón to Langston Hughes because "They are both important cultural mediators.[1] Who, one asks, explained so well to African Americans their position in American society as Hughes did in *The Ways of White Folks* (1931)? What Latin American writer has captured with such power—in so few lines—both the history of a nation and a sense of self and womanhood as did Morejón in 'Mujer negra'?" (4). According to Linda S. Howe, Morejón, "as an intellectual of cultural production," responds with "mechanisms and manners of speaking that simultaneously appear to be outside of, as well as within, the boundaries of cultural expression. Her ambiguous metaphors leave her intentionality up to the reader" ("The Fluid Iconography," 33). Howe describes a constant tension in Morejón's work that produces both politically committed and hermetic poems (32). This tension is particularly present in her poems and essays during the first fifteen years or so of the revolution, years marked by intolerance toward intellectuals. Examples are the censorship of Orlando Jiménez Leal's film *P.M.*, about the nightlife of Afro-Cubans, and the closing of the El Puente publishing house and group to which Morejón belonged and where she published her first two books (1965). Finally, these years were marked by the famous Padilla Affair in which Herberto Padilla was jailed in 1971 for his controversial collection of poems *Fuera del Juego,* published in 1968 (Luis, "Politics of Aesthetics," 35). According to Howe, a group of Afro-Cuban intellectuals met during the 1960s to discuss issues of race and to draft a "Black Manifesto" to be delivered at the opening of the World Cultural Congress in January 1968. Morejón did not belong to this group, but those who did were chastised and not allowed to attend the congress ("Nancy Morejón's *Womanism,*" 159).

Starting in 1975, with the First Congress of the Communist Party, there was an opening of sorts, marked by Castro's new relationship to the exiled community in Miami. This opening served as an opportunity for young artists like María Magdalena Campos-Pons to create iconography against the establishment, but this artistic generation of the 1980s finally opted for leaving the country. After the collapse of the Soviet Union, the Fundación Pablo Milanés promoted many black intellectuals and artists, but it too lasted only two years (1993–95). In 1993 Morejón left Casa de las Américas to become an editor at the Fundación, but she later returned to Casa. Howe states that Morejón's desire to work with the Pablo Milanés Foundation "demonstrates her determination to effect change in Cuba" (164). Overall, Afro-Cubans who remained in Cuba, like Morejón, are critical of times, from the 1960s to the 1990s, when the institutional government supported black independence movements yet did not allow its black intellectuals to speak openly about their Afro-Cuban identity (see Howe, "Nancy Morejón's *Womanism,*" 159–64).

I agree with Howe that Morejón's ambivalent intellectual attitude may be seen as a personal survival mechanism given the fact that she has chosen to continue living in Cuba. Her ability to survive and to continue producing throughout the years, always managing to uphold her integrity as a woman and as an Afro-Cuban, may be controversial, but it shows her to be an excellent mediator between her culture and her national identity. In speaking about the Cuban liberator and poet José Martí, the poet, critic, and editor Cintio Vitier describes him as Latin America's version of the committed intellectual whose criticism "takes place in the sphere of intellectual and artistic creation itself" (248).[2] Morejón follows within this same critical tradition as well as that of her more immediate predecessors, Nicolás Guillén and José Lezama Lima. Although at face value, these two great poets and thinkers appear to have produced contradictory versions of Cuban cultural identity, they, like Morejón, display a critical conscience inherent in their artistic pursuit. Ultimately, Morejón paves the ground for other Afro-Cuban women in the 1990s, such as filmmaker Gloria Rolando and artist Belkis Ayón who, because of intellectuals like Morejón, have been able to carve their Afro-Cuban identities in harsh economic times after the dreams of the Castro revolution waned (see Muguercia). In what follows, I focus on Morejón as cultural critic, an aspect of her work less well known than her poetry.

Nancy Morejón's poetry has been consistently acclaimed and warmly received by national and international readers alike.[3] Her selected poems gained international recognition in 1985 with the publication of the bilingual anthology *Where the Island Sleeps Like a Wing* by Black Scholar Press. This collection drew attention to the poet's concerns with placing women of the African diaspora at the center of Caribbean and Cuban historical memory. Her two most read and analyzed poems are "Mujer negra" [Black Woman] and "Amo a mi amo" [I Love My Master]. Other equally important poems depict the black working-class family as a haven for the poet during times of historical upheaval ("La cena" [The Supper]), racism inherent in United States society ("Un manzano de Oakland" [An Oakland Apple Tree]), and postcolonial struggles throughout the world ("En el país de Vietnam" [In the Country of Vietnam]). The collection, translated by Kathleen Weaver and endorsed by such prominent figures as Fernando Alegría, Audre Lorde, and Alice Walker, among others, pointed to Nancy Morejón as a distinguished revolutionary poet.

Her sustained work as a poet, translator, and cultural critic culminated in 2001 when she received the Cuban National Literature Prize. In her acceptance speech Morejón said: "Without respite, I have looked to give voice to a choir of silenced voices, which, throughout history, way beyond their origins, their race, and their gender, are reborn in my idiom. . . . History in capital letters has been important to me, and the history of small grandmothers was important, women prophets, the ones who embroidered the tablecloth where their own oppressors ate. A history of the lash, of migrations and stigmas that came by the sea and to the sea they return without apparent reason" (my translation).[4] With this statement about giving voice to those who have been silenced, Morejón joins the Latin American tradition of prophetic poets including Pablo Neruda, Nicolás Guillén, and Claribel Alegría, among others. But she emphasizes as well the silent histories of women whose domestic labor enhanced the lives of their oppressors, but who also established, silently, a tradition of creativity under duress. This tradition of women's labor has been lauded by many African diaspora women writers, including Alice Walker. Linda S. Howe, considering whether Morejón may be classified as a feminist for her emphasis on women's issues, states: "Morejón enlarges the context and, at the same time, reshapes the tradition of Caribbean protest discourse to embrace the Afro-Cuban woman's perspective. In this sense, we might say that a womanist approach, for Morejón, constitutes Black women controlling their own history and culture" ("Nancy Morejón's *Womanism*," 156; and *Transgression and Conformity*, 124).

Several critics of Morejón's poetry have pointed to the tension in her work between black woman's history and the domestic and intimate history of women from the African diaspora: "[T]here is always in her work that creative tension between the idea and the image, between the demon and the flower, between poetry that is socially and politically engagé and poetry that is deeply, profoundly lyrical" (DeCosta-Willis, 1). Her essays and books (*Pájaro* and *Recopilación*), her affiliation with institutions such as UNEAC (the Cuban National Union of Writers and Artists) and Casa de las Américas, the support of influential writers and intellectuals such as Nicolás Guillén and Mirta Aguirre, and the publication of more politically oriented poems, such as "En el país de Vietnam" and "Mitologías," allowed Nancy Morejón, figuratively, to sing herself out of literary silence" (DeCosta-Willis, 10–11). Although Morejón's role as international poet began with the publication of her anthology by Black Scholar Press, her role as a major literary figure in Cuba came as the result of her work as a journalist and literary critic. After a period of poetic silence between 1967 and 1979 (Howe, "Nancy Morejón's *Womanism*," 162), when her poetry found no outlets for publication, her *Nación y mestizaje en Nicolás Guillén* [Nation and Hybridity in Nicolás Guillén], which won the UNEAC prize for the Enrique José Varona essay in 1980 and was published in 1982, propelled her onto the national cultural scene.

Morejón's critical work on Nicolás Guillén allowed her to express her ideology as deeply rooted in the concepts of *mestizaje* and *transculturación*, which Guillén and Fernando Ortiz developed respectively. In this critical essay, as well as in her shorter cultural pieces, Morejón follows a long tradition of Latin American intellectuals, from Carlos Mariátegui to Juan Marinello, who formulated a critique of the concept of culture. In his essay "Literary Criticism in Spanish America," Aníbal González points to "a decided tendency to organize their works around the history of culture. Their interpretation of literary works was usually contextual, designed to show the links between literature, culture and society" (451). In her own journalistic essay "Comentando *Quirón o del ensayo*" [Commenting on Quirón, or Regarding the Essay], Morejón asserts that in writing *Nación y mestizaje* she drew on sources from literature, history, and sociology to formulate her own essays (*Fundación de la imagen*, 193).

I argue that Morejón writes essays to formulate a history of ideas that advances a coherent image of Cuban culture as hybrid, including European and African influences in equal measure, and that relegates concepts of race and gender to a secondary plane. This emphasis on hybrid culture informs her seemingly unwavering support of the Castro revolutionary agenda with its Marxist class analyses, linking economy and culture in the same manner as Fernando Ortiz did in his coining of the term *transculturation* in 1940. This is particularly the case with her cultural criticism of the 1970s and 1980s. In the 1990s she begins to reconsider her concept of race and self-identity in ways that were self-censored in her earlier writing.

Besides her work on major Cuban writers, artists, and musicians, written for such Cuban cultural journals as *Casa de las Américas, La Gaceta de Cuba,* and *Unión,* in the last two decades of the twentieth century her writing ranges widely, including UNEAC prize speeches, reviews of art shows, the promotion of the writing of contemporary or younger writers and artists, cultural criticism on Caribbean masters, and a personal account of her trip to South Africa.[5] Like José Martí before her, Morejón endeavors to define "national culture as highly refined end products of a laborious and deliberate historical process" (Aníbal González describing Martí, 439). In my analysis, Morejón's essays fall into two stages based on her necessity to establish herself as a cultural figure, first in the cultural environment in the 1970s when writers had to contend with Fidel Castro's "Words to the Intellectuals," and second as an internationally known poet and critic.[6] The first stage includes her essays written between 1969 and 1984 and anthologized in 1988 in *Fundación de la imagen* [Foundation of the Image] as well as her critical book on Nicolás Guillén. The second stage displays a greater diversity of topics and a freer disposition to engage issues of race and gender. Most of these essays hint at her own invisibility as a black woman writer (Howe, "Nancy Morejón's *Womanism,*" 157), notwithstanding her recognition as a cultural writer and an internationally known poet.

Morejón develops her idea of the poetic image, in both essays and poetry, under the tutelage of José Lezama Lima. I use her essays on art, in conjunction with the study of one of her poems from the 1993 collection *Paisaje célebre* [Celebrated Landscape] to establish Morejón's indebtedness to Lezama Lima as she defines her mature poetic image. I begin by presenting the essays that contribute to her definition of national culture after the 1959 Revolution and continue by analyzing a poetic image closely allied to intimate pictorial renditions that reveal a highly guarded subjectivity in her poetry. Throughout, I suggest that Morejón's tension between idea and image represents a survival strategy of sorts for a black woman poet who sought a place in Cuba's cultural landscape with its highly prescribed exigencies. She did not present a profile of ambivalence toward the nation, yet ambivalence is embedded in her work.

Fundación de la imagen, a title that reflects Morejón's indebtedness to José Lezama Lima, collects short journalistic essays published elsewhere from 1969 to the mid-1980s. In her essay on Lezama Lima, published first in *La Gaceta de Cuba* in 1970 and subsequently in *Fundación* (135–49), Morejón extrapolates from Lezama Lima's definition of the Cuban essay: "Why should the essay's methodology not nourish itself on the means of other literary genres, on other ways of approaching logical thought?" (148). Citing Hans Magnus Enzensberger, she defines the essay's methodology as multiple, including "moments of reporting and autobiography" (148). In her analysis of the works of Lezama Lima, Juan Marinello, Mirta Aguirre, and Luisa Campuzano, Morejón advocates for an interdisciplinary essay form, agreeing with Campuzano that Cuba's tradition of the critical essay erases differences between the literary and the nonliterary, in that the literary takes into account historical and political considerations and methodologies ("Comentando *Quirón o del ensayo,*" 195, in *Fundación,* 191–97).

In her essays on the antislavery novel, on the Cuban essay, or on Caribbean literature in general, Morejón advances her own ideas about *mestizaje*, the African diaspora, the value of popular literatures, and her apprehensions about feminism in her contemporary context. In these early essays, Morejón tends to make pronouncements about a subject by relying on the ideas of well-established intellectual figures in Cuban letters. On feminism, for example, Morejón states: "Mirta Aguirre does not propose a *feminine culture* in America, rather, on the contrary, she proposes an American culture where the equality of human rights between men and women has already given way to a political liberation that would lead to a more just society" ("Mirta Aguirre y su *Ayer de*

Hoy" [Mirta Aguirre and Her *Today's Yesterday*], 91, in *Fundación*, 78–102). This quotation illustrates how Morejón refuses to consider issues of gender in isolation; rather, she places the equality of women within a larger political and human rights context. In so doing, she differentiates her ideas regarding women's rights from those of Western privileged women and aligns herself with the struggles of women throughout the world who must consider the economic and social constraints that limit their lives. She also wishes to distance herself, in particular, from what may be considered "bourgeois movements" in the United States.

As cultural critic, Morejón constructs a complex idea of Cubanness that integrates the history and experience of its Afro-Cuban citizens, always mindful of their systematic exclusion, starting with the first conceptions of nation in the nineteenth century by thinkers such as José Antonio Saco, among others: "Cuba would be white and could begin being Cuban" (*Fundación de la Imagen*, 24). The relationship between being Cuban and being white excluded all others who were brought to the island as slaves and indentured servants. According to Morejón, this exclusion can now be rectified as a consequence of the revolutionary changes taking place in the nation since 1959. In her essay on *Cecilia Valdés* written in 1979, "Mito y realidad en Cecilia Valdés" (*Fundación de la Imagen*, 9–28), Morejón states: "In the case of Cuba, the socialist Revolution has determined in a diaphanous and tenacious way a decided vocation to find and proclaim the most legitimate roots of our identity" (15).

This essay serves as an example of how the author can begin with a literary topic and dedicate most of her writing to a historic, sociological, and economic analysis of the basis of Cuban culture starting in the nineteenth century: "The backbone of Cecilia Valdés will serve us as a nutrient source for promoting ideas" (10). For Morejón, as for other critics of this foundational antislavery novel, the myth of Cecilia Valdés represents the nation defined in terms of its monocultural economic system deeply dependent on slavery. Slavery, in turn, supports the Spanish colony whose society can be construed as a pyramid, with the slaves at the bottom and with white Creoles and Spaniards who partly control production and commerce at the top. This idea originated with Enrique José Varona and reappeared in César Leante's reading of the novel (see Méndez Rodenas, "Identity and Incest," 85–86). According to Morejón, even though Cecilia Valdés does not occupy the lowest rank of Cuban society, she represents its weakest link because "Cecilia doesn't want to be Cecilia" (17). The light-skinned mulatta does not want to be who she is, because like all Cubans who wish to ascend the social pyramid, she does not wish to be associated with the black slave who, in the worst sense of colonial dehumanization, represents nothing more than merchandise. Cecilia's human desire for a better life necessarily alienates her from her ancestors who, as Africans, are devalued in the emerging nation. The colonial system thus sets up an equivalency between a class struggle and a race struggle.

At the root of the novel's social construction, in Morejón's view, lies the practice of *blanqueamiento* (whitening) wherein the weight of "bettering" the race falls entirely on the mulatta. Thus, Cecilia grows up with the imperative of marrying a white man because she is three generations removed from her African great-grandmother. The message of alienation, to refuse to be black, to be Cecilia, gets passed down from generation to generation in a family unit of absent white fathers who deny their mulatta daughters their paternal name and of mothers who are increasingly light-skinned. By the end of the essay, Morejón has tied sex to alienation, which is incarnate in the figure of Cecilia Valdés. She concludes that even within a revolutionary society there are vestiges of a racism that is consciously rooted in the concepts of class and race. Throughout, Morejón subsumes issues of race and gender to class analysis, yet the implicit, overwhelming message of alienation based on the coincidence between slavery and the nineteenth-century concept of race foregrounds the function of racism in Cuba's past and present cultural landscape. The ultimate topic of the essay, the alienation of the black female subject perpetuated by an alienated family structure within a slave society, propels Morejón, the poet, to counter with the creation of an alternative female subject who, unlike Cecilia, hates her masters and rebels against them and their social constructions. "Mujer negra" [Black Woman], "Amo a mi amo" [I Love My Master], and "La cena" [The Supper] give back integrity to contemporary black women who grow up nurtured in a black family where mother and father shelter their children against social and political strife.[7]

Quietly and skillfully, while Morejón subsumes race within class in her essays, she foregrounds the issue of race in her poetry about black women. Even though Morejón often evades the issue of race in her early essays, in a personal statement published in *Afro-Hispanic Review*, a 1996 issue dedicated solely to the poet, she affirms: "The originality that may be appreciated in my poems, I believe, comes from my condition as a woman and my condition as black. Both conditions have added a very special substance to all that I have written in the process of the political convulsion that all of you recognize" ("Las poéticas," 7).

Morejón's reevaluation of Caribbean culture as influenced by the popular sectors of society is intrinsically tied to her analysis of Cuban identity based on class. Particularly in her essay on Juan Marinello's analysis of José Martí's works (*Fundación*, 68–77), Morejón emphasizes Martí's renewal of the Spanish language rooted in popular traditions: "Only speech, the radiant contact with the speech of the people, could save it (the Spanish language) from slow and certain death. América, through Martí's prose, infused a good portion of the blood of that necessary popular vitality" ("La huella de España en Juan Marinello" [Traces of Spain in Juan Marinello], 75).

Like Martí, Nicolás Guillén enriched his poetic idiom with the popular language of blacks in Havana, as well as with the Hispanic traditions of the Romancero. Guillén's incorporation of the rhythms of the *son*, with its roots in African and Hispanic musical traditions, and originating in the eastern provinces of Cuba, makes him an innovator in Cuban letters at the formal level. Morejón is also interested in the poet laureate's placing his poetry at the service of Cuba's working class: "The Cubanness of Guillén's poetry, then, does not reside exclusively in having brought the *son* into the literary or poetic arena. I believe that its unquestionable Cubanness must be understood, in another sense, in the contents to which his poetry alludes comprehensively, when he places many of his themes in the service of the purest essence of the popular soul" ("Mirta Aguirre," 86). Through Marinello's conception of Martí's language and Aguirre's analysis of Guillén's genius, Morejón defines the Cuban writer in terms of his enriching the Spanish language with the ingenuity of popular speech, and in terms of placing his linguistic gift in the service of the people.[8]

In the 1982 publication *Nación y mestizaje en Nicolás Guillén* [Nation and Hybridity in Nicolás Guillén], Morejón maintains Guillén's uniqueness as a national poet, because for him the concept of nation cannot be imagined without cultural *mestizaje*, without the integration of Spanish and African roots as they coexist and transform themselves in the Antillean context. Vera Kutzinski defines *mestizaje* as "miscegenation, racial amalgamation (as in *blanqueamiento*, whitening), creolization, racial mixing, inter- or transculturation," and as "the principal signifier of Cuba's national cultural identity" since its use by José Martí in "Nuestra América" [Our America] (*Sugar's Secrets*, 5). Derek Walcott objects to the term *miscegenation*, given its connotation that "there's something wrong genetically" (Moyers, 431); Edouard Glissant defines creolization *(antillanité)* for the Francophone Caribbean in *Caribbean Discourse* (220–36); and the critic A. James Arnold elaborates on the term in his essay "Créolité: Power, Mimicry, and Dependence." According to Morejón in *Nación y mestizaje,* for Guillén, poetic expression not only demands the transformation of language to incorporate the idiom of the black popular sector, but also a revolutionary attitude toward aesthetic considerations to encompass social and political dimensions (213). Because in his early poetry (the 1930 *Motivos de son* [*Son* Motifs]) he addresses black people with their language and their internalized racism, Guillén takes on the systematic undermining of cultural contributions by the Afro-Cuban in the gestation of the Cuban nation (Morejón, *Nación y mestizaje,* 99). According to Morejón, Guillén's avant-garde poetry responds to the anti-Machado revolutionary movement taking place in Cuba during the 1930s, with its mobilization of the working class in the political arena. His emphasis on *mestizaje* grows out of Afro-Cuban journalistic tradition in the early decades of the twentieth century, which, under the leadership of Gustavo Urrutia opened up a fruitful dialogue about "the black problem." Prominent figures such as Juan Gualberto Gómez advocated for the equality of the races in the concept of nation while Jorge Mañach opposed *mestizaje* and countered with the concept of harmony between the races. They both opposed the U.S. solution of separate but equal spheres. Ultimately, the dialogue favored what Morejón described as a bourgeois solution, the integration of blacks through education. This solution failed to take into account obvious economic and social factors such as racism that made integration merely through education impossible. What Guillén proposed in his poetry was a concept of nation as the ultimate expression of mass struggle (199).

As she did in her essay on *Cecilia Valdés,* Morejón uses Guillén's poetry as a springboard from which to clarify the contributions of Afro-Cubans to Cuba's cultural landscape. In *Nación y mestizaje* she raises Guillén's stature to prophetic dimensions, claiming that Guillén anticipates through his poetry the socialist nation that will become a reality with the 1959 Revolution. The titles of her chapters offer an indication of the nature of Morejón's critical discourse: 1. Transculturation and *Mestizaje,* 2. The Concept of Nation, 3. The Racial Question, 4. A Reading of "The Last Name," 5. In Spanish: The Antilles.

The first chapter focuses on Fernando Ortiz and Nicolás Guillén's transculturation and *mestizaje,* with a discussion of similarities and differences, arguing against Ortiz's view that Cuba's indigenous cultures suffered such a tragic demise with the arrival of the Spanish as to have left no significant trace in contemporary Cuban culture other than geographic and semantic terms. Another major difference between Ortiz's transculturation and Guillén's *mestizaje* lies in the moment when each process begins. Ortiz is silent on when transculturation began, although presumably it was at the moment of the encounter, whereas Guillén's *mestizaje* coincides with the emerging nation in the late eighteenth and early nineteenth centuries. While both agree in their concept of culture as plural-based primarily on the transformation of Spanish and African traditions—and both consider the economic basis at the root of the encounter and integration of cultures—Morejón points to Guillén's anti-imperialist ideology as one of the few ways of allowing the nation to transcend its neocolonial status. Ultimately, in Morejón's presentation, it was Guillén's equal valorization of the Spanish and African heritage that made it possible to return to blacks the civil integrity that they deserve as participants in the forging of the nation.

In her second chapter, Morejón illustrates the systematic erasure of the contributions of Afro-Cubans toward nation and culture. The author cites, as she has before, the influence that José Antonio Saco had in the exclusion of blacks in the forging of the new republic, since they were considered foreigners, immigrants. Given the ties between the United States and the new republic and the U.S. encouragement of a white-only rule, Guillén responds with his anti-imperialist message in *West Indies, Ltd* (1934). Only when working classes rule will Afro-Cubans find a place in society. In the chapter on race, Morejón emphasizes Guillén's struggle at the level of the working classes, an ideology commensurate with the poet's preference for a popular poetic language. Morejón, like Guillén, constantly relegates the concept of race to a secondary position to class, so that blacks may be seen as integrated into all levels of society, rather than as isolated according to race.[9] In her analysis of "El apellido: Elegía familiar," Morejón points to Guillén's integration of its African members into the early history of the nation. The tragic and ironic tones prevalent in the elegy lay bare the abuse of slaves and the erasure of their African names in favor of their Spanish ones. The last chapter places Guillén's contributions in the context of other Caribbean literary movements that recover black heritage. In Guillén's case, as opposed to Aimé Césaire's, for example, the Cuban poet is capable of rewriting Cuban history in a text such as the 1972 *El diario que a diario* [The Daily Daily], because he writes from a stance of a black man living in a liberated and not colonial nation. (The Africana critic Vera M. Kutzinski points to the limitations of this statement in "Poetry and Politics," 279). Morejón concludes by stating her preference for the label *Afro-Hispanic* rather than *Afro-Cuban* because the first affirms Guillén's *mestizaje* in the truest sense of the word. In her rather critical review of *Nación y mestizaje* (1983), for what I agree constitutes a quite ideological analysis of Guillén's poetry, Kutzinski states the following regarding Morejón's attention to her definition of terms:

> Although Morejón's insistence on the term "afrohispánico" as a most accurate description of Cuban culture may be brushed off as political rhetoric or criticized for its apparent, and perhaps inevitable, seductiveness, it helps remind us of the dire need for a more unified and precise terminology especially when dealing with such broad concepts as "American culture," "Latin American culture" or "Afro-American culture." Even more significantly, Morejón's book, partly because of the intensely ideological tone of her own rhetoric, alerts us to the political connotations of certain terminological constructs and choices and thus to the inevitably political nature of language and literature. ("Poetry and Politics," 278–79)[10]

Kutzinski's strongest criticism of Morejón's book lies in the Cuban writer's failure to attempt a critique of language in Guillén's poetry, particularly when Morejón analyzes "El apellido" (280). Kutzinski recognizes, however, Morejón's reluctance "to explore in greater depth the intricate relationship between language (and thus literature) and ideology, between both literary and political rhetoric and authority, in the context of a socialist regime" (280), given the obvious social and political context in which Morejón writes. Many years after Kutzinski's publication of her review in 1983, other critics, such as William Luis and Linda S. Howe, have pointed to Morejón's accommodations to the critical stages of retrenchment and openings in cultural terms in Castro's Cuba. Howe describes Morejón's role as "one of contradictions, setbacks, and measured success" ("Fluid Iconography," 30).

With *Fundación de la imagen* and *Nación y mestizaje en Nicolás Guillén*, Morejón explicitly favors a class analysis in the construction of a history of ideas as they pertain to Afro-Cubans. She emphasizes class, yet repeatedly points to the silencing of Afro-Cuban voices based on racist assumptions. I resort to a quotation by the critic Efraín Barradas, who studies Morejón's poetry as a revision of Guillén's: "Morejón can assume her negritude without having to declare it, but only because others before her—here Guillén plays a very important role—assumed it in an explicit and almost aggressive manner" (26; my translation). This statement may well be repeated in terms of Morejón's evasion of the issue of race in *Nación y mestizaje*. As she points to Guillén's solution of *mestizaje* as the way to counter this historical exclusion of blacks, she consistently proceeds with accounts of Afro-Cuban cultural contributions such as those of Juan Gualberto Gómez and Gustavo Urrutia, intellectuals whose history would remain silent were it not for the voice of black writers like Morejón. Almost two decades after she published these essays, Morejón, in a frank conversation about racial stereotypes in the mass media in Cuba with Cuban poet and journalist Pedro Pérez Sarduy, recently asserted that in spite of the social gains of the black popular sectors during the Castro revolution, it is still necessary to insist on historical and cultural contributions of Afro-Cubans as a way to struggle against racial prejudice: "I think there are many battles yet to be won. I think we have traveled in a good direction, and that should be recognized. The popular masses have won a space where the *mestizaje* Guillén spoke so much about, and which has been so important to me, has gained ground. I think that's important, but there's another space that has to be won, which is historical reflection, knowing more about our history of slavery and the black and mulatto population of Cuba. . . . We need to know a lot more" ("Grounding the Race Dialogue," 166).

The essays I consider, published from the mid 1980s to 2002 in *La Gaceta de Cuba, Casa de las Américas,* and *Revista Proposiciones,* reveal Morejón's desire to "know a lot more." These short essays record the cultural legacy of the African diaspora in Cuba and other Caribbean nations, and the topics include an homage paid to black Cuban singer Bola de Nieve in January of 1999, the opening of an exhibition of the books and journals published by Black Scholar Press in 1985, an article in praise of the *son* master, Venezuelan Oscar de León in 1984, and her remarks when awarding the Casa de las Américas poetry prize to the Martiniquean Nicole Cage-Florentiny in 1996. Other essays analyze films, theater, other Cuban writers, and the value of Cuban cultural institutions, such as Casa de las Américas. Morejón has also written essays on Cuban artists Manuel Mendive, María Magdalena Campos-Pons, Lawrence Zuñiga, and Alfredo Rostgaard, and on the American Melvin Edwards. Her essays on art provide a special case because in them she adheres to the methodology of artistic analysis and engages the canvases she views and analyzes in a poetic dialogue. An analysis of two of her essays on the Afro-Cuban primitivist painter Manuel Mendive, one published in 1969, the other in 2002, illustrates my point.

In "Manuel Mendive: El mundo de un primitivo" [Manuel Mendive: The World of a Primitivist] (*Fundación,* 150–62), Morejón follows most of the prescriptions for writing about art, including meticulous descriptions of the sculptures and canvases, defining *primitivist art* as prescribed by art theorists, establishing comparisons with such other primitivists as Gauguin, signaling similarities with Van Gogh's use of expressive color, and marking different stages in the artist's development. To support her analyses, Morejón includes quotations from the artist and describes life situations that signaled a drastic change in his use of canvas and color. Because in his art Mendive depicts the mythology of his Yoruba traditions as represented in Cuban practices, Morejón devotes time to clarifying the signification of his art as "a new poetry for our plastic arts" (*Fundación*, 150). Notably absent from this essay are sociological and political inter- pretations of the work, as in her analysis of Guillén's poetry. Moreover, as a writer, Morejón uses a poetic language that signals a dialogue be- tween the poetic imagination of the writer and that of the painter. She quotes Delacroix's idea on the subject: "I see prose writers and poets in painters" (150). Notice, for example, the cadence of the opening sentence of the essay, which, because it emphasizes parallelism with a verb in the infinitive, recalls similar sentences and poetic utterances by José Lezama Lima[11]: "To find the elucidating signs of a mythological cosmos, to enter the world of a painter like Manuel Mendive, presupposes an unusual state of marvel, enigma and new acknowledgments" (150).

In December 2001 Morejón delivered the address on the occasion of Mendive's receipt of the National Prize of (Plastic) Art. In "Elogio de Manuel Mendive" [In Praise of Manuel Mendive], published by *Casa de las Américas* early in 2002, Morejón describes Mendive's, and her own, Cuba: "That Cuba is in Mendive a secret shouted out loud, a thick underbrush of signs more than revealing" (147). With this description, Morejón alludes to Lydia Cabrera's *El Monte* with its cultural content and modes of signification (including silences that speak out, evasion, and the telling of lies that nevertheless arrive at the truth). In presenting a fellow successful Afro-Cuban cultural figure—Morejón won the National Prize for Literature, also in 2001—she engages a rhetorical tradition that proudly guards its secrets but celebrates its mode of signification. In the case of Morejón and Mendive, that poetic mode engages figurative lan- guage, silences, and the autobiographical. In describing Mendive's work, Morejón states: "six more legitimate creations go past us like doves, or like those kites that announce the end of the afternoon near Tallapiedra" (146). In describing her poetry, she confesses her indebtedness to Mendive: "Why not think and appreciate that some of my poems were born under the warmth of his brushes, under the wise tenderness of Matilde, his mother, and of the mischief of the ineffable Charlie, his older brother, and of Carmen, his tall, tall aunt, classic and tranquil?" (146). Here, as in her poem "La cena" [The Supper], creative endeavors are nurtured by the warmth of the black family unit. For Morejón and Mendive, the most cherished cultural values must be kept secret, divulged only through "a thick underbrush of signs more than revealing." Like Lydia Cabrera's informants, here, Afro-Cuban subjects choose to survive and retain their culture through what may be considered by others contradictory and ambivalent statements. Morejón expresses it best with the following words:

> Writing is nothing more than art and necessity, unable to be bribed by anything or anyone. My first thirty or so years of my craft as a writer have not been easy, but I do not complain because they have constituted for me an ineffable academy. The important thing is that word that may fix, in any way possible, an experience in my life. And I have had proof that silence has been, many a time, an incalculable source of literary foundations and even of certain formal efficacy. As an old Yoruba proverb states: "a great silence makes a great noise." (Cordones-Cook, 70)

In my view, Morejón proposes here, in a veiled manner, that the contradictions and silences in her poetic and essayistic career constitute a kind of autobiographical statement of an Afro-Cuban woman poet who in the first thirty years of her professional life saw it impossible to write explicitly about the things that mattered to her most: being a woman and being black.

When Morejón engages a poetic language in her critical writing about fellow Afro-Cuban artists, she follows in the tradition of José Lezama Lima (classified as "hermetic" by the socialist cultural apparatus), who was an avid promoter and critic of Cuban Baroque art as produced by such great artists as Víctor Manuel, Amalia Peláez, Mariano Rodríguez, René Portocarrero, Roberto Diago, and others.[12] As founder of the group Orígenes, which included both poets and writers, Lezama published their work in the well-known journal of the same name. His own conception of the poetic word is based on a system that conflates word and visual image. In his critical introduction to Lezama Lima's *La visualidad infinita* [Infinite Vision], Leonel Capote states: "During the forties, Lezama begins to configure his poetic system about the world. . . . With this system, he outlines a concept of life starting with poetry, finding its foundation in Tertuliano's phrase: 'It is certain because it is impossible.' Through the system in question, Lezama thought: 'metaphor, image, poem and poetry allied, they accomplish the impossible'" (28). Beyond his concept of the poetic image that transcends figurative language to include life experience,

Lezama Lima consciously incorporated the pictorial in his descriptions of landscape and home found in his novels *Paradiso* and *Oppiano Licario* (*La visualidad,* 15). He was intent on reforming art criticism by imposing his own creative intelligence to discover the new in a long tradition of Cuban art. Capote defines his art criticism style thus: "His criticism of Cuban culture defines itself as a clear prose with a propensity toward poetry" (14). In his criticism, Lezama Lima constructs poetic images in which he captures the qualities of light in artworks he admires. In this process he creates his own poetic rendition of the concept of light. In his analyses of Cuban art, Lezama Lima engages poetic concepts of time, space, light, color, and Cuban culture.

Elucidating Lezama Lima's concepts of light and landscape will be useful in this context to clarify how in her poetic landscapes in her 1993 work *Paisaje célebre*, Morejón conflates the concepts of pictorial image with simultaneity of time and space. When describing light in the works of Amelia Peláez, Lezama Lima states: "It seems as if the arrival of light on her figures offered her the circumstances of her living" (*La visualidad infinita,* 166). The capacity of the artist to reproduce the brilliance of Cuban light on objects also highlights the artist's and the viewer's self-identity as a creator as being dependent on that light. A beautiful rendition of Cuban light as portrayed by Víctor Manuel appears in stanza four of Lezama Lima's poem "Nuevo encuentro con Víctor Manuel" [New Encounter with Víctor Manuel]:

> Every day he showed us
> that light materializes in the splendor
> of bodies on the seashore
> or on the tedium of our fascination
> with leaves, looking in parks
> for the hand of man.
>
> . . . .
>
> He leaned out to look
> and he always saw an interminable fluency,
> but he never betrayed the possibilities of looking.
>
> *Poesía Completa,* 358 (my translation and ellipses)

Lezama Lima's disquisitions on light and on art occur both in his essays and in his poetry, erasing distinctions between writing art criticism and writing poetry. Moreover, for Peláez and Manuel, the depiction of light and artistic creation coincide in the act of looking. Later, I demonstrate how Morejón reproduces Lezama Lima's creative intelligence as she views Cuban art in her poem "Pogolotti."

In describing a canvas by Mariano, Lezama Lima states: "There, without closing in on space-time spirals, he finds the solution by simply painting the successive with the simultaneous" (*La visualidad*, 187). Mariano's ability to depict time as spatial simultaneity represents for Lezama Lima what is most Cuban, most American, in its widest sense of the word. Lezama Lima thus defines the Baroque as a most Cuban of styles: "For me the Baroque is our very own condition, it is a very American condition. I would say that two elements determine the conditions of our Baroque style, that is *simultaneity,* that is to say, what is successive for Europeans, for Americans it is simultaneous. . . . And then, another element of our very own Baroque is *the parody of styles*" (quoted in Capote, introduction to *La visualidad,* 49). Morejón engages Lezama Lima's idea of Cubanness as expressed in a simultaneous condition of artistic expression in poetry and in visual art in her poem "Pogolotti."

"Pogolotti" is representative of many of the poems in *Paisaje célebre* because it recalls the work of a Cuban painter, in this case Marcelo Pogolotti, and through the recollection of the images on his canvases, Morejón simultaneously enters into her own childhood memory of the now transformed neighborhood that bears the same name as the artist: Pogolotti. Heather Rosario-Sievert writes about Morejón's painterly sensibility prevalent in the entire book and says: "A more mature poet, however, views the changing panorama about her . . . and the eye/I of the artist adjusts, seeks other foci, seeks fragments of the past, placed in new landscapes, in *paisajes célebres,* and chooses, in masterful painterly ways, their placement at points of stillness, beauty, and magic, evoking an aesthetic sensibility and a visual echo of the audible nostalgia" (48). My reading of "Pogolotti" illustrates how Morejón, like Lezama Lima, creates a poetic image that puts into play a multiplicity of social, personal, and artistic considerations (also see Luis, "Politics of Aesthetics," 37). Morejón stated her indebtedness to Lezama Lima in conversation with Juanamaría Cordones-Cook: "Poets of my generation—not all of them, rather, a few—became overwhelmed by his metaphoric proposal, with his revision of the concept of the imago" (63).

"Pogolotti" is dedicated to Graziella Pogolotti, daughter of the painter, accomplished cultural critic, and friend of the poet. In her own essay about her father's contribution to Cuban painting, Graziella Pogolotti creates a discourse that includes the autobiographical, the analytical, and the ideological. According to the daughter-critic, Pogolotti depicts the

Cuban working classes with Léger-like figures to accentuate the anonymous and automatic nature of human labor in the early decades of the twentieth century. His canvases portraying human figures at work employ muted colors and strong lines to emphasize the perpetual motion of dehumanizing labor. A good portion of Graziella Pogolotti's essay explores the alienation that artists like her father suffered in depicting the working classes "during our neocolonial republic" (39). In one telling sentence, the daughter-critic offers the following image of her father: "He always retained in his memory, with surprising precision, the image of his city, the exact description of the streets, of the architecture of the houses, and above all, of the social drama of his country" (33). I quote this sentence, in particular, to suggest this is precisely what Morejón accomplishes in her poem.

Morejón devotes the second half of her poem to Marcelo Pogolotti's art because he depicted the unemployed dockworkers who lived in the neighborhood known as Pogolotti, which she visited as a child. Morejón describes these dockworkers in connection with Pogolotti's canvases in a Havana museum:

De pronto, muchos años después,
aquellas chimeneas,
aquellos músculos selváticos,
se dieron a la fuga para siempre
y fueron encontrados,
infinitos domingos después,
en los cuadros de Don Marcelo.
                    (27–28)

[Suddenly, many years later,
those chimneys,
those junglelike muscles,
took flight forever
and were found,
an infinity of Sundays later,
in the paintings of Don Marcelo.]
                (my translation)

In creating her own image of the working sector of the city après Pogolotti, Morejón produces a canvaslike image "reminiscent of Mexican murals" (27). The rescue of the image of those men and that cityscape matters to Morejón because, in an effort to safeguard Afro-Cubans from the cultural "depravation" of their Santería practices and from their poverty, such neighborhoods were demolished, and model, new construction rose in their place. Morejón's line "took flight forever" captures her pain at the loss of a rich culture, depicted by Lydia Cabrera's informants in *El Monte*, which happened to be undervalued by the revolutionary project of the 1960s.

The Afro-Cuban filmmaker Sara Gómez depicts the transformation of "marginal" neighborhoods in her 1974 docudrama *De cierta manera* [One Way or Another].[13] This "imperfect cinema," conceived by filmmaker Julio García Espinosa, mixes documentary and fictional film techniques (Fowler Calzada, 88). Sara Gómez dutifully records, via the use of documentary reels, conversations of actual residents about the necessity to restructure their community. Tearing down the old and building the new would improve their poor sanitary living conditions and allow inhabitants of poor neighborhoods to integrate themselves into a social program that would discourage Santería practices, practices that would alienate them from participating fully in Cuba's new civic life. The repetition of a shot in the film that depicts a wrecking ball smashing down tin-roofed wooden shacks and dilapidated old buildings reinforces the revolutionary statement of clearing away the old to build the new. There is no denying that the building of stable, architecturally sound housing greatly benefited the residents of poor neighborhoods. Yet along with the restructuring of the physical structures would also come the destruction of a way of life.

The dramatic development of Gómez's film traces the transformation of an Abakuá secret society member from a character who cares only about the perpetuation of the all-male, exclusionary society to one who participates in collaborative work, stops lying to hide his philandering activities, and establishes a romantic relationship based on the equality of the sexes. The Abakuá separatist becomes Che Guevara's New Man who relinquishes individual needs in favor of the revolutionary collective. The filmmaker Gloria Rolando comments briefly on the polemic nature of the film, given its dramatic story based on a biracial couple, on "the integrationist vision that Sarita had of Cuban society," and on the director's "sharp documentary eye to protect reality." Speaking about Gómez's complex presentation of what residents of the neighborhoods lost in the rebuilding of their households, Rolando states in particular: "[N]or is it a real solution to move the inhabitants from a marginal neighborhood, there is a tradition, customs, with all their positive and negative charge" ("Interview in *Mujeres*" [Women]).

What might have been destroyed by the wrecking ball in *De cierta manera*, Morejón safeguards in her own poem. "Pogolotti" begins with:

Antes de ser el nombre de un pintor,
de un gran pintor cubano,
Pogolotti, en mi infancia,
era una rústica ruta de malezas
que conducía a una casona alta.

(27)

[Before being a painter's name,
the name of a great Cuban painter,
Pogolotti, in my infancy,
was a rustic road filled with undergrowth
that led to a tall house.]

(my translation)

Morejón's description of this cityscape counteracts the alienating image of chimneys in the distance later in the poem. The cityscape echoes the type of image that Morejón used to describe Mendive's Cuba: "una densa maleza de signos más que reveladores" (a dense undergrowth of signs more than revealing) ("Elogio de Manuel Mendive," 147). The poetic image takes the viewer up the hill to a tall, large, and deep house, with a picketed yard filled with the colors and smells of calabashes, trumpet wood, and barbecued goat. This goat had no doubt been sacrificed in a Santería ceremony as depicted in Sergio Giral's film *María Antonia* and then cooked for the entire community to enjoy. For Morejón, Pogolotti was a Sunday kind of place where the extended community, under the tutelage of a *madrina* (godmother/santera), shared meals under the mango trees, where newborn babies were fed gifts of sugar and honey, and where women and children did not leave until the arrival of the working man Silvio. Along with the highly visual depiction of the site, Morejón provides the reader with the smells of fruit, flowers, and cooked goat, and the sound of the *madrina*'s voice:

En Pogolotti pasé tantos domingos
de quimbombó bajo los mangos,
de azúcares y miel para recién nacidos,
de "no se vayan todavía
que ahora viene Silvio
para que vea a las niñas."

(27)

[In Pogolotti I spent so many Sundays
of okra under the mango trees,
of sugars and honey for newborn babies,
of "don't leave yet
since Silvio is on his way
so that he may see the girls."]

(my translation)

Comforted by the "embrace of her godmother" (27) and the lush sights and sounds of the old house, the child gazes out to see the unemployed workers going out, depicted in the poem as if in the epic Mexican murals and Pogolotti's smaller-scale canvases. The joy of community makes the dehumanization of Afro-Cuban men more bearable, only because the poet accomplishes a distancing of the pain through artistic image. The poet Morejón who gazes at Pogolotti's canvases stands poised between the present of the artistic image and the past of her poetic vision, made simultaneous by the *madrina*'s embrace. The coincidence of artistic visual image and poetic word stands as Morejón's process in the rescue of a lost cultural memory:

entre el pasillo umbroso de un museo
y el patio de los chivos.

(28)

[between the shady hall of a museum
and the patio of the goats.]

(my translation)

Like Lezama Lima, who describes Cubanness through the viewing of Peláez and Mariano, through the simultaneous juxtaposition of her own poetic memory and the vision of Pogolotti's canvases, Morejón recovers the warmth and the pain of a lost childhood as she visualizes for the reader a large house up on a hill.

As Miriam DeCosta-Willis has so rightly stated in general about the poetry of Nancy Morejón, there exists a tension between her intimate and social concerns. Morejón herself has taken the time to address this tension: "Am I a social poet? Yes. Am I a lyric poet? Yes. . . . But you're going to find, at the same time, a metaphoric poetry indebted to the concept of image that José Lezama Lima held. In me, you are going to find as well a poetry of (racial) identity, indebted even more to the great poetry of Nicolás Guillén" (Cordones-Cook, 65). Even though Morejón goes on to mention the works of other poets as well, including Eliseo Diego, Emilio Ballagas, and Virgilio Piñera, I believe that the ambivalence in her poetry, sometimes more evident than in that of others, may best be explained by the tension created by her having read and revised in her own ways the poetry of Guillén and Lezama Lima.

In "Pogolotti" the poet displays a tension between her creation of a nurturing scene and the pain involved in the contemplation of the social alienation faced by an entire people. In her analysis of the poetry of Afro-Cuban women poets, Catherine Davies compares the poems of Nancy Morejón and Georgina Herrera:

> But these poems go further because they inscribe resistance against sexual, racial and class exploitation from a distinctively feminine, socialist, multi-ethnic perspective. At the same time, the two poets write themselves into the mythical-historical process, which informs their present-day identity. They create worlds with the poetic power of imagination. Morejón tends to privilege a Marxist dialectic and Herrera maternal bonding in an exploration of and identification with the interrelated histories, myths and politics of Cuba and Africa. (*A Place in the Sun?* 186)

Morejón's privileging of "a Marxist dialectic" aligns her with the poetry of her mentor Nicolás Guillén, who views art "as a social praxis" (Mullen, *Afro-Cuban Literature,* 134). According to Mullen, in Guillén, "the racial question is subsumed in a broader notion of *mulatez*" (134). Through her social analysis of "class exploitation" (Davies) in "Pogolotti," Morejón signals her indebtedness to the poetry of Guillén.

In this poem, that tension between Morejón's intimate and social concerns also achieves the simultaneity that Lezama Lima so treasured in the coincidence of word and visual image. However, it is through the concept of Guillén's *mestizaje,* so central to Morejón as she confirms in her interview with Pedro Pérez Sarduy, that a more coherent image of her as a cultural critic arises. If the concept of *mestizaje* endeavors to integrate African and European influences as they interact in the creation of a new cultural definition of Cubanness, then Morejón's critical idiom manifests its valorization of Afro-Cuban contributions through her critical studies of both Nicolás Guillén's poetry and Manuel Mendive's art. In each case, Morejón takes her literary lead from the two great masters of Cuban contemporary culture, Guillén and Lezama Lima. In literary terms, Morejón's *mestizaje* recuperates her African heritage by following Guillén's model of writing on behalf of those who have been silenced. By fashioning her own version of Lezama Lima's *imago,* she re-creates

Orígenes' version of Cubanness that emphasized her Hispanic heritage. If these two discursive veins seem at odds in her two essays on Mendive and in a poem like "Pogolotti," they flow seamlessly, giving us in poetic terms what is implicit in all of her essays: Nancy Morejón's best manifestation of her own cultural *mestizaje*, a cultural *mestizaje* that, as Davies so rightly affirms, springs from a "distinctively feminist, socialist, multiethnic perspective" (186). Ultimately, her critical and poetic idioms provide for us, her readers, a comprehensive vision of Cuban history, inclusive of her African heritage and mindful of the intimate, small histories of the *madrinas* who, under siege, perpetuated their Afro-Cuban culture.

AS A CULTURAL critic during the first three decades after the 1959 Revolution, Nancy Morejón was a trailblazer for other Afro-Cuban women, clearing a space for them in which to explore issues of gender and race in a much more open manner. In the 1990s, the filmmaker Gloria Rolando and the artist Belkis Ayón made strong contributions—toward the recovery of previously excluded Afro-Cuban history, in the case of Rolando, and toward addressing racist and sexist stereotypes of Abakuá culture, in the case of Ayón.

Following the example of Morejón, who emphasized the need to know more about Cuban culture, Gloria Rolando devotes herself to the promotion of African diaspora practices through the medium of video documentary. The Cuban filmmaker Gloria Rolando (born 1953), who has worked for ICAIC (the Cuban Institute of Art and Film Industry) for more than twenty years, is best known for a series of documentaries made in the 1990s. She studied music at the Conservatorio Provincial de Música Amadeo Roldán, and in 1976 she completed her studies in art history at the University of Havana and began working at the ICAIC. She did postgraduate work at the University of Havana on Caribbean literature in 1987 and at the Casa de las Américas on slavery in 1988 ("Gloria Rolando's Biography").

At the Black Women Writers and the Future conference (New York, October 1997), Rolando stated that for the moment she had chosen the documentary for its testimonial value and to "reveal chapters of the African Diaspora" ("Gloria Rolando: Speech at Black Women Writers and the Future Conference"). Her first documentary in 1991, *Forever Present: Oggún [Un eterno presente: Oggún]* features the life and talent of Cuban singer and founder of the Conjunto Folklórico Nacional, Lázaro Ros. In an interview, he relates the *patakines* (Yoruba legends) of Oggún, the deity of metal, war, progress, and civilization, and of Ochún, the deity of love and river waters. Concurrently, Rolando inserts scenes representing the *patakines,* using song and dance. Finally, *Forever Present: Oggún* films a *toque,* a Yoruba ceremony, over which Lázaro Ros presides in one of Havana's colonial inner patios. In Rolando's second documentary in 1996, *My Footsteps in Baraguá,* she interviews members of a Cuban West Indian community composed of people from Jamaica, Tobago, and Barbados. The documentary weaves personal interviews with scenes of worship in which participants pray in English, as well as scenes of them playing cricket and celebrating the Maypole dance.

The director's third documentary in 1997, *The Eyes of the Rainbow,* dedicated to all women who wish for a better world, portrays the life of Black Panther Assata Shakur from her childhood to her political involvement in the United States to her exile in Cuba. Accused of shooting a policeman in the United States, she sought asylum in Cuba, where she has lived for the past several decades. This documentary alternates between interviews with Shakur in what appears to be a military fortress and dance scenes honoring Oyá, the warrior *orisha,* who aids in remembrance and is the keeper of the cemetery. In keeping with Shakur's African American heritage, much of the musical background for the film consists of spirituals arranged by Sweet Honey in the Rock and Julius William. The film also includes newsreel footage about the civil rights movement in the United States. While speaking about the Black Panthers, Shakur demands amnesty for all political prisoners.

In much of her testimony, Shakur praises the Cuban nation for having welcomed her in her liberation struggle and for dealing with people of the African diaspora with respect and admiration. While sitting facing the Bay of Havana, Shakur speaks of Cuba's natural beauty; while sitting with a group of women in a living room, she praises the accomplishments of the Castro revolution regarding education and health care; and while singing Cuban music, she comments on how slaves on the island were able to maintain and transform African musical forms through the use of drums and songs in the Yoruba language. Through Shakur's testimony, Rolando makes her own views known about her own country and culture. The mechanism of allowing one African diaspora woman to speak for the other implies a collective experience for women of African descent across national boundaries. Such a use of superimposition of voices and images is prevalent in this documentary and is much more developed in Rolando's next film in 2001, *Las raíces de mi corazón* (Roots of My Heart).

In addition to allowing a Black Panther to speak about her activism, imprisonment, torture, and exile, Rolando uses this documentary to foreground Assata Shakur as an example of black women's struggles and hardships in the past and in the present. Early in the interview, Shakur speaks about her grandmother as a figure who stood by her throughout her six years in prison and as a woman whose dreams announced Shakur's subsequent escape from prison. Shakur states: "My grandmother has always had dreams and they have always come true." The grandmother visited Shakur at the Yardville Unit for Women where she was imprisoned for life and told her that she had had a dream of dressing her granddaughter as a woman. Being dressed implies being prepared to join the outside world.

While speaking about her years of detention, Shakur recalls her survival strategy of identifying with those who came before her. At different times she states: "Being African is a matter of a history, of a people, not of being black"; "I feel like a marooned woman, an escaped slave. I'll never forget what my people lived through." Her experience as a woman in jail acquires universal connotations when she must decide whether to have a sexual relationship with another prisoner and then whether she would keep the child (this while being kept in a men's prison). Of this experience, Shakur states: "In prison we decided to have sex, to be human. I now know what it would have been like for slaves to consider having children." Toward the end of the documentary, Shakur speaks of her separation from her loved ones, especially her mother. "Separation has been very hard on my family," she says. "It is a real part of being African, of being slaves. . . . Today my mother died. My homage to her: to carry on her tradition. I hope that I can live up to my mother's examples and my ancestors' expectation of me. I have a duty to all those who came before to continue the struggle, to love, to be giving." The film closes with an explanation of her name: "My name is Assata (she who struggles) Olubala (for the people) Shakur (in honor of the forces of good)."

In all three documentaries, Gloria Rolando makes extensive use of song and dance elaborately filmed in the woods with dancers wearing African and African diaspora garb. In all three, song and dance serve to place the lives of the subjects being interviewed within a larger cultural and mythical context. *Forever Present: Oggún* brings to life the story of Oggún, the *orisha* to whom Lázaro Ros has dedicated his life. There is a moving scene of Oggún in the forest working with hammer and anvil when the beautiful Ochún comes to offer him honey in her calabash. In *Footsteps in Baragua*, prayer, song, and dance attest to the survival of culture even when uprooted from its land of origin. Much of the film is dedicated to dancing, with the camera playing with the speed of the film to focus on people's faces, on the rippling of a full skirt representing the waves of the Atlantic (Yemayá, the deity of the seas). In *The Eyes of the Rainbow,* Oyá links Assata Shakur's liberation struggle against racism to a long tradition of female warriors. The presence of Ochún, the deity of sensuality, represents the life force that allowed Shakur to conceive a child while in prison.

In *Forever Present: Oggún* as in *The Eyes of the Rainbow,* Rolando's subjects are presented in dramatic settings to emphasize their leadership capabilities and their pride as members of the African diaspora. In *Footsteps in Baragua,* members of the community of all ages are interviewed at home, in their gardens, and during mealtimes. In this documentary, the director resorts to family photographs, newspaper clippings, and people's testimonies to reveal the migratory nature of workers who moved from helping construct the Panama Canal to joining the Cuban workforce in sugar plantations and mills. It also records the importance of migrant workers in Cuba's sugar industry in the first half of the twentieth century.

In general, Gloria Rolando mines all artistic resources available in documentary filming in her struggle to record forgotten histories. In her speech at the 1997 Black Women Writers and the Future conference, Orlando stated: "Many of our ancestors shed their tears, but many others never shed theirs because they converted those tears into rage, into rebellion and history. This history, which many times remains forgotten or distorted by a Eurocentric bibliography[,] is precisely our principal source of creativity as much for literary works as for the world of images. Oral literature, the personal histories of our people are the obligatory references to penetrate into this inexhaustible universe of the collective memory."

Gloria Rolando's statement serves as the best transition into her most recent short film, *Las raíces de mi corazón* [Roots of My Heart]. While fictional, it is in keeping with the intent of her earlier documentary work. The specific moment in history explored in this film concerns the 1912 massacre of the Independientes de Color, when the military forces of Cuban president José Miguel Gómez killed more than 6,000 Afro-Cubans. They had risen in arms when their established political party was banned on the grounds that organizing along racial issues was racist as well as contrary to the Cuban constitution.

Aline Helg's book *Our Rightful Share* traces the historical participation of Afro-Cubans from the time of the revolutionary wars (1868–78 and 1895–98) to the 1920s, well after the 1912 massacre. Helg's book is one among several that have collected journalistic records highlighting Cuba's debates about the rights of citizens along the racial divide.[14] Until recently these debates had been portrayed in historical analyses only from the Eurocentric point of view. It held that all Cubans shared the same rights and opportunities as set forth in the Cuban constitution. The fact that blacks and whites fought alongside each other during the Wars of Independence was taken as proof that racism did not exist on the island. However, after independence, when only those of European descent received military promotions and civil service jobs, blacks began to organize along political lines. When in 1908 Evaristo Estenoz founded the Independents of Color, whites in power launched a fierce campaign to label the Independientes as racist. The party was banned in 1910. Estenoz reorganized politically by trying to prove that the banning was unconstitutional, but to no avail. He directed uprisings by the Independientes de Color against American sugar interests in the Oriente province. President Gómez ordered the massacre to prevent an American intervention. After a formal celebration in Central Park in Havana to declare the racial war a thing of the past, the Massacre of 1912 fell into oblivion. In *Las raíces de mi corazón* Gloria Rolando translates into visual images those forgotten events in Cuba's historical record, using journalistic sources, revisionist history, oral memories, and personal stories. With this film, she endeavors to eradicate the silence and distortions surrounding the massacre.

At the core of the official historical record in the early 1900s lies the accusation that the Independientes de Color were racist, since Cuba was officially considered an integrated nation. *Las raíces de mi corazón* begins with a scene that shows that, to the contrary, racism remains a reality in Cuba even at the beginning of the twenty-first century. Zaida, older and white, and obviously in a place of authority, has summoned Mercedes, an Afro-Cuban woman in her early thirties, to her office. The topic of conversation is Mercedes' next journalistic assignment. Zaida recommends that Mercedes concentrate on women's fashions of the early twentieth century. Mercedes would rather investigate the political role of her ancestors during that same period. The women argue, the boss accuses her inferior of dreaming:

Zaida: Black issues are not appropriate at this time.
Mercedes: You don't realize that my dreams are part of the history of our
   country.[15]

From the very first scene, racism in Cuban society becomes the focal point, with a consciousness that the personal and the historical, that dreams and reality, are inseparable in Rolando's creative endeavor.

As the action develops, the protagonist's and the filmmaker's "investigative reporting" go hand in hand. Both Mercedes and Rolando avail themselves of multiple means to arrive at "the truth." The historical, personal, and mythical strands are interwoven to portray the complexity of the art of recovering lost truths. Rolando portrays this process in a scene in which Mercedes sits at a friend's house and discusses her predicament: Should she follow her superior's mandate or work on her own project? While the women discuss the issue, Mercedes' hair is being beautifully braided. The camera focuses on Mercedes' head as hands pick up a single strand of hair and braid it with two others. The new hairdo enhances Mercedes' beauty. Consequently, she receives comments throughout the day about the transformation she has undergone. Comments such as "You look like a queen with that hairdo" and "How beautiful you look with that hairdo" become leitmotifs throughout the film as Mercedes meets friends, mother, and lover.

Much of Cuba's racism at the birth of the nation was based on fear both of the black *brujo* (witch) who allegedly stole white children as sacrificial victims and of the black *ñáñigo* (member of the Abakuá secret society associated with crime) who was closely linked with rape of white women. Transforming the image of the black in Cuban society is most important in trying to overcome that racism. In her book on race in Cuba, Helg states: "race was a fundamental social construct that articulated the hierarchy of Cuban society. . . . There were two social groupings distinguished from each other by physical appearance, and one group was dominant against the other. The barrier maintaining this hierarchy was founded on physical differences characteristic of continental space (Europe versus tropical Africa), including skin color, hair texture, and facial features, as well as on cultural differences such as social customs and religious beliefs. In rough terms, it established the superiority of persons of full European descent over those with partial or full African descent" (Helg, 12–13). Paramount in overcoming that hierarchy even today is the need to dissociate physical features from racist fears. When Rolando focuses on the beauty of Mercedes after her hair has been braided in an African manner, she not only emphasizes the pride of looking like one's ancestors but also creates an image of the black person as looking like a "queen," as being able to occupy those spaces in Cuban society that have been denied to blacks.[16]

Moreover, I suggest that this braiding scene is a key to understanding Rolando's artistic methods. The scene becomes one of nurturing as the friend asserts, "Fight for your project." When Mercedes leaves the house, she is determined to unveil the secrets in her family, secrets that will lead her back to the massacre of 1912. In *Las raíces de mi corazón* Rolando braids multiple cinematic and cultural resources to get at the root of historically kept secrets. Women's work—to braid and to investigate in collaboration—produces beauty and pride in being Afro-Cuban.

What then are the forces in conflict and in collaboration as Mercedes pursues her truths? At the personal level, the secrets in her family have been perpetuated to respect the memory of a great-grandmother, María Victoria, who had a child out of wedlock. A surviving great-aunt, Cecilia, has provided the photographs, letters, and newspaper cuttings from which Mercedes must reconstruct her past. Mercedes' mother speaks of silence as a way to forget the pain of the past, while Mercedes insists on her investigation in order to recover a family's and a country's history. In order to respect the memory of those who have passed and alleviate the pain, older generations forget; younger ones honor them by remembering. Ultimately, Rolando's film is also about the nature of memory and its representation through artistic means.

Once family members begin to collaborate with Mercedes in her pursuit, the forces of her dream take center stage. Even though the film takes time to establish Mercedes in the context of the outside world—her work, her friends, her relationship with her two children as she picks them up from school—it is in the interior of the house and in the realm of her dreams that real knowledge arrives. The song at the beginning of the film highlights this interiority and brings together the purposes of protagonist and filmmaker and provides the title to the film:

Una mujer pregunta   [A woman asks
si es posible   if it is possible
si el día y la noche   that day and night
comparten el delirio   could share the delirium
de la imaginación.   of imagination.

Una mujer se envuelve,   A woman gets involved,
se abriga con su historia,   comforts herself with her story,
tan sólo cuando escucha   only when she listens to
vivas siempre   the always vibrant
las raíces de su corazón.   roots of her heart.]

                                      (my translation)

Gloria Rolando, "Mercedes (Monse Duany) Looks Over the Family Album,"
from *Las raíces de mi corazón*, 2001.

Imagination in the form of dreams, and the roots of one's heart provide
the creative process that leads to the truth. Such a process entails listen-
ing and looking into oneself. One of the most poignant scenes in the
film takes place when Mercedes and her mother sit at a table where the
mother separates debris from dried grains of rice while Mercedes looks
at the evidence of her great-grandmother's involvement with José Julián,
an Afro-Cuban who died in the 1912 massacre. As in the braiding scene,
steps toward self-discovery take place within the context of domestic-
ity. As the women talk, black-and-white scenes of black men hanging
from trees flash onto the screen to the accompaniment of drums. Since
such flashes do not disturb the peaceful exchange between the women,
they seem to be intended for the audience, who can begin to anticipate
a period of self-discovery as the truth begins to break into Mercedes'
consciousness in the form of images. In contrast to the gruesome black-
and-white scenes, the interior of the house is muted by the yellow glow
of lamps in the room. Mercedes has just awakened her mother, who had
fallen asleep in a rocking chair. For Afro-Cubans an empty rocking chair
allows the ancestors to take their place in familiar surroundings. As the
mother leaves the chair, it is left vacant for María Victoria to come and
inhabit Mercedes' familiar spaces. After this intimate scene of conversation, Mercedes receives from the hands of her mother the pendant that

José Julián gave María Victoria. It had been given as a promise that they would marry after his return from the insurrection in Oriente. Mercedes places the pendant next to the couple's photograph on her dresser and sits in bed with all the documents she has received from her mother and great-aunt. Material objects serve as mnemonic devices for acquisition of memory during the waking hours.

While asleep and in her dreams, Mercedes enters into a different kind of collaboration in order to unlock María Victoria's past. Two major figures in African diasporic mythology intervene in Mercedes' dreams. The first is an African woman who may represent a combination of Yemayá (the deity of the seas and in particular of the Atlantic), of Ochún (the deity of sensuality, motherhood, and river waters) and Oyá (the keeper of cemeteries, the warrior woman, the keeper of memory). The second is the Old African, the spirit of the night, who represents collective memory. In the dream sequence, filmed in color and in black and white in hazy hues, the figure of the African woman enters the house and goes into the bedroom to take Mercedes into the realm of the seas where they dance together. At one point it is difficult to distinguish one from the other. The African woman wears an elaborate African dress of yellows and blacks, while Mercedes dons a simple tie-dyed dress of bright blues, also in the African tradition. Through hair and dress, Mercedes fully assumes her African traditions.

During the dancing, a male voice-over repeats refrains: "Dreams may come either at night or during the day," "Truth lies between reality and dreams," and "Listen to what the roots of your heart tell you." It is the voice of the second mythical figure in Mercedes' dreams, the Old African, wearing a wide-brimmed hat, smoking tobacco, and walking through the woods with the aid of a mahogany cane with faces turning in opposite directions. As the spirit of the night who poses questions, the Old African personifies the life of old memories still with us. His voice repeats, "Not all appearances are true," and "Things have two faces." From time to time, images of his walking through the woods are interposed with those of Mercedes asleep in her bed.

During her waking hours and in collaboration with the women in her inner circle and with mythical African ancestors in the realm of dreams, Mercedes achieves a vision of the past: the screen Mercedes sees in her dreams projects a couple dancing on a back porch to a *danzón* (a popular Cuban dance derived from the traditional habanera). The young man, José Julián, wears a white linen suit; María Victoria a white-laced dress lined in blue taffeta. As is evident from the restrained moves of the *danzón,* they are clearly in love. At the end of the dance, they go from the sunken porch up some stone stairs that obviously lead out onto the street.

A close-up intervenes: Mercedes and her mother speak about José Julián's departure and disappearance. The family has speculated through the years that perhaps he was married to someone else, that he went back to Tampa, Florida, where he and his family had become part of the Cuban tobacco industry that supported Cuban independence. No one has said that he could have been killed in the massacre. The scene then returns to the porch where María Victoria reads a letter from José Julián while sitting in a rocking chair. He speaks of the reorganization of the Independientes de Color, of his work with Estenoz, of his imprisonment, of his father's being able to bail him out of jail, of his promise to marry María Victoria in Cuba when blacks have equal rights. There is a short sequence in black and white of men fighting in the mountains of Oriente. Then of José Julián and María Victoria making love in a room adorned with blue curtains. Both sequences are in slow motion. Candles from María Victoria's bedroom in Oriente and from Mercedes' room in Havana are superimposed. The voice of the Old African returns with his refrains: "Keep the secrets of fire," "Life is slow, but death is immediate," and "Things have two faces." From the sensual images of the couple making love, the camera jumps to black-and-white scenes of the massacre. A woman is killed in the woods. People are in flight, then fall to the sound of rifle fire. Mercedes is seen reading the newspaper announcing the extermination of "the racist dissidents." A female voice reads the headlines in an ironic tone while the muffled screams of María Victoria are heard in the background. The Old African walks among the dead. A dirge is heard. The figure of the African woman returns to Mercedes' living room. The sequence closes with images of candlelight and the sound of hurricane-force winds.

Throughout the dream sequence there is an attempt to erase the boundaries between dream and reality (with the superimposed images of Mercedes and the African woman), past and present (with the juxtaposing of Mercedes and María Victoria's realities), and the personal and the historical (with images of Mercedes sleeping and scenes from the massacre). Yet there is a difference between the roles that María Victoria and Mercedes play. María Victoria witnessed history but participated in it only in an indirect manner. Mercedes also witnesses history through her research and in her dreams, but she goes on to represent a double of the African woman who leads others in imagining forgotten truths and dreams. In this respect she stands in for Gloria Rolando who, as artist, translates both personal and Cuban history into the cinematographic image. Whereas María Victoria suffered her losses with tears and later silence, Mercedes directs her personal life in purposeful ways. At the professional level, Mercedes goes against her boss's mandate and refuses to ignore her dreams. At a personal level, she divorces her husband and reaches out to Armando, a lover who celebrates her braids with pride and encourages her to take her discoveries out into the world: "Let's bring all of this into the open air, let's give it life" (meaning the photos, the letters, the newspaper cuttings). In one scene, they have the following exchange:

Mercedes: Do you believe one can know things from dreams?
Armando: My grandmother used to say: Lies may run for a long time, you can grab truth in a day, it doesn't take long.

Within the context of the film, the day of which Armando speaks is the twenty-four-hour period that constitutes the dramatic length of the fifty-minute film. In the mythical realm of dreams, the keeper of collective memory is the Old African; in domestic life, that keeper is the great-aunt. Likewise, Mercedes' mother has played the role of the African woman as facilitator between truth and Mercedes' inquisitive imagination, which is personified by the Old African and his refrains.

Before going out into Central Park with Armando and her children, Mercedes puts on María Victoria's pendant. She relights the candle before the couple's photograph. All four go to the plaza in front of José Martí's statue. The film points to the irony of a place where the ideals of a leader who dreamed of a country for all races should also be the place where in 1912 Cuban president José Miguel Gómez held a banquet to celebrate the elimination of "the racist insurrection" quelled under his military power. It is also ironic that leaders from Gómez to Castro have appropriated Martí's ideals of racial equality between races as if they had actually been realized after Cuba's multiple revolutionary processes. As Mercedes' children play, she and Armando sit and view present-day Cubans of both genders, both whites and nonwhites cross the plaza in slow motion. The unpronounced question arises: Is Cuba a nonracist country now?

While enormous positive changes for Afro-Cubans have happened since the 1959 Revolution, racism persists. Clearly, within the context of the film, little changes in present-day Cuba in regard to safeguarding the memory of Afro-Cubans: Mercedes' boss encourages her to forget her family history. Only the braiding of the hair and the production of the cinematic image have transformed the creator and, it is hoped, the viewer. The voice-over of the Old African pronouncing the phrase "Once awakened, truth refuses to sleep again" clearly points to the director's belief in the power of film to transform its audience and Cuba.

The film ends on a historical note. Black-and-white images of the dead revisit the screen. A male voice calls out the names of those who died in the cause for independence: Antonio Maceo, José Maceo, Mariana Grajales, as well as those martyred in 1912, among them party leaders Pedro Ivonnet and Evaristo Estenoz. The question gets asked repeatedly a capella: "José Miguel (Gómez) why did you kill so many innocent blacks?" In a call-and-response manner, the names are pronounced, and "inocente" follows. At the very end, the screen goes black, and white letters summarize the historical events.

With *Las raíces de mi corazón,* a short fictional piece, Rolando has held to the purpose of her documentaries, which vowed to rescue the history of the African diaspora. The end of the film clings stubbornly to the portrayal of historical events as preserved in the African diasporic practice of call and response. By closing this way, Rolando points to the force of African diasporic cultural practices as being essential in the face of racist adversity. Actual events of the massacre are visualized in black-and-white to heighten and differentiate them from the personal story portrayed in color.

Before concluding, I must contextualize this film in a tradition of Cuban film by other filmmakers, such as Umberto Solás in *Lucía* (1968), in which women's stories intersect with Cuba's three revolutionary movements. Scenes between women in Rolando's film recall scenes in *Lucía*—for example, the gossip scenes between women on the streets. Rolando's use of personal histories to arrive at national history through the interplay of photography hearkens back to Sara Gómez's documentary *Retrato de familia* [A Family Portrait], and Rolando dedicates her film to Gómez. Rolando's use of cinematography to reinterpret Afro-Cuban history recalls Sergio Giral's 1974 *El otro Francisco* [The Other Francisco] and Tomás Gutiérrez Alea's 1976 *La última cena* [The Last Supper]. Many of the scenes of blacks dying in the fields are reminiscent of Sergio Giral's treatment of the runaway slave in *El otro Francisco*. With *Las raíces de mi corazón,* Gloria Rolando positions herself within a well-established tradition of Cuban cinematography that acts as revisionist history. What distinguishes her film from the tradition is her complete departure from the strategies of the "Imperfect cinema," which sought to combine documentary with fictional methods to arrive at a new version of history.

The self-consciousness of those endeavors is absent from Rolando's 2001 film.

Las raíces de mi corazón responds to a more contemporary project in the media arts to interject the image of the Afro-Cuban into more popularly accessible media. This project must also consider the economic hardships in contemporary Cuba that prohibit epic cinematic productions as in the past. In an interview with Mathilde Mansoz and Barbara Aranda, Rolando expresses the following views:

> The general economy of the country suffers a great deal and that has consequences on cultural life. In spite of it all, one continues to try producing films. Recently, several alternatives have arisen. For example, the National Union of Writers and Artists has created a small production group to perpetuate the tradition of documentary film. That is testimony of a will to continue. Many aspects of Cuban culture and traditions are the object of that documentary tradition through, for example, the presentation of historical figures. ("Interview de Gloria Rolando")

Gloria Rolando's expressed interest in presenting historical figures is innovatively treated in *Las raíces de mi corazón,* intersecting as it does with a feminine sensibility that strives to valorize the role of the domestic, of oral traditions, and of the mythical in the filmic process. The fact that braiding hair can be made to symbolize the cinematic creative process and that an emotional sensibility is valued enough to appear in the title of the film points to a film production that finds insufficient the mere revision of history as a primary focus. In *Las raíces de mi corazón* Gloria Rolando shies away from hierarchies and gives equal and contemporaneous value to several strands in braiding her message: the personal, the mythical, the historical, oral traditions, and such cultural practices as song and dance. In this beautiful film, image, sound, the written word, and oral traditions play equal parts in getting at the full picture, at the full cultural truth. Despite the economic hardships involved in creating this film, Gloria Rolando has achieved full maturity with her own revision of both the African diaspora culture and Cuban history.

WHILE GLORIA ROLANDO recaptures Afro-Cuban history by weaving, as if into an African-style braid, the historical, the personal, and the mythical, the artist Belkis Ayón rescues the artistic signification processes of Abakuá society to deal with contemporary Cuban issues of racism and sexism. As Eugenio Valdés Figueroa states in *Siempre Vuelvo: Colografías de Belkis Ayón* [I Always Return: Collographs by Belkis Ayón] in 2000, "her discourse is marked radically by a sexual conscience that turns out to be polemical (final page).[17]

The myths and rituals of the all-male Abakuá Secret Society, their theatricality, and their symbolic representations have tended to influence Cuban arts in the nineteenth and twentieth centuries (Castellanos and Castellanos, *Cultura Afrocubana*, vol. 3, 256). In this vein, the Afro-Cuban artist Belkis Ayón (1967–1999) produced large-scale collographs that departed from Abakuá iconography, particularly from the creation myth of Tánze and Sikán. Born in Havana, Ayón attended the San Alejandro School of Fine Arts (1982–86) as well as the Higher Institute of Art (1986–91). In 1998 she was elected vice-president of the Association of Plastic Artists of the UNEAC. She had multiple one-person exhibitions in Cuba, the United States, Haiti, Germany, Italy, the Netherlands, and Canada and won several prizes in Cuba, Puerto Rico, and the United States (*Siempre Vuelvo*), including the Distinción por la Cultura Nacional [Cuban Prize for National Cultural Distinction], 1996; the Premio, Bienal de San Juan del Grabado Latinomericano y del Caribe [Biennial of San Juan Prize for Latin American and Caribbean Engraving], 1997; and artist-in-resident posts at the Brandywine Workshop in Philadelphia, the Tyler School of Art in Temple University's Printmaking Department (also in Philadelphia), and the Rhode Island School of Design's Printmaking Department in Providence, 1999.

As a preamble to my analysis of Ayón's artistic expression, the words of Cuban artist and critic Tonel (Antonio Eligio Fernández), who links the works of the Cuban ethnographer Lydia Cabrera to that of Belkis Ayón, are instructive:

> It's significant that a woman, an artist, has insisted on elaborating the iconography of a belief system that by definition excludes her. It immediately recalls a previous figure of Cuban culture: that of Lydia Cabrera, who during the first half of this century managed to record and process very valuable testimonies from practitioners of the Abakuá religion. In her investigation, Belkis seems to share some of Cabrera's ethnographic vocation, as well as some of that extravagant patience Cabrera had when approaching the *ñáñigos* "without fear or condescension (Cabrera)." (Fernández, 62; my translation)

Accordingly, without Lydia Cabrera's prior ethnographic research into the Abakuá Secret Society, it would be impossible to satisfactorily analyze Belkis Ayón's large-scale collographs.

According to Cabrera in the 1970 work *La sociedad secreta Abakuá: Narrada por viejos adeptos* [The Abakuá Secret Society as Narrated by

Its Old Initiates], the central mandate to an initiate of the society consists of keeping the secrets of the association's origins and practices. The all-male Abakuá Secret Society was first founded in Cuba in the Havana port of Regla in 1836 by slaves from the Calabar region of present-day Nigeria. Its members are popularly known in Cuba as *ñáñigos*, after the name of their highly ornamented public dancers, who represent the return of the dead for participation in earthly rituals. They are also commonly known as *diablitos*, little devils. In their belief system, members of the society enjoy the benefits of an alliance with the supernatural, as well as safe passage of their spirit into the afterlife upon death of the body (Castellanos and Castellanos, vol. 3, 205). They also receive material and spiritual protection from their fraternity.

The most guarded secret since the Abakuá society's inception concerns its myth of origins. In it, the figure of Sikán, daughter of the king of the Efor peoples, went to retrieve water from Oddán, the river that separated the Efor from the Efik. Abasí, the Supreme Being, saw fit to divulge his powers to her, a woman, and not to a man of the Efor. As Sikán placed her calabash of water on her head, she heard the Supreme Being's powerful voice (breath, life). Frightened, she fled to her father, who kept her in a secret place and commanded her not to share her story with anyone. Ultimately, Sikán divulged the Efor secret to her husband, an Efik prince. Consequently, the Efik demanded that the Efor share Sikán's secret with them. A battle ensued and was settled with the provision that Sikán's life be sacrificed by hanging from the sacred palm tree. Her body was dismembered and her flesh and blood consumed by the first members of the society (Cabrera, *La lengua sagrada de los náñigos* [The Sacred Language of the Ñáñigos], 483–86, 168–72).

The voice of the sacred fish Tánze, which had been caught in Sikán's calabash, can now be heard in the sound of the sacred Ekue drum, made from the wood of a palm tree found by the Oddán River and covered by the skin of Tánze. The skin of the sacred fish transforms the drum into a sacred object. Because the drum did not at first have as powerful a voice as when Tánze was alive, Sikán's blood and eyes were applied to its skin. Sikán's and Tánze's eyes become the symbols of the Abakuá society, symbols of the supreme mystic vision (Cabrera, *La sociedad secreta*, 107, Castellanos and Castellanos, vol. 3, 241). But even Sikán's sacrifice did not invest the drum with the original powerful voice. Eventually, the skin of a goat, representing Sikán herself, was superimposed on the skin of the sacred fish; only then was the powerful sound that Sikán had heard reproduced (Cabrera, *La sociedad secreta*, 113).

In *La sociedad secreta Abakuá* [The Abakuá Secret Society], Lydia Cabrera presents the myth of Tánze and Sikán in its multiplicity of versions (83–122). Cabrera's multiple informants agree that so many versions may cause confusion. Ultimately, however, they enrich the tradition: "so many versions enhance traditions notably" (119).[18] In some, Sikán's father and husband object to her being sacrificed; in others they do not (95, 96). In some, Sikán speaks out just as she is to be sacrificed; in others, she remains silent (90). In some, Sikán was sacrificed because she had seen Tánze—a fact that she denied and the elders confirmed (86). In some, she is a maiden; in others, a married woman (96). In some, it is said that she could not divulge the secret to her husband because she was confined in the woods, unable to speak to anyone for months (97). In some versions it is written that whoever receives Tánze will be sacrificed. In most, Sikán is punished for her betrayal and is led to the palm tree to be sacrificed by her father. In these versions, her father had promised that he would lead her to a place where she will view the mystery and become powerful (105). Sikán realizes she is about to die only when her blindfold is removed just prior to her hanging. In other words, *she* is betrayed.

The figure of Sikán represents both the mother of the creation myth and the sacrificial victim who ensures the perpetuation of the myth. The spirit of the Supreme Being, in its incarnation as the fish Tánze, and the spirit of Sikán are united in the sacred drum, Ekue. Because Sikán divulged Abasí's secret, all women are barred from membership in the society despite the fact that she represents the mother of the Abakuá: "The spirit of the Sikanekue walked along the river to meet the great ones and become a great one herself; she left in order to return, to be worshiped and to give life. To give birth to *obonékues*. To be a mother who reveres her children. We are born of the water and we shall return to it. Water is the mother of the spirits" (108).

Because of the multiple variations, Sikán surfaces as an ambiguous figure representing both the mother of the original secret and the betrayer of it. Because she has been chosen, Sikán enters into the realm of the sacred: "And Sikán Sina Yatán, whose ears were penetrated by the Voice, never guessed that at that moment, her head was already sacred thanks to the breath and the contact with Ndibo; nor did she guess that she, a woman, would be the Bearer of salvation, of the Strength who would exalt the men of Efor" (84). It is thanks to her having heard the sacred voice that the Efor become powerful. The accusations against her center on her inability to follow the paternal mandate—that is, not to view Tánze and not to divulge the secret of his power, his sacred voice. She refuses to abide by the command to keep silent, a desired attribute of the female gender in patriarchal societies. Gender determination also appears in the myth in the fact that Sikán encounters the sacred in the exercise of one of her domestic duties, fetching water. Lydia Cabrera describes her duties thus: "As was the habit of the laborious women of the Calabar, who worked so much, maybe even more than the men, every day Sikán went to fetch water for the chores and needs of her house" (83).

In addition to the multiple oral and written versions of the Abakuá myth of origin, the society possesses an *anaforuana,* a complex visual system of sacred symbols that are used to evoke sacred figures, events, places, myths, rites, and mythological transformations. The symbols, it is believed, create and give power. For example, white is associated with death, yellow with life. Thus, what has not been drawn with white and yellow chalk cannot have reality, cannot be sacred. The Abakuá are masters of symbolic substitution. Lydia Cabrera has compiled these symbols in her 1975 work *Anaforuana: Ritual y símbolos de la iniciación en la sociedad secreta Abakuá* [Anaforuana: Ritual Initiation and Symbols of the Abakuá Secret Society]. As with the myths, there are multiple symbols that represent Sikán, her sacrifice, and her power to be reborn in the sacred drum (71–83). For all important Abakuá rituals, the symbols evoke the initial rituals performed in the Calabar region. They identify the Cuban present with the Calabar past, material reality with the mystical. To represent Sikán's sacrifice, a goat is killed so that its blood may be used to bring to life the sacred drum's voice. In the sacrificial rituals, as well as in the *anaforuanas,* Tánze, Sikán and the goat are interchangeable.

Belkis Ayón evokes Sikán's betrayal in her collographs, which are transgressive in that they give voice to the female interpreter, to the female artist within a ritualistic system that forbids the presence of women. They replicate Sikán's life in their refusal to remain silent. Moreover, Ayón's art symbolizes and therefore makes real what was forbidden to Sikán, the ability to view the mystery. While Ayón interprets Abakuá iconography, she presents myths in their human and cultural complexity, taking into account the multiplicity of versions of the myths. What seems to interest Ayón is also at the core of Abakuá beliefs: the synthesis of the real and the sacred, the domestic and the mystical. In a November 1993 interview with David Mateo, Belkis Ayón noted the obvious relationship between Abakuá narratives and human existence. Her research into the relationship between Abakuá myths and Christian religiosity resulted in the representation of what she describes as "personal saintliness" (Mateo, "I Always Come Back"). As Lydia Cabrera and Jorges and Isabel

Castellanos have pointed out, Abakuá Secret Society avails itself and is open to comparisons with Christian symbols (the role of victimization, communion as representation of the original sacrifice, fish as emblem of the sacred, human victim and animal as interchangeable forms of sacrifice, the flesh transfigured as spirit).

What interests me most is Ayón's replication in her art of the Abakuá religious sensibility, that is, their mastery at symbolic substitution. At the heart of the Abakuá Secret Society lies its power to effect transformations from the real to the sacred, from the past to the present. This power is best captured, I believe, in its *anaforuanas,* its symbolic representations. For the Abakuá, representations are understood in their visual as well as dramatic senses. A powerful example of this power lies in the *anaforuana* that represents the transformation of Tánze, the sacred fish, into Ekue, the sacred drum (Cabrera, *Anaforuana,* 110–11). This transformation implies a progression: of spirit into voice or breath, then into material fish that is caught and dies, then into the material skin representative of the resurrection of the voice (spirit), then into the skin of Sikán in the form of sacrificial goat skin, that is Ekue, the sacred drum. This drawing of the transformation of Tánze into the Ekue represents a fish with a three-point tail (the three Efor tribes) that gives shape to the Ekue drum. The surface of the drum replicates Tánze's and Sikán's eyes, crowned by the four initial leaders of the Abakuá Secret Society.

It is most telling that, like the Abakuá, Ayón manipulates symbolic substitution by tracing her own silhouette for all the human representations in her canvases, particularly that of Sikán. In her interview with Mateo, she stated that "Sikán's legend is a theme I have been working on since I was a student at San Alejandro, and what has always drawn my attention is the female character as victim, though from a rather generic standpoint, hefting the connotations that could be derived from such a situation" (Mateo, "I Always Come Back"). Is it the ambiguity of Sikán's character as victim that interests Ayón? Or is it that the multiple versions of the Abakuá myth of origin afford the artist a myriad of interpretations of the social and mythical position of women in the passage from Africa to the Caribbean?

Moreover, since the artist uses her own figure as the model for her representations of Sikán, does Belkis Ayón project an artistic fusion of the autobiographical with the mystical? The artist contends, "I see myself as Sikán, as a bit of an observer, an intermediary and one who reveals: departing from my studies and my experiences, I invent her imagery since I am not a believer. But Sikán is a transgressor, and as I see her, I see myself" (Ayón, *Dossier, 1986–1999*, 5). Regarding her figures, Ayón has also stated: "It is true that I am the model for my figures. Together with me they pass from one stage to another continuously; they even lose weight when I do. They are characters I submit because I like the idea of deciding their fates. They are the only alternative to getting even. In other words and using livelier terms, my figures are, in fact, the only way to make amendments, though I live a less mythical life. I exist in a far more objective perspective and [am] much more practical (Mateo, "I Always Come Back"). Modeling her figures on her own image allows Ayón to pass similarly from one stage to another, to make amendments, and decide her own fate. At the heart of this methodology lie the concepts of transformation, revision, and artistic control. Her art, like Abakuá religiosity, depends on mystical and continuous transformations to allow figures to be transported between the past and the present.

In addition to referring to a remote African past, Ayón's collographs present a means for interpreting Cuba's present situation for blacks in light of the country's more recent past, that is, the first two decades of the twentieth century. For an analysis of the place of Afro-Cubans since the time of independence, I rely on the work of Aline Helg in her book *Our Rightful Share*. It is one among several that have collected journalistic records highlighting Cuba's debates about the rights of Cubans along racial lines (see also Aviva Chomsky's essay). Helg presents and analyzes the role of the Cuban press in the early twentieth century in fomenting racist attitudes that would make it impossible for Afro-Cubans to fully participate in the economic, social, and political levels of the newly established nation.

After having filled the ranks of the revolutionary army in the wars of 1868–78 and 1895–98, Afro-Cubans expected to become civil servants, and for those who served as generals in the army, to become members of the political elite. Such expectations based on José Martí's ideals of founding a nation in which citizens of European and African descent would enjoy equal rights were never fulfilled. Although his dream never became a reality, his writings were used as proof of racial equality in the new nation. This equality had supposedly been founded by white landowners who emancipated their slaves and by the coexistence of blacks and whites who fought side by side against the Spanish. Afro-Cubans' expectations were never fulfilled in the new republic because of fears on the part of the ruling elite that if Afro-Cubans occupied important positions in politics, Cuba would become another Haiti, a nation in which the French were exterminated or forced to leave the country after Haitian independence in 1804. Ultimately, Afro-Cubans did not enjoy their "rightful share" because of fears aroused by the journalistic promotion of such supposedly threatening figures as the black *brujo* (male witch) and the black *ñáñigo* who would snatch white children for use as sacrificial victims of "atavistic" rituals, and who would rape white women.

Afro-Cuban journalists tried to defend against such racist portrayals. Helg writes: "In fact, *El Nuevo Criollo* [*New Creole,* newspaper edited by Rafael Serra 1902–9], which promoted bourgeois values . . . responded to mainstream racist interpretation of brujería only in a defensive way. . . . It accused the white press of utilizing black brujos and *ñáñigos* to stigmatize all Afro-Cubans. . . . Only a counterdiscourse praising the wealth of Cuban's African cultural heritage and black participation in building the nation would have given Afro-Cubans the strength to face up to negative stereotyping" (Helg, 136). It is only after the cultural contributions of poet Nicolás Guillén in the 1930s, painter Wifredo Lam in the 1940s, and many Afro-Cuban writers, artists, and filmmakers after the 1959 Revolution that Afro-Cubans create a counterdiscourse highlighting the wealth of Afro-Cuban culture. Belkis Ayón's collographs are prominent in this counterdiscourse.

An analysis of four of the artist's works shows her mastery at symbolic transformations with the intent to honor the past and to inform the present. The first, *Sin título* [Untitled, Woman in Fetal Position; 1997], displays the silhouetted figure of Sikán, from the back, in white, crouching and holding Tánze, the sacred fish, behind her back. The central figure, all in white, sits as if on a gray grass surface that in places shows Tánze's eyes. The grass surface is surrounded by the river waters. The darkness surrounding the white figure floating on the water may be symbolic of a child about to be born, about to cry out. She could very well be uttering Sikán's defiant statement: "Abasí's will gave me what they have taken away from me! It is mine!" (Cabrera, *La sociedad secreta,* 90). Four other figures are immersed in the dark gray river water, which has a textured background of scales, representing Tánze. At each corner of the large rectangular piece (77 ½ x 54 ½ inches), there is a figure of Sikán, all in shades of gray and black. In the left top and bottom corners, she is depicted covering her eyes and holding her ears in response to the powerful voice of Tánze, as if to abide by her father's command not to view the mystery. In the upper right corner, she appears with arms raised above her head and with clenched fists. In one of the versions of the myth, when Sikán is about to die, she exclaims rebelliously: "Even though I may die, I will own the Ekue, Ekue will always be mine" (Cabrera, *La*

Belkis Ayón, *Sin título*, 1996. Colograph, 196 x 139 cm.

sociedad secreta, 100). The last image is just of Sikán's white face, which gives the impression that she is drowning in the river waters. This figure may depict Sikán at the moment before death or perhaps after she has been hanged; her eyes and mouth seem to cry out for help. In one of the versions of the myth, she is strangled and decapitated, and her eyes are placed on the Ekue drum, superimposed on Tánze's skin. Often the *diablitos* will represent Sikán with a mask with bulging eyes and protruding tongue to signify her suffering (Cabrera, *La lengua sagrada,* 485).

Like the Abakuá myth, Ayón's canvas portrays multiple aspects of Sikán's story. Yet *Sin título* goes beyond replicating the Abakuá myth of transformations. Because all five figures appear contemporaneously on the piece, the artist underscores the complexity of Sikán's experience and its mythic significance. By depicting three figures in white rather than gray, Ayón emphasizes the connection between two stages in Sikán's life: before and after she has divulged Abasí's secret. Ayón draws a contrast between a compliant Sikán entirely in gray and a rebellious one—her eyes and fists are white. The use of white and gray on the otherwise very dark background emphasizes the defiant and victimized facets of the Abakuá mythical figure. The central one, modeled after Ayón's body, humanizes the myth; the other more iconographically mythic figures sink into the waters and fade into the background. Ayón makes her rebellious statement by superimposing her contemporary image of herself onto the mythic past. Past and present merge in the timeless present of the canvas, just as they do in the *anaforuanas*.

The central figure of Sikán/Ayón defiantly holding the fish Tánze can be interpreted as representing the power to give voice to that which has been silenced by patriarchy and by social and political conventions. One of the best-kept secrets in Cuban society, early as well as late in the twentieth century, concerns the nature of its racism. Cuban presidents, from José Luis Gómez in the second decade to Fidel Castro in the final decades, have claimed that equality exists among the races, citing the teachings of freedom fighter José Martí, whose ideas regarding a free society for all did not become a reality for Afro-Cubans after independence in 1902. Instead, his writings have been used to suppress any dissent on the part of Afro-Cubans. As already discussed, the worst suppression was ordered by President Gómez in 1912 when more than 6,000 Afro-Cubans were massacred as racists for taking up arms after their political party Independientes de Color was declared unconstitutional. Following Castro's revolution, Afro-Cubans made economic and educational advances and entered almost all sectors of society, except the political sphere, where mostly whites still occupy positions of power. It is only as recently as the 1990s that sociological studies have begun to document a persistence of racism instilled at the level of the family (see Caño Secade and *La Gaceta de Cuba* 1 (2005), dedicated to the topic of nation, race, and culture).

The situation of black women in Cuban society as victims of sexism and racism has been perpetuated in the stereotype of the mulatta as licentious and treacherous, yet silenced by society. A recent example can be found in the testimonials of multiple black women in present-day Cuban society in Rolando Díaz's 1999 film *Si me comprendieras* [If You Understood].[19] Ironically, while women in all sectors of society are allowed to tell their stories in personal interviews, a fictional frame of the film has a director seeking out women for a dance chorus in a traditional Cuban musical, where most women are portrayed as highly sensual. In Belkis Ayón's work, sexism finds dramatic treatment in the 1999 work entitled *¡¡Déjame salir!!* [Let Me Out!]. This collograph truly represents woman as mythical victim, but not as a passive victim by virtue of the voice featured in the title. Sikán's face is caught in a series of dark concentric circles, along with the sacred fish Tánze and the sacrificial goat. The circle, the Ekue drum, fuses the power of all three figures in its loudly resounding skin. But unlike the Abakuá circle, which stands for the perfect union of the spirits, Ayón's gray and black canvas (39 x 29 ½ inches) places Sikán at the center and allots only marginal space to the fish and goat figures. Sikán's hands, which frame her face, seem to be touching the drum's surface in an effort to go beyond the black skin in which she has been trapped by her mythologically ambiguous position as virgin/woman or traitor.

Belkis Ayón, *¡¡Déjame salir!!* 1997. Colograph, 100 x 75 cm.

When viewed in conjunction with the 1998 *Acoso* (Harassment), *¡¡Déjame salir!!* acquires a more contemporary meaning. In *Acoso*, Sikán's hands, or Ayón's, in my interpretation, hold a hurricane, with the eye of the storm proceeding toward the top right of the canvas. Sikán's eyes and body are caught up in the powerful winds and gyrate within the circle. At the symbolic level of Ayón's representation, the knowledge and

Belkis Ayón, *Acoso*, 1998. Colograph, 100 x 75 cm.

possession of Abakuá iconography earn her "the right to belong to the society and communicate according to its conventions" (Matibag, *Afro-Cuban Religious Experience*, 122). As an artist who possesses Abakuá symbols, Ayón is capable of presenting a critique regarding the victimization and exclusion of women from within the Afro-Cuban culture. Here, the artist also brings into focus the harassment that women, black and white, suffer in the Caribbean, where machismo, racism, and hurricanes are a common occurrence. In this canvas, the artist's black and white hands seem to be clearly in control of the forces of the wind, rather than being trapped inside the drum as in *¡¡Déjame salir!!* Nevertheless, because of the furious power of the concentric winds, the viewer is aware that its powerful force threatens to slip from the artist's hands. Ann Jones, curator of a Cuban artists show at the Barbican Centre in London in 1999, entitled *Trabajando p'al Inglé* [Working for the English], poses two questions regarding Ayón's treatment of the foundational Abakuá myth: "But, does the artist realise that by proposing such drastic modification of the essential nucleus of the Ñáñigo myth, she is also questioning the reason for the existence of such a society? Her novel and original version of the myth is also a subversion. She is proposing to nullify the male predominance within a brotherhood exclusively constituted by men. But is not the Abakuá's society an irritating emphatic model of our own society, of any human society?" (29).

The fourth canvas, also in whites, blacks, and grays, the 1998 work *Resurrección* [Resurrection], depicts multiple figures of Sikán, with a white, central figure of a woman rising above all the rest. In this work, Abakuá symbols are present (such as the circle with the eyes), but it is the Christian image of the Resurrection that stands out, with the woman rising up to heaven and leaving the suffering images behind. The fact that the resurrecting figure is rendered in white makes it ambiguous, since in Abakuá iconography the color white represents death. The work evokes the sacrifice and Resurrection of Christ, but with a woman at the center. The size of the piece (11 x 9 feet) emphasizes the importance of the subject and recalls monumental paintings by Michelangelo, El Greco, and Bosch depicting the sufferings of humans in the underworld and Christ's glory in heaven.

Ayón's interest in silhouetted figures endows her collographs with a movement and a drama that I associate with the mannered yet mystical canvases of El Greco. Of her figures the artist states:

[During my studies at the elementary school] . . . Without my being aware, I started growing [sic] a kind of trauma with drawing and painting, and because of that, I started searching for types of figures that would be credible but not abundant in anatomical exquisiteness. Later, I found out that this moderation in details gave added protection to the mystery of the images and that I should keep insisting on the poses, the gestures, the eyes, trying to avoid certain definitions. (Mateo, "I Always Come Back")

Beyond the social interpretation of the feminine figures in Ayón's work, it appears true that the artist also used her work for autobiographical purposes, working through traumas to gain control over them, to go beyond them via a liberating death/resurrection. The issues that she takes up, which are central to the Abakuá society, focus on the exclusionary social place of women in society as well as on women's victimization in male-centered societies. Her collographs mine the transformative aspect of African iconographic practices that conflate past and present. Her large-scale works employing shades of black and white bring to the forefront the silent-no-more issues of gender and race in Cuban society. Moreover, her use of Sikán as transformative figure allows her to propel her rebellious message into a present where her silent (because it is visual) yet powerful voice exploits the flexibility and endurance of African cultural practices such as that of the Abakuá. Ayón has stated, "I create images for the most varied stories of the myth, motivated by its lessons about human questioning, about the struggle for its conservation and survival" (quoted in Acosta de Arriba, "Imágenes desde el Silencio" [Images from Silence], 3). With her self-representation as Sikán at the center of her collographs, Belkis Ayón, like Nancy Morejón and Gloria Rolando, has called attention both to an insidious racism in her country and to her rich African heritage, while placing herself at the center of contemporary Cuban artistic production.

4 The Autobiographical Poetry of Excilia Saldaña

IN THE LAST of a series of autobiographical poems, the Afro-Cuban poet Excilia Saldaña (1946–1999) declares: "Hace falta la transfiguración del monte" [The transfiguration of the sacred wilderness is necessary] ("Vieja trova sobre soporte CD ROM," 22). Since early in her career as a poet, Saldaña defined herself as a black Caribbean woman poet: "I am a woman and my work carries that stamp implicitly. . . . And I don't want to only write as a woman, but as a Black woman" ("Excilia Saldaña," 198; ellipses mine). Because she consciously writes within an Afro-Cuban tradition, the word *monte,* meaning "forest" or "mountain," also carries the connotation of "sacred wilderness," the place where Afro-Cuban deities reside and where communication between human beings and their ancestors occurs. When Saldaña proposes the transfiguration of the sacred wilderness, she appeals as well to the Christian tradition, the word *transfiguration* meaning "the change in the appearance of Jesus in the mountain" (*Webster's New World College Dictionary*). With the line "Hace falta la transfiguración del monte," Saldaña reveals her cultural *mestizaje/transculturación,* concepts that her predecessors Nicolás Guillén in the 1930s and Fernando Ortiz in the 1940s defined as the reciprocal influence of African and Spanish cultures in the creation of the hybrid nation that is Cuba.

As a poet, Saldaña also uses the word *transfiguration* to mean a change in shape or form, a going across, beyond, through the figures and forms of language to get at the meaning of the word *monte.* Since "Vieja trova sobre soporte CD ROM" is an autobiographical poem, the word *monte* can also be read as the place where the life of the poet finds figurative expression. *El monte* is variously the place where Christ faced his demons, proclaimed his ministry, and assumed his sacred identity; where the *orishas* (Afro-Cuban deities) communicate with humans; where, as a linguistic site, the poet defines the self. In the following pages, I explore Excilia Saldaña's attempts at self-figuration within the Cuban tradition of *mestizaje* through a series of autobiographical poems. Before going on to my analyses, a brief overview of the poet's life and works is in order.

Excilia Saldaña (1946–1999) was a Cuban poet, translator, educator (Universidad Pedagógica de Santa Clara) and editor of children's literature (Editorial Gente Nueva in Havana). She grew up in Havana in a black middle-class family composed of her paternal grandparents and her parents. She was raised primarily by her grandmother, Ana Excilia Bregante, a fact the poet has recorded in her children's book *La noche* [Night], as well as in her autobiographical poem *Mi nombre: Antielegía familiar* [My Name: A Family Anti-Elegy]. For several years, starting in 1959 when Fidel Castro assumed power in Cuba, Saldaña was estranged from her family owing to her revolutionary views. She received her university degree in Hispanic American literature and specialized in journalism and publishing. In 1967, at the age of nineteen, her collection *Enlloró* won a mention in the prestigious Casa de las Américas Prize, but the poet declined its publication because of the poetry's immaturity. At the age of twenty-two she married and had a son, Mario Ernesto Romero. The marriage lasted five years. Throughout her life she suffered from severe asthma, which ultimately caused her death. She lived and worked mainly in Havana and traveled throughout Europe and the Americas. Besides her central dedication to being a poet, Excilia Saldaña was committed to the education and training of primary and secondary school teachers. She cherished her recognition throughout the island as one of the most accomplished writers of children's books.

Saldaña received the Nicolás Guillén Distinguished Poet Award given by the UNEAC (the Cuban National Union of Writers and Artists) in 1998, as well as several awards for her children's writing: Ismaelillo Prize (1979), La Rosa Blanca Prize (1984, 1987), and La Edad de Oro Prize (1984). Her major literary works include several books for children, a collection of aphorisms, a lengthy erotic letter, and three major autobiographical poems. These extensive poems show Saldaña's repeated attempts to draw her personal and poetic portrait, always in dialogue with the rich Hispanic literary tradition dating back to Sor Juana Inés de la Cruz, San Juan de la Cruz, and Quevedo, and to the more recent voices of José Martí, Federico García Lorca, Vicente Huidobro, and Gabriela Mistral, among others. In her effort to inscribe her own name at the center of Cuban letters, Saldaña also alludes to the prophetic voices of Pablo Neruda, Walt Whitman, and William Shakespeare.

Most central in the definition of her poetic voice, however, stands the poetic mastery of Nicolás Guillén, who established for Cuban letters the integration of Hispanic and African traditions in the poetic idiom. Like Guillén, Saldaña plays with the traditional meter and rhyme of Hispanic poetry in conjunction with the rich narrative treasure and strategies found in Yoruba and Bantu cultures as transmitted by Cuban blacks in legends called *patakines* (as in her children's book *Kele Kele*). Saldaña's mastery at appropriating and integrating universal poetic traditions as a black woman of the Caribbean is evident in her collection of aphorisms, *El refranero de la Víbora* [Collection of Refrains from La Víbora], and in her "Cartas eróticas" [Erotic Letters] contained in *In the Vortex of the Cyclone*. From her lullabies (*Jícara de miel* [Honey Gourd]) to her auto-biographical poems, Excilia Saldaña places the figure of her grandmother, Ana Excilia Bregante, at the center of her poetic inspiration. Particularly in *La noche* and *Mi nombre,* the grandmother reaches mythical dimensions to represent the experience of black women in the African diaspora as keepers of memory and as nurturers of both white and black children in the Caribbean context. Behind the figure of the grandmother looms large that of Mariana Grajales, mother of Cuban independence general Antonio Maceo, as well as unacknowledged black women in Cuba's history. Ultimately, in Saldaña's poetry, the personal is closely tied to the historical and the mythical.

In this autobiographical prose poem from Excilia Saldaña's collection of children's poems, *La noche,* the personal becomes the mythical:

Nací el 7 de agosto de 1946, a las seis de la tarde cuando el sol se preparaba para dar paso a La Noche. Entonces llegó ella: dé los brazos adolescentes de la madre pasé a los suyos hechos para ser abuela: mi abuela. Pero, ahora, cuando la miro en los retratos veo una mujer sin edad, rolliza y saludable como buena hija de mulata caribe y de isleño. Ya no está, sólo me quedan unas manillas de oro, una jarra rota y el perfil de mi hijo: mas, ¿no es acaso la memoria presencia del corazón? Ella es. Tengo mi nombre extraño y suyo, y los recuerdos: inmarcesibles, nuestros.

En la casona de la Víbora o bajo el portalón de Santa Fe, aprendí su palabra y su silencio. Y la mejor parte de mí. (Back cover)

I was born August 7, 1946, at six in the afternoon when the sun was about ready to give way to Night. Then she arrived: from the adolescent arms of my mother I went to hers, arms made to be grandmother's: my grandmother. But now, when I see her in photographs, I see an ageless woman, ruddy and healthy like any daughter of a Caribbean mulatto woman and of an islander. She is no longer; some gold bracelets, a broken pitcher and the profile of my son remain. But, isn't memory the presence of the heart? She lives on. I have my strange name which is hers, and the memories: unwithering, ours.

In the old house of La Víbora, or under the huge porch in Santa Fé, I learnt her word and her silence. And the best part of me.[1] (Back cover)

The gesture of the infant's being handed over into the grandmother's arms signifies not only the giving of the baby to the grandmother's care, but also the gesture of the child's being handed into the Afro-Cuban tradition. This transition from the personal to the mythical sphere is made concrete with the image of the photograph bearing "an ageless woman," born out of the figure that reinvents the origin of Cuban culture, the mulatto woman, product of the imposed mixing of the Spanish and the African.

The gold bracelets and the broken pitcher, fragments of the past, represent the grandmother's presence, as does her profile recast in Saldaña's son. In this prose poem, Excilia Saldaña positions herself as the link to a past that—but for the memories engraved in the poet's imagination—could be erased. The future depends on the poet's ability to nurture it with her own words.

The grandmother's image in the poet's name, "my strange name," and in the sounds and silences of the grandmother's voice, has given Saldaña "the best part of me," her poetic idiom. The poet-grandchild receives the oral tradition on both domestic sites and public sites, in the house and on the porch. In her poetry, female traditions are literally handed down with a loving gesture, from the interior to the exterior, and are given oral and written voice.

With this prose poem from *La noche,* Saldaña puts into place a series of concepts that she repositions throughout her poetry: memory, self-identity as tied to national history, the assumption of the grandmother's name, and the definition of family founded in the relationship of granddaughter to grandmother, skipping one generation and erasing the patriarchal line. The only male present is the child-son, who exists, at least physically, as a mirror of the grandmother's profile.

In a statement about sexism in Cuban society and her relationship to her then eight-year-old son, Saldaña expresses her belief in "the new man": "I want my son to grow up to be a man who will understand that 'his woman' is above all his comrade, his friend, his equal. I'm sure he will because both myself and the State are working toward this. Although my son is only eight years old, he very much respects the fact that I write and he's my best critic when I'm writing for children. We have a project for the near future. I'm sure he will be the kind of man Che dreamed of, and besides being my son, he'll be the friend I choose to have" ("Excilia Saldaña," 198). Besides embodying the grandmother in his profile, the son, in his relationship to his mother, the poet, embodies as well the image of Ernesto Che Guevara's concept of "the New Man," committed to nation and community at the expense of the personal. In Saldaña's view, the new man, her son, must be a companion and collaborator to the women in his life. The son, like the grandmother, becomes a figure who supports and collaborates in the poet's endeavors (these ideas are fully developed in *Mi nombre*). In Saldaña's rendition of the family in *La noche*, a book dedicated to her grandmother and to her son, the concept of family gets revised from that of the nuclear, middle-class family to which Saldaña supposedly belonged, to that of a future family based on mutual support between the sexes, and to that of a mythical family in which the supportive son and the wise grandmother replace the patriarchal figure.

In "Autobiografía" the reader surmises that the father's absence in Saldaña's family portrait in *La noche* correlates with his deplorable behavior:

mi padre un muchacho extravagante
(así decían cuando el hijo
de familia resultaba un cabrón)

my father was a playboy
(that's what they called them in those days
when the son of the family was a no good bastard)
("Autobiografía," *In the Vortex of the Cyclone*, 200, 201)

Extreme sarcasm dominates the tone of "Autobiografía" from beginning to end. The father, "hijo de familia," meaning from the middle class, is qualified as *extravagante*. ("Hijo de familia" also hides the more vulgar expression "hijo de puta," son of a bitch.) *Extravagante* obfuscates the father's less-than-model behavior of smoking marijuana, gambling, and screwing around ("fornicara"). *Extravagante* points also to society's condoning of such behavior on the part of privileged males who are not at all blamed for their irresponsibility: "en fin no fue su culpa" [well it wasn't his fault] (201). Saldaña thus exploits the sexism present in Cuban society before the Castro revolution ("así decían entonces") through the sarcastic portrait of her father. The portrait of the mother is no more flattering as she appears trembling and reduced to the representative image of a womb:

> imagínese las circumstancias
> mi madre temblante
> el hueco
>
> imagine the context
> my trembling mother
> the proverbial cavity
> (201, 202)

With these few lines the concept of the nuclear family as a supportive social unit is shattered.

In her study of *Mi nombre: Antielegía familiar,* "Cross-Cultural Home-bodies in Cuba," Catherine Davies analyzes the model of the Caribbean family as presented by Saldaña: "[T]he disconcerting encounter of two cultures (African/European) figured in two types of corresponding domestic organization: the subculture of the flexible Caribbean household and the dominant culture of the middle-class or socialist nuclear family" (180). "The flexible Caribbean household" often headed by grandparents or by the grandmother alone attains mythical status in Saldaña's depiction of the grandmother as a nurturing being in *La noche,* whereas in "Autobiografía" the middle-class unit represents the degrading prototype of two young beings who come together to reproduce and then abandon their responsibilities. These two poems catalog the personal and historical consequences for Caribbean women of being reduced to a reproductive organ. While Saldaña, in her poetic creation of the family, reflects on personal experience, she also recalls fragmented family structures during slavery when children were cared for by older women so that their mothers could be returned to the forced-labor market.[2] While enslaved, black women acted as nurses for white children, *criolleras* in Cuba, at the expense of nurturing their own. This role, as we saw in chapter 1, was depicted by Cirilo Villaverde in *Cecilia Valdés* in the character of María de Regla (see particularly chapters 8 and 9, section 3), described by William Luis as central, given her prominence at the beginning and the end of the novel and her knowledge of the Gamboa family secrets (*Literary Bondage,* 116). Black women who bore the burden of heavy work as well as that of nursing children, both white and black, also transmitted oral traditions from one generation to the next and helped to divulge secrets their owners would rather have kept hidden.[3] In *La noche* and "Autobiografía," Saldaña rejects mother and father (the European nuclear family) and embraces the grandmother (Caribbean household) as the figure who will engender the poetic self. Saldaña's identity emerges from the words and the silences of her grandmother, here representing female survival during times of slavery: "aprendí su palabra y su silencio" [I learnt her word and her silence] *(La noche)*.

In "Autobiografía" self-definition rises out of loss and anger:

quiero decirle que los pájaros azules están en muda
quiero decirle que hay un luto injustificado en esta madrugada de hastío
que hay tanta ira de dioses
y tanto y tanto perdido
y tanto,
y aún más

I want to tell you the blue birds are moulting
there's unjustified mourning this tedious dawn
the gods are so angry
and there's so very much lost
and so much,
and even more

(202, 203)

The poem, which begins in a conversational tone—with the declaration that it is not worth keeping secrets anymore, that one must begin by telling all—ends pregnant with what has been left unsaid, "y tanto y tanto perdido / y tanto, / y aún más." Sorrow and anger have been made explicit, yet the source of those emotions is kept secret. The end repeats a contradictory phrase found throughout the poem, "quiero decirle" [I want to tell you], which conveys both a desire to unveil secrets and the impossibility of doing so. The actual autobiography rises out of the tension between voicing and silence, between family expectations ("mi madre, médico / mi abuela, maestra" [my mother, a doctor / my grandmother, a teacher] (200, 201), and what the poet considers worthy of her telling ("de mi pequeña vida anónima" [about my small anonymous life] (200, 203).

The poet's anonymous life of "coleccionando balas y sellitos" [collecting bullets and stamps] (202, 203) alludes to the postrevolutionary children's activity of collecting bullet cartridges already spent by the revolutionaries. Yet it also places the child within a larger context than that implied by her "small anonymous life." From the outset, the poet's date of birth is coupled with a catastrophic world event, the bombing of Hiroshima, which occurred a year and a day before her birth. Her birth, positioned alongside one of the most violent events wrought by human-kind, results from the poet's insistence on life even in the face of abortive measures. The verb "nací" [I was born] is repeated three times: once in relation to Hiroshima, once in relation to abortion, and once in relation to the fact that her father was an extravagant young man.

A product of self-perseverance, even before birth, Saldaña portrays her birth within less than propitious contexts. Her self-portrait, more-over, appears less than exemplary:

Crecí gorda y bizca
abominablemente tonta
samaritana por vocación

I grew chubby and cross-eyed
abominably silly
Samaritan by vocation
(200, 201)

Alongside this self-portrait, which Saldaña renders with sharp sarcastic brushstrokes and pigments of sorrow and anger for having been unwanted before birth, she also records a violent domestic scene in which the father slaps her because of her revolutionary beliefs. What is most salient in the portrayal of the event appears in parentheses: "(sabe usted lo que eso sig-nifica / cuando nunca se ha recibido una caricia?)" [can you understand what that means / when there's never been an embrace?] (202, 203). In a Borgesian ironic mode, Saldaña places the essential, the absence of love, in parenthesis so as to appear to undermine what is being said. With this scene, Saldaña creates a portrait of herself as one who rises in the absence of paternal love and counters the violence of paternalism at the moment in which she shouts Castro's revolutionary slogan, "¡Patria o Muerte!" [Homeland or Death!] (202, 203). With this slogan Saldaña supplants the figure of her extravagant middle-class father and replaces it with that of Fidel Castro, the proponent of a classless society. Even though Saldaña the young woman found her voice in opposition to her father within the context of the 1959 Cuban Revolution, at the end of "Autobiografía" Saldaña the poet persists in voicing a sense of loss "y aún más" [and even more]. The open-endedness of the poem signifies a reluctance toward closure, a gesture that Saldaña will repeat several times until what has been kept secret will resolve itself in a poetically satisfying way.

Catherine Davies has already addressed the performative nature of Saldaña's autobiographical enterprise in *Mi nombre,* "a performance which consistently resists closure" ("Cross-Cultural Homebodies in Cuba," 188). This impulse to resist closure is evident in three of Saldaña's main poems, "Monólogo de la esposa," *Mi nombre: Antielegía familiar,* and "Vieja trova sobre soporte CD ROM." This resistance is consistent with Afro-Cuban modes of signification—and includes repetition as a strategy within a religious structure in which all signs and symbols reiterate a primordial act.

Lydia Cabrera's *El Monte* [The Sacred Wilderness] elaborates the Afro-Cuban modes of signification that find expression in Saldaña's poetry. According to Cabrera, as we saw in chapter 2, the narratives of informants who wished her to reach understanding of Afro-Cuban culture always divulged a resistance to cultural disclosure.[4] This resistance was made evident to her through their use of digression, contradiction, and dramatic simulation of inauthenticity. These strategies were meant to test the listener regarding her respectful interest in their culture. Narrative structures thus implied a dialogic mode based on the listener's real interest. In order to illustrate the signification process, one of Cabrera's informants offered the following strategy: "Walk along a long road to go on amassing the truth, piece by piece, which is scattered everywhere" (Cabrera, 137). "Walk along a long road" necessarily implies repetition of fragments of cultural secrets and events before real disclosure may ensue.

In his study of Afro-Cuban religious experience and its manifestation in Cuban narratives, Eugenio Matibag also pinpoints repetition at the heart of "its discursive-practical foundation" (*Afro-Cuban Religious Experience,* 16). He explains: "For the symbols, motifs, and figures of Afro-Cuban religions, signification means not only repetition but also repeatability: all signs 'written' and 'read' in religious practice are so executed within the structure of reiteration, in a process that recognizes as authentic what is an imitation or repetition of an original or primordial act remembered in the religion's mythology" (16–17). Through repetition of a primordial act Saldaña wishes to enact the process of signification in her autobiographical poems. The "secret" scene displaced in the two poems already discussed is that of incest. Its qualification as a primordial act, in literary terms, stems from Villaverde's *Cecilia Valdés,* in which incest with a half brother rather than the father defines the catastrophic beginnings of the Cuban nation. For Afro-Cuban women, the primordial act refers to the period of slavery when the master or the master's son raped female slaves, mulattas, who in most cases had been engendered by the master himself.

To assist in understanding Saldaña's iterative gesture as a process of getting at a personal and cultural truth through a "structure of reitera-tion" (Matibag), I turn to Leigh Gilmore's study, *The Limits of Auto-biography: Trauma and Testimony,* in which the critic studies texts on the border of classical autobiographical paradigms.[5] Gilmore confronts the problematic of articulation of trauma, the "self-shattering experience of violence, injury, and harm" (6). In her conclusion, the critic ties the concepts of trauma, representation, testimony, and memory in ways that correlate closely with Saldaña's poetic performance: "The truthfulness of knowledge about the self and trauma as it arises in relation to self-representation immediately confronts the issue of judgment. The associa-tion of autobiography with representativeness, confession, and testimony suggests some of why this should be so. So does the history of identifying memory as a central and vulnerable location of identity, and trauma as a threat to the self due to how it injures memory" (144–45). Central to each of Saldaña's autobiographical poems lies Gilmore's concept of "identifying memory as a central and vulnerable location of identity." At the opening of each poem, personal definition through the traumatic event of incest is transferred or, rather, transfigured into a metaphor of memory that must be cajoled into releasing its past truths for judgment. The poetic self comes forth as either witness or advocate in the judgment of the crime committed in a now distant and silent past. The highly meta-phoric opening of all the autobiographical poems under discussion an-ticipates for the reader the difficult task involved in the remembering and condemning of the incestuous act. The speaker divulges not so much a crime, but rather a process of knowledge. Gilmore expresses it as follows: "I use 'knowing' to suggest a process, even an ethic, that is not directed toward a judgment in which the subject is 'known,' but through which it models an engagement with what is difficult, compelling, intractable, and surprising. The knowing subject works with dissonant materials, fragmented by trauma, and organizes them into a form of knowledge" (146–47). In this respect of recording a process wrought with difficulties as well as a truth, Gilmore's description of "a form of knowledge" differs little from Afro-Cuban signification that seeks to record a primordial act through multiple attempts at delaying disclosure.[6]

In the following pages, I first analyze Saldaña's metaphors for her in-jured memory and then present the poet's apparently evasive strategies in an effort to arrive at a hidden truth. I conclude by showing how the poet's repeated attempts at defining poetic voice is intimately connected to an erotic sensibility.

"Monólogo de la esposa" [The Wife's Monologue] provides one of Saldaña's most beautiful and complex metaphors for memory:

Los crespos de la noche cuelgan del cielo.
Se esparcen por los hombros de la casa las guedejas
del silencio.

Yo las peino. Suavemente yo las peino:
Soy la anónima alisadora de las ondas del sueño,
también soy una niña acuática
trenzando y destrenzándome
la cabellera del recuerdo.

The curls of night hang from the sky.
The long tresses of silence are loosened on the shoulders of the house.

I comb them. Softly I comb them:
I am the anonymous one who smoothes the waves of sleep.
I am a watery child, as well,
braiding and unbraiding
the tresses of my memory.

(*In the Vortex of the Cyclone*, 12, 13)

The curls, long tresses, and waves—as metaphors for night, silence, sleep, and memory—locate the difficult task of remembering trauma in the domestic sphere, the house, where the wife, the anonymous one, or the child reenacts the "braiding and unbraiding" of the overwhelmingly "long tresses of silence . . . loosened on the shoulders of the house." These loosened curls of night (oblivion) fall upon the shoulders of the house with uncommon force. Moreover, the gesture of braiding and unbraiding displays the action of a troubled self doing and undoing a task that connotes the soothing of an injured memory. Were it not that the curls, then long tresses, then waves, require an increasingly ominous task of combing, the gesture described here is quite soothing: that of a young woman softly caressing and combing her hair. To counteract the insistence of sleep and silence, the poetic "I" moves from the soft gesture of smoothing the tresses of memory to storming at them: "A veces me paro en los acantilados del hogar / y los aciclono hasta convertirlos en cumbres borrascosas" [At times I stand on my home cliffs / and storm at them until

I turn them into my own wuthering heights] (12, 13). Thus, the force of the hurricane (*aciclono,* to storm like a hurricane) and the soft winds may "blow upon all lies," "blow upon the truth" ["soplar sobre la mentira," "soplar sobre la verdad"] (12, 13). Along with hurricanes come lamentations; along with soft winds, persistence. The metaphoric construction of "the tresses of my memory" displaces the trauma, "lamentations," from the self to that of the figure of memory (the tresses) and focuses on the structure of reiteration, "persistence," as the poetic locus of injury.

In *Mi nombre: Antielegía familiar,* the figure of an injured memory manifests itself at the beginning of the poem, as well, this time, as through the traumatic process of irrupting questions (questions as attempts by traumatic, repressed memories to surface into consciousness):

> Los recuerdos levantan la mano como colegiales:
> > Al pase de lista
> sólo del preferido no hay respuesta.
> El ojo insolente,
> > ¿dónde se oculta?
> ¿Dónde, la voz rajada y hueca?
> El sinsonte temeroso del pecho.
> > ¿Dónde?
> ¿Dónde está el que soy? ¿Qué olvido me malcría y tutela?

> Memories raise their hands like schoolchildren:
> > At the roll call
> only the teacher's pet does not answer.
> The insolent eye,
> > where is it hiding?
> Where is the voice cracked and hollow?
> The breast's trembling mocking bird.
> > Where?
> Where is the one that I am? What obliviousness indulges and protects me?
> (*In the Vortex of the Cyclone,* 78–81)

In *Mi nombre* reiteration manifests itself in the personification of memory as eager children wanting to divulge their knowledge while the poetic self seems to remain lost in indulgent and protective space that obliviousness affords against the traumatic event. This intermittent play between divulging information (on the part of the children) and the suppression of answers to questions that intuit insult or injury ("insolent eye," "voice cracked and hollow," and "trembling mocking bird") portrays in figurative terms what psychologist Jennifer Freyd terms "knowledge isolation." Knowledge isolation denotes "how information about abuse becomes unavailable to consciousness while other contemporary memories of the abuse are preserved" (quoted from *Betrayal Trauma* in Gilmore, 27–28). This avoidance of knowledge because of its painful nature even in the face of eager desire to know is represented in "Monólogo de la esposa" with the image of braiding and unbraiding the tresses. Moreover, in this stanza from *Mi nombre*, the self is described in the third person as some other "one": "¿Dónde está el que soy?" [Where is the one that I am?] in a questioning mode. This use of the third person within a question establishes a poetic distance from the search for self-definition, where trauma and poetic voice should inhabit the same space, at least symbolically, with the use of the first person singular.[7]

In the third autobiographical poem under discussion, "Vieja trova sobre soporte CD ROM" [An Old Love Ballad in Support of CD ROM], Saldaña revisits "el misterio de la casa" [the mystery of the house], already established in "Monólogo de la esposa." In *Mi nombre* she ends the introductory section of the poem with a series of questions closing with a simple "¿Pero yo quién soy?" [But who am I?] ("Vieja trova," 23).[8] With this third poem in search of figurative strategies with which to address her trauma, Saldaña opts for an openness signified by the use of the first person that results from returning once more to the site of transfiguration: "¿Quién soy yo en la pobreza de este retorno?" [Who am I in the poverty of this return?] (23). The poverty of this return anticipates the father's biography, recorded at the center of the poem with a mixture of poetry and prose, as well as a heavy dose of sarcasm as in "Autobiografía." Prior to the mundane autobiographical question, "Who am I?" Saldaña literalizes her search and presents herself as firmly planted:

> He venido a la luz,
> para dar testimonio de la luz,
> de esta mi Isla perfecta.
> Estoy en mi sitio

> I have come to the light
> to give testimony of the light,
> of this my perfect Island.
> I am in my place

(23)

If poetic voice speaks from the place of the house/Island, a house invaded by the mystery of the night (silence), what then is the poet's place after having revisited the site on numerous occasions?

In "Danzón inconcluso para Noche e Isla" [Unfinished Danzón for Night and Island] (*In the Vortex of the Cyclone*, 112–15), Saldaña plays variations on lines from the nineteenth-century Cuban liberator and poet José Martí: "Dos patrias tengo yo: Cuba y la noche" [I have two homelands: Cuba and night]. In her poem, Saldaña develops an image of the island as a bird's wing that lifts the bird as it wakes from sleep and breaks the cage of night to rise and sing. Saldaña ends with a revisionist trope of Martí's verse:

> Soy la noche. Soy la isla
> Dos patrias en mí que las contengo
>
> I am the Night. I am the island.
> Two homelands contained in me
> (114, 115)

If in her three autobiographical poems Saldaña inhabits a house haunted by silence and mystery, in "Danzón inconcluso," home is the island of Cuba in the fullness of its history—both revolutionary and literary (through the connection with Martí)—and in its metaphoric physicality as bird's wing. If Martí identifies himself with homeland and night as liberator and poet, Saldaña makes the metaphoric leap of incorporating into her own soaring being both night and island via her voice, "un canto de espaciosa anchura" [a song of slow expanse] (112, 113). In light of the closing in which the poet equates her being with night and island, the opening verses may be construed as self-portrait:

> La Noche
> goza de la isla dormida. Inocente. Frágil
> como un pájaro fatigado del que sólo se sabe que vive
> por el ala
>
> Night
> enjoys the sleeping Island. Innocent. Fragile
> like a weary bird known to be living only
> because of its wing
> (112, 113)

The island/bird/poet is fragile and weary but for the agency of the wing/poetry/poet's own voice that allows her to assume her place, her home, at the center of the Caribbean basin, and of Cuba's national and literary history.

When at the beginning of "Vieja trova sobre soporte CD ROM" Saldaña professes to give testimony to her perfect Island, she situates herself at the center of Cuban literary tradition via José Martí. She begins by reiterating images that have appeared in her previous autobiographical poems. These include night, silence, the mystery of the house, the family, the bird's wing, and the island. In a stanza in which she asks "¿Quién soy?" [Who am I?] ("Vieja trova," 23), the answers brought in by the force of echo are bird, house, night, and damsel. Yet she qualifies each answer with another series of questions implying the speaker's inability to fly, endure, be reborn, and chatter. In what amounts to Saldaña's last iteration of her experience of trauma, she begins the poem with an erotic dimension:

> Penetra la noche el misterio de la casa
> cual pájaro en sexo de doncella

> Night penetrates the mystery of the house
> like a bird in a damsel's sex

> (22)

These lines allude to Jupiter's transformation into a swan in the seduction of Leda as found in Ovid's *Metamorphoses* (Ovid, 139–40). In "Vieja trova" it becomes evident that the father resembles Jupiter in his many infidelities. The image of the swan is also linked to hermaphroditism, bringing together the masculine and the feminine, with the neck and beak as the masculine, and the bird's body as the feminine (Cirlot, 322). Accordingly, as the opening image of the poem, the swan announces the poet's task as being both masculine and feminine, both active and passive.[9] The erotic dimension of this poetic gesture is evident as well in "Danzón inconcluso" where Saldaña employs an image of a bird in heat (114, 115). In "Vieja trova," the search for knowledge in its flight to expression is intimately tied to sexual desire. And to reach understanding through desire, the poet searches for a house resembling the jingle bells of silence, "una casa parecida a los cascabeles del silencio" (22), a house like a turtle's shell (in Afro-Cuban legend, the turtle is a figure of the trickster), a house defined in Afro-Cuban terms: "el *ilé* de los *oricha* esclavizados" [the sacred house of the enslaved deities] (22). Reaching understanding in what Saldaña terms "la sabiduría más pequeña" [the smallest wisdom] involves finding the house/home where the injuring trauma took place, while standing in a Caribbean figurative haven. This *ilé* of the *oricha*, however, does not suffice. Just before the poem gives way to the father's biography, it defines another figurative space from which to speak:

> Estoy sentada sobre el yin y el yang, de las mutaciones:
> "Ve al pozo y bebe,"
> "Llégate al abismo y déjate caer"
>
> I'm seated on the ying and the yang of mutations:
> "Go to the well and drink,"
> "Reach the abyss and let yourself fall"

(23)

The poet sits on a sphere of feminine/masculine mutations that dictate for her to drink from the waters of the well and to let herself fall into the abyss. In this last of three autobiographical poems, the work of memory involves a leap into hell (in *Mi nombre* the house is the first stop in hell) while drinking from the waters of desire.

"Vieja trova sobre soporte CD ROM" qualifies the poetic endeavor as giving testimony. This desire to give testimony constitutes a gesture present in all three autobiographical poems and locates the construction of memory within the realm of jurisprudence. Already in "Autobiografía" the poetic voice repeats the phrase "quiero decirle" [I want to tell you], in an implicit dialogue with either reader or judge to make explicit the subject's sense of loss and anger. However implicit, the poem declares that an injustice has been committed. Poetic expression redoubles as a survivor's voice that insists on raising questions, and as the voice of her advocate who cross-examines possible witnesses to the crime. In "Monólogo de la esposa," the poetic voice figures as a lawyer searching for evidence, while in "Vieja trova" the poet turns prosecutor of the purported rapist. The conclusion of all three poems presents the female subject as triumphant survivor, not as victim. In all three, the poetic voice declares the search for a forgotten secret that must be unveiled. At the center of each of these three poems, the "I" finds the figure of the father. In "Monólogo de la esposa," the father stands as flamenco dancer; in *Mi nombre,* the "absent" father, the enemy, declares his presence through the terror that the women in the house experience; and in "Vieja trova sobre soporte CD ROM," the father is the gambler who rapes to win. As the poet softly combs the tresses of her silence, she increasingly divulges the emotions that had been announced at the end of "Autobiografía": sorrow, terror, and anger.[10]

In "Monólogo de la esposa" the poetic voice clothes itself as the wife who searches for the man who took her virginity: "que se acerque el que tomó mi doncellez" [let the one who took my virginity come forth] (*In the Vortex of the Cyclone*, 24, 25). In order to find the first who stained her hands with blood, the wife, much like a minister from a court of law, summons all the men from her past: "los convoco a la hora nonata a una asamblea" [I summon you to an assembly at an unborn hour] (20, 21). By turning the men from her past into "mis muertos" [my dead ones] (24, 25), Saldaña conjures the fears that haunt her, but she also displaces any answer to her persistent questions—"¿Quién es el primero?" [Who is the first?] and "¿Quién me doró las manos de sangre?" [Who gilded my hands with blood?] (26, 27)—into a later moment in the poem: "Mas la respuesta no estaba entre los muertos" [But the answer was not to be found among the dead] (26, 27).[11]

The displacement of the answer to these multiple questions allows the poet to draw a self-portrait already anticipated in "Autobiografía": "Crecí gorda y bizca / abominablemente tonta" [I grew chubby and crosseyed / abominably silly] (200, 201). But, although in "Monólogo de la esposa" the subject remains cross-eyed (a trait of the poet herself), she no longer appears silly ("tonta"). Her poetic strength relies no longer on mere sarcasm; rather, it appeals to the mastery of intertextuality. The explicit dialogue with the reader found in "Autobiografía" now finds expression in the interchange between texts from differing poetic traditions, the Afro-Cuban and the Western. In "Monólogo de la esposa," Saldaña presents us with a self-portrait (24, 25) that positions the poet at the intersection of her Afro-Cuban tradition within the tradition of Ruben Darío's *Modernismo* in a revisionary gesture. I quote Catherine Davies from "Hybrid Texts:"

In this section Saldaña borrows from two famous lines in Darío's 'Sonatina', where *the fair-haired, blue-eyed princess* is 'guarded by a *hundred black men* with their hundred halberds / *a hound* that never sleeps and a colossal dragon'. In Saldaña's poem Darío's princess (which the bride wants to be before she kills her father) has been replaced by the cross-eyed mulatta who is guarded and served not by black men but by white men, and not by a European hound and dragon but an indigenous Cuban 'sijú' (owl) and an African-Cuban 'otá' (sacred stone). This clever reversal of Western aesthetic paradigms and the insertion of a black Cuban identity into a canonical poem which epitomizes Hispanic *modernismo* (the cultural movement which emulated the conquest culture of the European cosmopolitan élites) is effected by the female subject who refuses to be sub-altern (that is, subjected to another). (212)

Besides effectively rewriting one of Darío's most anthologized poems to place herself at a newly defined center of the Latin American literary canon, Saldaña repositions the so-called oral, traditional Afro-Cuban aesthetics alongside that of *Modernismo*'s founder and master. Moreover, she emulates Afro-Cuban narrative practices that counterbalance hierarchical arrangements by providing multiple versions of a primordial act or of the profile of a deity *(patakín)*. In a sense, self-portraits revised multiple times within Saldaña's oeuvre reproduce the Afro-Cuban *patakines,* which represent moments in the lives and transformative portraits of Afro-Cuban deities in their various manifestations *(avatares).* In "Monólogo de la esposa," as in much of Saldaña's poetry, "autobiography as an intertextual system of meaning is an expansive and expanding network of associations that reaches across the boundaries of texts and lives" (Gilmore, 116).

Saldaña's rhetorical gesture of drawing on more than one system of signification is not unlike that of Lydia Cabrera, who, in *El Monte,* when revalorizing the practices and traditions of the Abakuá, the most maligned of Afro-Cuban groups, appeals to both European and Afro-Cuban sources to establish the Abakuá as "the Masons of Africa" (199). Most importantly, however, by situating Afro-Cuban oral traditions on a par with *Modernismo*'s efforts to displace the center of Hispanic poetic production from Spain to Latin America, Saldaña exposes the silences of Latin American literary history in failing to valorize "traditional" aesthetics as paradigmatic rather than exotic. I turn to Stephan Palmié, who, in his study of Afro-Cuban modernity and tradition, asserts that what colonial rationales have placed in opposition—modernity (of which *Modernismo* is a part) and Afro-Cuban traditions—must instead be seen as "puzzling forms of hybridity once subjected to the test of concrete historical situations" (19). He focuses on the presentation and reevaluation of "regimes of knowledge" understood by the West as "anomalous, irrational, unrealistic, or simply implausible" (20). When in "Monólogo de la esposa" Saldaña appeals to her dead ones as specters, she refers not only to the men in her past but also to what Palmié calls the revenants or ghosts of Afro-Cuban culture. By making often devalued and therefore absent narrative practices come alive in the context of a poetic idiom fully conscious of Hispanic poetic mastery, Saldaña gives voice to her dead ancestors, the Masons of Africa, as well as to their rhetorical strategies, as necessary sources in her poetic endeavor. Saldaña's self-portrayal, in the best tradition of Latin American literature from Sor Juana Inés de la Cruz (in her sonnets) to Jorge Luis Borges (in "Borges y yo"), centers on the self-reflexive act of literary production.

Throughout "Monólogo de la esposa," Saldaña depicts the process of traumatic disclosure as wrought with difficulties. Immediately after concluding the task of self-portrayal, the poet expresses the desire to see the eyes and the hands of the one who took her virginity. That search is to be pursued "aunque un sol de alacranes me coma la sien" [even though a scorpion sun eats at my temples] (24, 25). A litany of questions follows with no answers. The Wife turns her back on her dead ones and goes out into the public sphere to interrogate multiple members of society in her search for answers: "Entonces salí a la calle a preguntar" [Then I went out on the street to ask] (26, 27). For a litany of ten stanzas, the poem follows a formulaic pattern based on traditional popular verse in which the initial stanza of going out on the street leads to questioning the shopkeeper, the plumber, the carpenter, the artilleryman, the cook, the missionary, the ministries, and so forth. In each instance the Wife's asking for her injured identity results in insufficient paradoxes that evade the subject of incest. Even though no answers are forthcoming, the Wife continues to insist on questioning because, at least poetically, it is possible to "enjoy a kind of pleasure in the narrative organization of pain" (Gilmore, 22). Throughout, the search for the traumatic event goes hand in hand with the autobiographical impulse:

> Entonces salí a la calle a preguntar
> en las oficinas y en los ministerios.
> Y llené papeles y redacté autobiografías.
> Y conté mi vida desde el fin hasta el comienzo.

> Then I went out into the street to ask
> in offices and ministries.
> And I filled out papers and edited autobiographies.
> I told my life from the end to the beginning.

> (30, 31)

To minimize the vertigo (26, 27) and the pain (a scorpion sun eats at my temples), the search for identity is grammatically distanced via use of the third person: "¿dónde está la niña linda?" [where is the pretty girl?], "¿dónde está la muchacha confiada?" [where is the confident young girl?], "¿dónde está la mujer segura?" [where is the secure woman?] (30, 31). The search for identity presents itself at different stages of the subject's life in autobiographical fashion, much in the same way that *patakines* present specific moments of a deity's life. But the interrogation of her dead ones and of the patriarchy in their multiple social functions does not yield answers. It cannot yield answers because, as in "Autobiografía," male representatives of society, whether they be confronted in the private or the public sphere, prefer to ignore or make excuses for the violence perpetrated on women by the patriarchy (Gilmore, 50–53). The available avenues of jurisprudence fail the female injured subject at all three different stages in her life. The representation of the incest scene only becomes evident after the subject opens the gate of memory with the key shared by Caribbean women in the poet's past: "la frágil carabalí" [the fragile Carabalí woman]; "y la adusta castellana" [and the austere Castilian] (32, 33). By likening her own experience to that of African and European women, Saldaña inserts her personal history into a collectivized experience. Personal and collective traumas must be recorded so that women suffering the injury may be transformed from victims to survivors (Gilmore, 47).

Toward the end of "Monólogo de la esposa," Saldaña records the scene of incest in a most symbolic manner, marking a regression in memory by first seeing the Wife who returns from the bloody corner to find the father, then by witnessing how the young girl is forced to participate in the dance, and finally by depicting the little girl dancing with the father in an afternoon of games and incest:

Soy yo. La Esposa.
Del rincón de la sangre vuelvo.
Allí encontré a mi padre
         en una tarde de juegos:
que no es mulato, dice,
         sino gitano de baile flamenco.

   La Señorita Hija
   entrando en el baile;
   que lo baile, que lo baile;
   y si no lo baila
   le doy castigo malo;
   que la saque, que la saque.
   Salga usted, que la quiero ver bailar . . .

Y me saca el Padre
                y me da la vuelta
y me gira en el humo
                y me cerca en la siesta.
        En los vapores del ron,
        la niña fue sólo hembra.

"La niña se ahogó en el pozo
entre sapos y culebras"
—gritan por toda la cuadra
Nené Traviesa y Cenicienta—.

.   .   .   .

¡La niña no tiene niña.
Ay, tarde de incesto y teas!

It is I. The Wife.
From the bloody corner I return.
There I found my father
                in an afternoon of games:
Who is not mulatto, he says,
                but rather a flamenco gypsy dancer.

        The Maiden Daughter
        entering the dance;
        let her dance, let her dance;
        and if she doesn't dance
        I'll punish her bad;
        lead her out to dance, lead her out.
        Let her come out, I want to see her dance . . .

And my Father leads me out
and he turns me around
and he whirls me in the smoke
during the siesta he circles me 'round.
        In vapors of rum,
        the girl was only a maiden.

"The girl drowned in the well
amongst bull frogs and snakes."
Naughty Little Girl and Cinderella
yell all around the block.

. . . .

The girl has no girl.
Ah, afternoon of incest and flambeaux!]
                    (34, 35, and 38, 39; my ellipses)

The poet here portrays the recovered scene, depicted in three pages of children's rhymes, in which the subject is represented as multiple (the wife, the maiden daughter, and the girl) and as contradictory (the girl has no girl). Incest forces the child to become a woman and vice versa. As consciousness travels back in time, the command of self-definition expressed in the first person gets buried in the third person of the young maiden and the little girl. The hitherto absent father in the poet's memory appears as a mulatto who wishes to pass as flamenco gypsy dancer. By displacing the figure of the black father, and replacing it with that of the Spaniard, Saldaña centers personal experience in the context of Caribbean history. Yet she insists on the particulars, the drunkenness of the father (in vapors of rum) and the overwhelming nature of the event (the girl drowned in the well). Moreover, the poetic round brings back the personal, but as object of the father's dance (he turns me and he circles me 'round) rather than as subject of the search (There I found my father).

The splitting of the self as subject and direct object also finds representation in the figures of Nené Traviesa and Cinderella. Even though the girl child characters are present in the poem to react to the girl's fate, they also stand as doubles of the violated girl, product of the splitting of consciousness that trauma engenders in the subject in its attempt to survive an unspeakable event. Both characters are orphans, having lost a mother. Both disobey a parental mandate: Cinderella goes to the dance and marries the prince; the Naughty Little Girl reads and accidentally tears the rare book of children's stories that her father had forbidden her to touch. Nené Traviesa is a character in a José Martí short story for children anthologized in *La edad de oro* [The Golden Age]. When Nené, in the father's absence, finally topples the large, ancient collection of stories from its pedestal, she is able to lie on the floor and liberate all the characters that were trapped within its pages. Out of it come up several exotic men who represent the multiplicity of races in the Cuban nation—the white man, the Indian, the Chinese, the Arab, and finally the black man. All, except the last, rise out of the book dressed to represent the cultures from which they come. The black man, however, is naked, and Nené assumes that's why her father forbade her to touch the book: "[E]l otro es negro, un negro muy bonito, pero está sin vestir:

¡eso no está bien, sin vestir! ¡por eso no quería su papá que ella tocase el libro!" [The other one is black, a very pretty black man, but he's without clothing: That's not good, without clothing! That's why her father didn't want her to touch the book!] (Martí, 76; my translation). The story ends with Nené Traviesa caught by her father as she's holding two torn pages from the prized book, claiming to be a bad girl and feeling shameful. In "Monólogo de la esposa," by referring to Nené Traviesa, Saldaña metaphorically tears up the pages from Martí's children's story with the intent of revising them.

Implicit in Martí's story is the assumption of guilt on the part of the little girl who disobeys and then associates her act of defiance and guilt with the black man's nudity. Martí's not so innocent portrayal of the black man, like Caliban in Shakespeare's *The Tempest,* lays bare the nation's, and perhaps his own, assumptions about the black man who is bereft of culture and therefore must be represented as naked. Moreover, the underlying threat in *The Tempest,* beyond Caliban's desire to depose Prospero, is freely expressed by Caliban himself when he states that he would populate the island with little Calibans as engendered in violence with Miranda, Prospero's daughter. In Saldaña's poem, her father is no Caliban. Rather than stand up to Prospero as the black man, he cloaks himself in the garb of the flamenco gypsy dancer. But despite his assumption of the colonizing garb, as Franz Fanon writes in *Black Skin, White Masks,* the father still assumes the role of the black man as a sexual threat to women in the Cuban nation. Is Saldaña thus accusing her father of acting out his internalized racism when he rapes his daughter? This question remains unanswered until the end of "Vieja trova sobre soporte CD ROM." Like Nené Traviesa, in "Monólogo de la esposa," the child assumes the guilt and shame imposed by her father, Martí, and the nation:

> La niña ha resucitado
> en un charco de vergüenza.
> (¡Que no, que no quiero verla!)

> The girl has returned to life
> in a puddle of shame.
> (But no, I do not want to see her!)
>   (38, 39)

To survive the shame that the girl feels, Saldaña shuns the sight of the shamed girl by referring to one of Spain's most famous poets, Federico

García Lorca. When Saldaña cries out, again in parentheses, her pent-up emotion "(But no, I do not want to see her!)," she quotes from Lorca's famous "Lament for Ignacio Sánchez Mejías." The Spanish poet refers to the blood shed by the famous matador, whereas Saldaña points to both the blood on her hands and to the shamed girl. Lorca, well known for his *Romancero gitano,* a collection of poems about Spanish gypsies, may have also been reluctant to see the blood being spilt during the Spanish Civil War. Saldaña, by quoting within her own lamentation, a line about the death of a matador that repeats incessantly in Lorca's lament, implicitly proclaims a death sentence against her father.[12]

As the lengthy poem comes to a close, the poetic voice asks what power could exorcise for the father the memory of his act? The answer comes: "Soy yo. La esposa" [It is I. The Wife] (38, 39). His capacity to forget imposes on the daughter a splitting of the subject "I" between *reason* and *emotion:* "Feraz de tierras me sé . . . / pero zafra soy de miedo" [Fertile of lands I know myself to be . . . / but I am the harvester of fears] (38, 39). This contradiction between reason and emotion within the self is repeated in six stanzas, until the self beckons the Husband who with the Wife will begin "la Cópula del Universo" [the Copula of the Universe]. This last stanza denotes a consensual sexual union against the imposed act of incest. The copula, in grammatical terms, refers to the verb *to be,* with its capacity to unite the subject with its attributes. In poetic terms, "Monólogo de la esposa" ends with the integration of the poet's past selves, the girl and the young maiden, in the character of the wife. She, in turn, invites a husband to cleanse her hands and to come together in new beginnings.

The end of "Monólogo de la esposa" prepares the poetic ground for the act of naming, an act that revisits the terror of the house imposed by the father, but an act, like the Copula of the Universe, that equates the autobiographical gesture with poetic creation. In his excellent article on *Mi nombre: Antielegía familiar* [My Last Name: A Family Elegy], Conrad James points to the fact that in this poem Saldaña appeals to both male (Nicolás Guillén) and female (Ana Excilia Bregante, the grandmother) traditions in the construction of the autobiographical enterprise as manifesto: "[T]he autobiographical manifesto offers full potential for the staging of resistance" (James, 51). When Saldaña separates herself from her paternal name, she also rejects her status as a bourgeois member of society in favor of her revolutionary zeal, which Guillén upholds. She, in fact, asks the grandmother to join her:

Ana Excilia Bregante,
ahora,
niega esta casa,
niega la usura de la bolsa y la fiambrera

Ana Excilia Bregante,
now,
deny this house,
deny the profits of the purse and the pantry

(104, 105)[13]

The grandmother refuses to leave the house, but eventually, after forbidding her son to enter it, she offers it as a haven for her granddaughter. But because personal memories revert to the home as the space of trauma, in this poem the house becomes the place from which the poetic subject must be exiled. Incest literally thrusts the speaker of the poem into the public sphere.

Extricating herself from home is concomitant to erasing the paternal name, Saldaña, and exalting the maternal one, Excilia (James, 65). Even though Ana Excilia Bregante represents the paternal line, in Saldaña's autobiographical statement in *La noche,* the paternal grandmother becomes the poet's mother. The gesture of naming, like the gesture of receiving the child after birth in *La noche,* is placed in the domain of the grandmother:

Excilia,
tú,
siempre Excilia:
nombre de mi nombre:
nieta,
guardiana:
compañera

Excilia,
you,
always Excilia:
name of my name:
grandchild,
guardian,
compañera

(104, 105)

Right after being named, in a bold poetic gesture, Saldaña equates being exiled from home and paternal name with the force of a hurricane that propels her to personal survival through poetry, an act consequentially tied to the poet's act of procreation:

> Desterraron mi nombre y me desterraron.
> Me condenaron a llevarlo
> > de puerta
> >
> > en
> >
> > puerta
> siendo la que se fue o a la que han ido.
> Insomne de mi cama, ayuna de mi mesa.
> La casa ya no existe:
> > nadie la vela;
> en el vórtice del ciclón
> sólo se admite al que tenga vocación de ventolera:
> Libre estoy del espacio
> > de la libertad primera
> para encontrarme el origen
> > en el hijo que me engendra.

> They banished my name and they banished me.
> They condemned me to bear it
> > from door
> >
> > to
> >
> > door
> being the one who left or the one who also was left.
> Insomniac of my bed, keeper of the fast at my table.
> The house no longer exists:
> > nobody watches over it;
> in the vortex of the cyclone
> only those with a vocation for gusts of wind are admitted:
> I am free within the space
> > of the first freedom
> to encounter my origin
> > in the son who engenders me.
>
> > > (104–7)

The rejection of the paternal name ties the personal to the communal struggle against the Batista dictatorship because it brings together the rage against the father for having committed the incestuous act and for having rejected the daughter's revolutionary fervor: "un nombre que huele a pól-vora y cólera" [a name that smells like gunpowder and cholera] (98, 99). The young woman acts as subject when she leaves the house, yet she is also acted upon by the violence that has been inflicted upon her: "siendo la que se fue o a la que han ido" [being the one who left or the one who also was left]. Here active and passive voice mirror the copula that ends "Monólogo de la esposa," in which poetic voice effects the action of an active subject and a passive object. The subject's absence from the house obliterates it (by extension, according to Conrad James, the destruction of the house connotes the destruction of privileged patriarchal structures, 58). The poet, positioned in the vortex of the cyclone, also recalls the opening of "Monólogo de la esposa" where the "I" stands at the cliffs of the house and storms at it to "blow upon the truth" (13). Positioned in the space of remembrance, in the eye of the storm, the poet is capable of controlling the gusts of wind that blow upon lies and truth. The ability to pronounce and order her own freedom from lies creates a new origin in which the father is absent, and the act of naming flows from the lips of the father's mother, thus skipping a generation. In personal terms, the grandmother engenders the granddaughter, who in turn engenders a son who represents the "new man," rather than the old child, father, repre-sentative of a previous society.

Even though following the poetic line, Saldaña is engendered by Guillén through her indebtedness to his "El apellido: Elegía familiar"; with these verses, Saldaña skips several generations and refers to the poetry of José Martí. By finding her poetic origin in the son who engenders her, Saldaña refers to Martí's collection of poems to his son, *Ismaelillo*. In "Musa Traviesa" [Naughty Muse], the poet's muse, capable of flight, becomes his son: "Es un diablillo / con alas de ángel" [It's a small devil / with angel's wings] (30). At the end of the fifth stanza, Martí concludes with "¡Hijo soy de mi hijo! / ¡El me rehace!" [Son of my son am I! / He remakes me!] (35; my translations). In a pronouncement about her indebtedness to her poetic heritage, Saldaña begins by saying, "As a writer, I feel indebted to everyone," and ends with "And to Martí, of course" (introduction to *In the Vortex of the Cyclone*, 2–3). In the same statement, she expresses a particular link to those whose poetry displays the "love that they have toward children" (3). As she considered herself quite dedicated to the production of poetry for children, and as her books for children—such as *Kele Kele, La noche, Jícara de miel*—indicate, Saldaña constructs a link to Martí's poetry in his commitment to children in *La edad de oro* and *Ismaelillo*.[14] By referring to *Ismaelillo*, and in particular "Musa Traviesa," in which Martí ties his poetic imagination to the naughty flights of his son, Saldaña equates her poetic enterprise with that of Martí. In the case of Martí, his son remakes him; the son is the "hacedor" (maker), a word often used to connote the maker of poetry. It is important to know as well that Martí wrote *Ismaelillo* as a consequence of being separated from his son during his exile in Venezuela because of his revolutionary activities (Introducción 12). For Saldaña, a poet who has been exiled from her paternal name and her home, the son displaces the absent father, whom she has herself exiled from her poem, and becomes the one who engenders the poet.

In the absence of the father, "el proxeneta" (pimp) (80, 81), the autobiographical impulse to uncover the mystery of the house is driven by fear:

En la casa todos tenemos miedo.
Aunque sólo yo arrostre el crimen de burlarme de su cerco:
Cimarrona de los parques,
        apalencada en el colegio
con mi guámpara de risa
        y mi garabato nuevo:
sin tierra en mi propia tierra:
huyendo cada día del bocabajo
        y el cepo.
Y para colmo sin el consuelo
        de los ángeles.
Porque en el aire del trópico los ángeles no contestan.

In the house we are all afraid.
Although it is I only who defies the crime by mocking its boundaries:
A fugitive slave of the parks,
        hiding out at school
with laughter, my small machete,
        and my new scrawl:
without land in my own land:
fleeing each day from the facedown beating
        and caning.
And to top it all, without the consolation
        of angels,
    without the pity
        of angels.
Because in tropic air angels do not answer.

                             (82, 83)

Unlike her mother and her grandmother, the poem's speaker dares disobey the injunction to keep silent and therefore commits the crime of breaking the boundaries of bourgeois respectability that surround the house. Instead of the father paying for his crime of incest, the daughter, and poet, must pay for her audacity of making it public. The young girl must then find refuge in the parks and the school, which in the poem reproduce the sites of slavery, rebellion, and punishment. Appealing to the angels of Catholicism would not avail the subject with any salvation, since the Catholic church and patriarchy are more concerned with keeping propriety than with castigating the sins of the father. A subsequent stanza refers to the difficulties in finding a breath of fresh air for a severe asthmatic like Saldaña living in the tropics:

> donde estoy siempre
> en el centro
> ebria de gritos y maldiciones, suplicando
> lo que a los otros sobra:
> un trago noble y silencioso de aire
> que calme el ulular que llevo dentro

> where I am always
> at the center
> drunk with screams and curses, asking for
> what others have in excess:
> a gulp of air, noble and quiet
> to calm the howl I hold inside

(84, 85)

The self-respectability of her middle-class status and the lack of air with which to speak conspire against the poet who nonetheless chooses to howl and be punished for it.

To counteract the lack of pity on the part of the angels, Saldaña appeals to her African heritage, conceiving herself as "cimarrona" [fugitive slave] and choosing to trace her name "en la copa de la ceiba" [in the crown of the ceiba] (92, 93), at the top of the most sacred of trees. The speech act demands the free availability of air that the poet so much lacks:

> Sopla indiferente,
> sopla traviesa,
> sopla ingenua
> ahora que tienes para ti sola la demencia de las palabras

Blow indifferently,
blow mischievously,
blow candidly
now that you have for yourself alone the dementia of words
(94, 95)

At the end of the stanza marking the discovery of words to express her trauma, Saldaña equates the explosion of her personal expression with that of the Castro revolution in the image of the island as a bonfire (95). For Saldaña, expression of her injured self takes place in the context of slave rebellion before the independence of the nation and in the context of the revolution against bourgeois values concurrent with her own struggle against her father, a man from the middle class.

Within the Afro-Cuban context, particularly in Bantu terms, the act of naming is equivalent to calling into being that which is being named. In his analysis of the poem "Sensemayá," by Nicolás Guillén, Eugenio Matibag defines the Bantu word *nommo*:

> The ritual act of invoking Sensemayá's eyes and tongue and death in words "means" (or imitates or anticipates) killing the snake in reality. Guillén's poem demonstrates the "magical" power of the word as name or naming, a concept that is signified in the Bantu word *nommo,* which bears certain similarities with the Lucumí aché. The creative nommo literally means "name" in Bantu, but also "word," *verbum.* It connotes the identification drawn between the person or thing and the name of the person or thing. . . . Naming the snake, one calls the snake itself to presence and commands it. (158–59)

When Saldaña equates her summoning of words through breath with an act of slave rebellion, she rejects the equivalent act of creation through the word as conceived in the Judeo-Christian tradition (in tropic air angels do not answer). As in the Bantu tradition, when Saldaña names herself, alone, she is magically bringing herself into being through the poetic word: "El verbo que organiza el caos" [The verb that reorganizes chaos] (92, 93). As Conrad James and Catherine Davies have rightly stated in their respective essays on *Mi nombre,* Saldaña ends the poem by rejecting her surname and the poetic male tradition of naming given to her by Nicolás Guillén, a tradition that only deals with the poet's patriarchal line. Instead, she relies on a metaphoric multiplicity of names that relate her feminine concept of being with the elements and aspects of the sacred wilderness *(el monte)* most directly related to the seven powers of the Afro-Cuban pantheon. Examples of these are: "Mi nombre / de caldera y trueno" [My name / of cauldron and thunder], referring to Changó, and "Mi nombre / de río y miel" [My name / of river and honey], referring to Ochún.[15] The final line in the poem, "Mi nombre / para precipitarlo como una lluvia sobre el cántaro de mi archipiélago" [My name / to precipitate like rain on the *cántaro* of my archipelago] (110, 111) equates name and being with the island of Cuba.

Whereas in *Mi nombre* Saldaña postpones the act of self-naming until the end of the poem, delaying with a lengthy portrait of her grandmother (100–105), in "Vieja trova sobre soporte CD ROM," Saldaña asks, "¿Pero quién soy?" [But who am I?] (23), and then embarks on a portrait of her father for the next six pages.[16] If in *Mi nombre* Saldaña liberates herself from the fear that prevails in her parental household in order to name herself, in "Vieja trova" she exorcises the rage against the father in order to proclaim herself music: "Pero yo seré la música" [But I will be music] (33).

The biographical account of her father's life acquires a legalistic tone when the poetic voice states, "He venido a la luz / para dar testimonio de la luz" [I have come to the light / to give testimony of the light] (23). In a series of questions before presenting herself as giving testimony, she asks, "¿Qué regaño de la familia, anulará mi triunfo ante los doctores?" [What family reprimand will annul my triumph before the tribunals?] (23). (In Spanish, the word *doctores* implies lawyers.) Thus, the beginning of the poem anticipates the verdict against her father, depicted as a gambler, a pimp, and a rapist. The entire biographical section uses a mordant sarcastic tone in which "el hijo del farmacéutico" [the pharmacist's son] elevates the art of gambling to a fatal mandate of destiny, and he, the absolute gambler, is depicted as divine. The scene acquires the parodic intent of a religious awakening in the following melodramatic gesture: "El hijo del farmacéutico abrió los brazos y cayó de hinojos: él era un avatar, una de las evoluciones del Juego Absoluto" [The pharmacist's son raised his arms and fell kneeling: he was a transformed being, one of the evolutions of the Absolute Game] (26). The alleged philosophical recognition happens as the young man works in his father's pharmacy during a moment of absolute boredom (26). In the following passage, Saldaña establishes an intertextual game between her own parody of the father and Jorge Luis Borges's short story "El Aleph":

Mareado, tembloroso, el hijo del farmacéutico intentó incorporarse. Se apoyó en el mostrador tanteando la madera deslucida por años de ácidos y mixturas. Pero, entonces, ocurrió el verdadero milagro: sus dedos se hundieron en una celada del comején y se deslizaron hacia el corazón de un mundo desconocido de sapiencia. El tiempo fue bajando sus pulsaciones. Se detuvo. El espacio se espesó como un buen chocolate. Las leyes conocidas desaparecieron: un abaniqueo de soledad cósmica y aleluya lo sobrecogió: Literalmente levitaba. El hijo del boticario volaba como S. Giuseppe de Copertino por sobre morteros de talco boratado y ungüentos multicolores. Toda la inefable delicadeza de su ser pendía del techo como un murciélago. Allí, luego de alcanzar su radio schwarzchild, nada humano le fue ajeno. *Alea jacta est.* ¡La suerte estaba echada! Fundaría su propia mística. Que juego porque no juego. (26–27)

[Dizzy, trembling, the pharmacist's son tried to get up. He leaned on the counter examining the wood discolored by years of acids and mixtures. But then, the true miracle happened: his fingers sank into a termite trap and slid into the heart of a strange world of knowledge. Time slowed its pulsations. It stopped. Space thickened like a good hot chocolate. Known laws disappeared: a fluttering of cosmic loneliness and alleluias overwhelmed him: Literally, he levitated. The pharmacist's son flew like S. Giuseppe de Copertino above all the mortars of medicated powder and multicolored ointments. All the ineffable delicacy of his being hung from the ceiling like a bat. There, having reached his Schwarzschild radius, nothing human was unknown to him. *Alea jacta est.* The lots were cast! He would found his own mysticism. I play because I don't play.] (my translation)

The "miraculous" moment, the intellectual coming of age, occurs when the character slides into an unexpected space (a termite's trap) where he witnesses a world of unprecedented knowledge. Time, space, and the laws of the universe cease to display their accustomed familiarity, and the pharmacist's son, hanging from the ceiling like a bat, becomes all-knowing.

Saldaña's scene replicates a similar one in Borges's "El Aleph," in which a mediocre poet claims to have discovered an aleph, a visual sphere containing all knowledge, in the basement of his house. He becomes alarmed when the house is threatened with demolition, and he will no longer be able to write. He produces his poetry entirely by rendering literally what he observes. It also contains its own interpretation. The character "Borges," on the other hand, witnesses the aleph and comprehends the impossible nature of the poetic enterprise when the poet tries to contain what he sees and experiences within the chronologically determined linguistic code. Ultimately, he declares the aleph to be false and suggests that the true aleph may be audibly perceived in a column in an Egyptian mosque as a constant murmur. As I briefly explain in my article on "The Aleph," the audible aleph gives the reader the metaphor for Borges's fiction, an exercise in perceiving and reinterpreting the multiple references contained within the literary canon. But even in Borges, where the literary enterprise may supposedly be reduced to a game in literary cross-references, the personal lurks close by. In "El Aleph," it is Borges's character's loss of Beatriz, his object of desire, that prompts him to maintain a relationship with the mediocre poet. Borges, giving guarded ironic vent to his emotional expression of loss, leads "Borges" to the exposition of his poetics.[17]

Echoing Borges, Saldaña presents the reader with an unforgiving portrait of her father. Her biography describes him as operating one of the most successful bordellos in the Antilles and wills for him the punishment of his own regret: "cuando agonice en el horror y la maldición de una pasión interminable, incestuosa y prohibida, masturbándose ante el asco del espejismo de su propio espejo" [when he agonizes in the horror and malediction of a passion interminable, incestuous and forbidden, masturbating himself when faced with the disgust of mirroring his own mirror] (28). If in "Monólogo de la esposa" incest is depicted as the dance between daughter and father and in *Mi nombre* as a round (84–85), in "Vieja trova" the event finds expression in prose, allowing for the poet's rage to be made explicit in her accusatory depiction of a life filled with mediocre excess. By pronouncing a legal, almost god-like sentence of regret against her father, Saldaña prescribes the worst of hells for his future. The poem fulfills this hell as it describes his death, a massive explosion like a supernova (a stroke), a death that gives birth to a female universe, "un universo palabra tatuada con tinta y sangre; un universo juego" [a word universe tattooed with ink and blood; a game universe] (28). With these words, Saldaña describes her own poem as a word universe, echoing Borges in "El Aleph" and herself in *Mi nombre:* "mi nombre-palabra, / mi nombre-poema" [my word-name, / my poem-name] (92, 93). "Vieja trova," like the audible aleph in the Borges story, configures a layering of voices as in a game to disclose the maker's identity through the resonant poetic voice. Only upon the death of the father does the poet feel free to liberate her word. This liberating gesture portrays the ludic nature of her father's life as a poor mirror to that of his daughter's. In the daughter's life, gambling finds expression as a Borgesian game of literary reconfiguration.

After witnessing the bitter depiction of the father's life and death, the reader understands better the dedication of "Vieja trova," which, counteracting the fierce attack on the father in the body of the poem, forgives with gratitude and mercy: "A Asdrúbal Luis Saldaña, mi padre, y a Consuelo Molina, mi madre, con mi perdón y mi agradecimiento. Con mi piedad" [To Asdrúbal Luis Saldaña, my father, and to Consuelo Molina, my mother, with my forgiveness and my appreciation. With my mercy] (22). By first exorcising her anger through sarcasm, and not through irony as in Borges, and by then sentencing her father to regret his incest, Saldaña forgives. With this dedication, Saldaña reinserts the figures of mother and father in her poetic universe. The figure of the mother appears only briefly in the poem as

> la madre
> de
> la nieta
> de
> mi
> señor
> abuelo
> —el padre de mi padre,
> el hijo del farmacéutico
>
> [the mother
> of
> the granddaughter
> of
> my
> lord
> grandfather
> —the father of my father,
> the son of the pharmacist]
> (129)

Rather than portray her mother as the guardian of the home in the complex manner that she portrayed her grandmother in *Mi nombre,* Saldaña circumvents her direct line of parentage through a series of relationships meant to distance her mother from herself. Having accomplished that task, the poet must proceed to execute the integration of her own self against the threat of her impending death.

Throughout the biographical exposition of her father, Saldaña resists answers to the question "Who am I?" Only after she completes the father's portrait does the poet expose herself as "la hechizada, la temerosa, la asustada / como aquel jueves de la pasión" [the haunted one, the fearful one, the frightened one / just like that Thursday of passion] (29). The poet portrays herself as throbbing, as a heartthrob, aware of a reality that does not cease, yet she throbs in the flow of the mirror staring through the teeth of death: "a través de los dientes de la muerte" (29). From here until the end of the poem, Saldaña returns to a series of autobiographical images that may only be seen as such in retrospect. When referring to the mirror, she recalls Alice, wondering what is on the other side of it, as well as her own poem "A través del espejo" [Through the Looking Glass] (*In the Vortex of the Cyclone*, 44–47). This poem begins with an epigraph by the Cuban poet Eliseo Diego: "Escribo todo esto con la melancolía / de quien redacta un documento" [I write all this with the melancholy / of one who drafts a document]. "A través del espejo," like Lewis Carroll's book, revels in paradoxes ("the slippery / horror of hope" [47]), anxiety and melancholy, along with images of loneliness, and pain: "No hay prisa, / pongo el dedo sobre mi propia llaga" [There is no hurry, / I place my finger on my own wound] (46, 47). The central paradox of the poem reigns in the tension between the melancholy of drafting a document and the horror of the wounded self. At the end, the image jumps out of the looking glass as the figure of the Sphinx, a complex metaphor pregnant with unanswered riddles: "Rostro de reina y lomo de felino". [Queen's face and feline back] (48, 49). "There is no hurry," a line from the Chilean vanguard poet Vicente Huidobro in "Altazor" (representing the image of the poet as Icarus), encapsulates Saldaña's poetic enterprise as the withholding of secrets through images throbbing with the anxiety and pain of having been victimized by her father.

After the image of the mirror exposing death, "Vieja trova" proceeds with the narrative formula of a griot: "Hubo una vez una niña que fundó un secreto bajo los helechos" [Once there was a girl who founded a secret under the ferns] (30). With this narrative voice, Saldaña founds the temple of her poetry on a secret (much like Sikán in the Abakuá legend), under the shade of the greenness of the forest *(el monte)*. At the very end, in italics, Saldaña closes with the device of the entire poem having been recited to her by the keeper of the cemetery: "Esta es la historia que contóme un día, el viejo enterrador de la comarca" [This is the story told to me one day by the old gravedigger of the region] (33). Thus the title of the poem "Vieja trova" [Old Ballad]. By ending with the Afro-Cuban source of poetry as storytelling in the realm of death, Saldaña sets to recover all the selves she has imagined up until this moment:

—Una niña,
una muchacha,
una mujer.
Tres eran tres y las tres eran una—

[—A girl,
a young maiden,
a woman.
Three were three and the three were one—]
(30).

The poem, thus far composed in lines of varying lengths, begins to employ a regular pattern of five-syllable lines that address Saldaña's asthma and the severe physical complications she suffers from it—all this in verses with a joyful rhythm, ending in the assonant letter o:

Estoy muriendo
de hipo y pulmón,
pero agonizo
del corazón,
que pongo y piso
yendo y viniendo

[I'm dying
of hiccups and lungs,
but I agonize
from the heart
which I put out and stump
coming and going]
(30, 31)

With the rhythms inherited from Nicolás Guillén's *sones*, Saldaña makes light of her dying condition and of her heartfelt pain and keeps going, hanging on to life by returning to the selves she left behind. In fact, this light poem, inserted within the much darker subject of the rest of "Vieja trova," recalls another unlikely self-portrait in her collection of children's lullabies, *Jícara de miel*. "Lullaby for an Elephant Out for a Stroll" tells of an elephant, very elegant and wearing a turban, who tramples in the mud but seems unconcerned. The last stanza found in *In the Vortex of the Cyclone* ends with:

"Luego me barro
todo este embarro."

Y tan campante
sigue adelante

"Later I'll trouble
with this mud-messy jumble."
And, just as buoyant,
he proceeds to advance
(48, 49)

This lullaby is composed of five syllables per line and also emphasizes the comings and goings, both dark and light, of the subject's life.

In the next few stanzas of "Vieja trova," Saldaña recalls her selves from *Kele Kele,* her collection of *patakines* for young adults, in which through the depiction of female deities in the Yoruba pantheon, she managed to portray herself as well. The verses that cue the reader to look to *Kele Kele* are

Volvamos a empezar.
Yo no digo que sí, yo no digo que no, yo digo, niña mía que
yo soy
la criatura aquella a quien la muerte orfanó

[Let's begin again.
I don't say yes, I don't say no, I say, my dear child that
I am
that creature whom death orphaned]
(31)

These lines refer to the *patakín* "Las tres suspirantes" [The Three Sighing Girls], in which the poet child confronts Ikú, death, and overcomes her with her song.[18] In this *patakín* Saldaña establishes an intertextual dialogue with sonnet 145 by Sor Juana Inés de la Cruz, in which the Mexican Baroque poet portrays herself by revising a poem about the transitoriness of life and beauty by her predecessor Luis de Góngora. In Sor Juana's sonnet, the image of death, which had been represented by Góngora's sonnet 166 as earth, smoke, shadow, and naught, becomes cadaver, dust, shadow, and naught. Following in Sor Juana's footsteps, Saldaña has the cadaveric figure of Ikú threaten to turn the girl into dust, oblivion, naught. Like Sor Juana, Saldaña opts for a more prosaic representation of death but then portrays the young poet-to-be as defeating Ikú with a voice that resembles that of a swallow *(golondrina)*. Starting in *Kele Kele,* Saldaña begins to create figurations of her poetic self by following the examples of female precursors (Sor Juana and Ana Excilia Bregante) and rejecting that of males (Guillén and her father).

From such an early depiction of the child as a capable antagonist to death, Saldaña, in "Vieja trova," enters into a dialogue between the grandmother and the grandchild reminiscent of both *La noche* and *Mi nombre,* quoting herself as she goes. As the poem reaches its conclusion, with the repetition of the line mentioning the child, the young maiden, and the woman, Saldaña separates herself from them: "Ellas eran mi tiempo. Pero yo soy la eternidad" [They were my time. But I am eternity] (32). The poet finds her eternity in the reiteration of her most memorable verses, including the image of herself combing her hair in "Monólogo de la esposa": "la que se sentó bajo su pelo / a trenzar las aguas, el llanto, el abandono, las promesas" [the one who sat under her hair / to braid the waters, tears, abandonment, promises] (32).

Unlike the other three selves that Saldaña leaves behind, the poet wakes from the dreams of the promised Utopias and offers her last Cuban supper: "lechón-asado-naranja-agria-hoja-de-guayaba-humo-cruje-el-pellejo-chicharón-en-boca" [roast-pork-bitter-orange-guava-leaf-smoke-crackle-crisp-pork-rind-in-mouth] (33). To complement the food, she invites her past selves to pick up instruments and play, in essence, to prepare the stage for her poetic voice: "Pero yo seré la música / y ustedes el ruido" [But I will be music / and you the noise] (33). At the end of her last autobiographical poem, Saldaña concludes by revisiting her multiple selves. She utters the last note, in the full knowledge that her ailing but triumphant self reaches to a past of griot narratives and to a future of communication technologies. Her poetic voice, with the support of a CD-ROM, will carry her truth, anticipated in one of the poem's two epigraphs: "La praxis es el criterio de la verdad" [Praxis is the criteria of truth]—V. I. Lenin. Her life was, is, and will be the praxis of her own self-figuration, a praxis grounded in historical and personal contingencies and integrating the best of Western and African poetic modes of signification. Her truth is firmly planted in the transfiguration of the sacred wilderness, in the past injured self of Caribbean experience, and in a transcending voice that resounds with the voices of her revenants (Palmié): Sor Juana Inés de la Cruz, Darío, Lorca, Huidobro, Guillén, Borges, and, of course, Martí.

Thus far, I have analyzed how Excilia Saldaña negotiated the healing of her past selves through reiterations of her autobiography, finally forgiving her parents and integrating the fragments of herself through the praxis of poetry. I now conclude by looking at how Saldaña gives agency to the black woman as erotic subject. I have already mentioned the intimate relationship that Saldaña establishes between poetic endeavor and erotic desire, particularly as it manifests itself in "Monólogo de la esposa," in "Danzón inconcluso para Noche e Isla," and in the opening verses of "Vieja trova sobre soporte CD ROM." While in these poems the subject's sexuality finds expression through erotic desire as necessary to poetic production, only in a series of erotic letters, the longest of which, "Mi fiel" [My Faithful One], is published in *In the Vortex of the Cyclone* (58–77), does Saldaña actively construct an eroticized female subject.

The unpublished collection of erotic letters, addressed to several nameless male objects of desire, were written in the fiftieth year of the poet's life to constitute an erotic memoir. In "Mi fiel" the female subject who writes in the first person repeatedly enters into memory to depict the black woman as actor in lovemaking, described from the outset as a plundering *(saqueo)* (60, 61). She enters into memory as a victorious representative of the black race: "Y entro en el recuerdo con los brazos en alto, triunfadora, saludando a todas las mujeres de mi raza que desde las gradas me vitorean" [And I enter into memory with my arms on high, triumphant, greeting all the women of my race who from the stands call me victorious] (60, 61). In this extended prose poem, the object of desire is a young white lover who passively receives the caresses and the sexual gestures of the black woman to the point of arousal. The poem is quite explicit: male genitalia are described metaphorically as a flower that rises and wilts to the will of the black woman's hands: "yo sólo quiero asir tu flor, adornarme con ella el pelo, los hombros, la cintura" [I only want to assault your flower, adorn my hair with it, my shoulders, my waist] (64, 65).[19] As the poem progresses, Saldaña empowers the female subject by turning the white lover into her slave: "Y entro en el recuerdo aherrojando tus tobillos; cautivos de mis manos los rodeo de cadenas de hierro y sueños para que no escapes" [And I enter into memory shackling your ankles with my two hands, fettering your ankles with iron and dreams so that you do not escape] (60, 61). With this erotic letter, Saldaña effects an unprecedented reversal of master/slave roles so that the black woman, not the white man, controls the erotic situation. The female subject enters into memory with her passion, rather than as the object of the white man's passion: "Y entro en mi recuerdo, no con tu pasión, sino con la mía" [And I enter into my memory, not with your passion, but with mine] (66, 67). Even at the moment when the white lover makes love to the black woman, the black woman wills it: "Y entro en el recuerdo y hago que tus manos entren en la fiesta que es mía y tuya" [And I enter into memory and make your hands enter into the feast that is mine and yours] (72, 73).

In their introduction to the anthology *Recovering the Black Female Body*, Michael Bennett and Vanessa D. Dickerson state the purpose of their volume is "to amplify the counterhegemonic discourse of African American women writers who attempt to recover their bodies—to take back their selves and reappropriate and reconstitute a body that has often been hypereroticized or exoticized and made a site of impropriety and crime" (5). Unlike the image of María Antonia in Sergio Giral's film that fills the cinema screen with a spectacularly sensual body, in Saldaña's self-portraits the reader encounters a cross-eyed young girl whose body appropriates the sweetness of the by-products of the Cuban sugar-cane industry. In her autobiographical poems discussed in this essay, Saldaña responds to the assaults on her body as the "site of impropriety and crime," with a consciousness of a long history of abuse, starting with the violence of slavery and continuing to her present through the scene of incest. But in "Mi fiel," rather than being shackled by her past, poetic voice enslaves the object of her desire.

Rather than reject the sight of her violated body as found in "Monólogo de la esposa" with the phrase, "But no, I do not want to see it," in "Mi fiel" the subject enters into memory with her eyes open and with a willingness to look: "No, no cierro los ojos, sino que los abro: quiero ver y ver y mirar" [No, I do not close my eyes, rather, I open them: I want to see and see and contemplate] (58, 59). The subject sees and looks at her own body here described from head to foot, creating a metaphor for each part of her body that places it within the context of her Afro-Cuban heritage as well as a Western heritage. Since the list is lengthy, I quote only a few of the images: "mis piernas de ceiba suntuosa, y mis curvas de azúcar cruda" [my sumptuous silk-cotton tree legs, and my crude sugar curves], "mi pecho de trapiche" [my sugar mill breasts], "mi ombligo de güira cimarrona" [my runaway calabash bellybutton], "y mis senos de miel, canela y anís" [and my breasts of honey and cinnamon and anise] (72, 73). These metaphors draw from the Cuban historical tradition of the sugar-cane industry, from the Afro-Cuban tradition of runaway slaves and female deities, and, finally, from the Judeo-Christian tradition of the *Song of Songs*. This detailed description of a black woman's body had already been anticipated in *Mi nombre* in the following short stanza where the speaker enjoys looking at her body:

A través de la mulatez del melado
                    oteo un cuerpo:
me regodeo
        en el cañaveral inédito del pubis,
        en el penacho de la cabeza,
        en el desmoche de las axilas,
        en el breve trapiche de los pechos,
        en las piernas espesas,
        en el tacho de bronce del ombligo,
        en la centrífuga de los ojos,
        en los dientes refinos.

Through the *mulatez* of the honey-colored syrup
                    I survey a body:
I take delight
        in the unpublished canefield of the pubis,
        in the plumes of feathers on the head,
        in the shavings of the underarms,
        in the sugarmill of the breasts,
        in the thick legs,
        in the bronze bowl of the bellybutton,
        in the centrifuge of the eyes,
        in the refined teeth.
                            (90, 91)

In *Mi nombre* the young woman discovers her body and delights in it, conscious of its positioning in the slave trade and in the sugar-cane industry. In "Mi fiel" the lover's hands traverse her body and turn her breasts and her entire body into "a pulsating harp that vibrates, a painful concert of chords, a Gregorian danzón, a mystic rumba, a guaguancó" (73).[20] The body turned musical instrument and dance makes explicit a desire that draws on European and African traditions. Ultimately, the female subject becomes music through the poetic word: "Soy la nota inaudible de la música de las esferas" [I am the inaudible note of the music of the spheres] (72, 73).

As if making explicit the copula of the universe anticipated at the end of "Monólogo de la esposa," "Mi fiel" ends with sexual climax and its subsequent peace: "Ya. Una y otra vez. Ya. Así. Ya. Viniéndonos. Ya. . . . Hasta la paz . . . ¡Ya!" [Enough. Once and once more. Enough. Yes. Yes. Enough. Coming. Enough. . . . Until peace . . . Enough!] (74, 75). In this prose poem, the black woman exorcises sexual violation through ownership of the sexual experience. In the next-to-last paragraph, Saldaña employs a series of metaphors that in the past signaled fear and passivity. As actor of her own copula of a liberated universe, the poet is able to pronounce: "Terminó el peligro. Un mundo signa y ejecuta la luz de las palabras. El espejo emigra su revés. Es el recuerdo de antes del comienzo. La suerte está echada." [Danger is over. The world signs and executes the light of words. The mirror migrates to its other side. It is the memory prior to the beginning. The die is cast.] (76, 77). After having testified to the light and after having observed her body in full light, Saldaña controls the fate of the dice, of the erotic game that she herself has fashioned in the reincarnation of two bodies in sexual union. These bodies, masculine and feminine, like the swan about to raise its mortal song, stand as the new metaphor for the poet's healed poetic memory.

5 Possession and Altar-Making

María Magdalena Campos-Pons

MULTIMEDIA ARTIST María Magdalena Campos-Pons, born in Matanzas, Cuba, in 1959, emigrated to the United States in 1990 and embarked on a three-installation project entitled *History of People Who Were Not Heroes*, reflecting on her family's history and her displacement as a member of the Afro-Cuban diaspora. The three installations making up the project are called *A Town Portrait* (1994, 1998, Lehman College Art Gallery, Bronx), *Spoken Softly with Mama* (1998, Garden Hall Video Gallery, Museum of Modern Art, New York), and *Meanwhile, the Girls Were Playing* (1999, MIT List Visual Arts Center, Cambridge, Massachusetts).[1]

Clearly, because Campos-Pons places at the center of *History of People Who Were Not Heroes* a strong emphasis on modes of expression rooted in Santería practices, she becomes another strong player within the context of the island's rich Afro-Cuban cultural heritage.[2] The iconography and cultural practices of "the syncretic faith derived basically from Yoruba beliefs," known in Cuba as Santería (Mosquera, "Strokes of Magical Realism," 147), became prominent in the modernist period with the monumental contributions of Cubist painter Wifredo Lam and have continued to flourish in more recent works by artists Manuel Mendive, José Bedia, Ana Mendieta, Belkis Ayón, Marta María Pérez, and others.

Filmmakers Sara Gómez, Gloria Rolando, and Sergio Giral have recorded the history, myths, and cultural practices of the wide-ranging cultural groups that make up today's Afro-Cuban population (Yoruba, Congo, Dahomey, Efik/Efo [Niger Delta], Jamaica, the Bahamas, Haiti, and others). Such films as Gómez's *De cierta manera* [One Way or Another], Rolando's *Los hijos de Baraguá* [My Footsteps in Baraguá], and Giral's *El otro Francisco* [The Other Francisco] have become classics of Cuban cinema. In *María Antonia* (1990) Giral structures the film's narrative around a series of flashbacks that return to the narration of a *santero* who interprets the protagonist's life. In this film, Ifá divination, an orally delivered prophesy that mediates between an individual's desires and that individual's fate as interpreted by the Yoruba priest, coincides with narrative plot, with the *santero* symbolically assuming the role of the director.[3] By making evident the discursive practices of an ancient African tradition, Giral becomes both *santero* and director.

Campos-Pons is also such an artist/*santera*. As my analysis of several of her installations shows, she uses the African diaspora cultural practices of possession and altar-making, which she embeds in contemporary performance. This mixture of tradition and modernity, family history, Santería practices, and contemporary art theories is not new for Campos-Pons. Already in 1990, in conjunction with fellow artist Magali Espinosa, she explored in conceptual terms the value of performance as an expressive medium because of its ability to bring together different artistic languages. She believes that the resulting unique object creates new effects not inherent in the discrete idioms that it synthesizes, and allows a rupture from them. The ensuing spectacle ultimately reveals the logic of its composition while simultaneously defining the history of the culture that engenders that composition (see Campos-Pons and Espinosa).

Campos-Pons's mixed-media installations *Spoken Softly with Mama* and *Meanwhile, the Girls Were Playing* serve as the artistic culmination of the theoretical constructs that the artist had conceived eight years before. It is these two pieces—together with other installation pieces *Abridor de caminos* [Guardian of the Roads], *Sustenance,* and *Secret,* which I believe function as developmental antecedents to *Spoken Softly with Mama* and *Meanwhile, the Girls Were Playing*—on which I concentrate in this essay. First, however, since her life figures so greatly in her works, a brief biographical introduction to Campos-Pons is both necessary and integral to understanding her work.

María Magdalena Campos-Pons is a Boston-based Cuban artist. She grew up in a town built around former slave barracks in the province of Matanzas. Her father is an herbalist steeped in Afro-Cuban tradition, and her mother toiled for many years as a domestic worker (public conversation between the artist and curator on the occasion of the opening at the Museum of Modern Art [MoMA]). These essential elements of the artist's family history find full expression in the installations I analyze. Campos-Pons received her training at the National School of Art (1980) and the Higher Institute of Art (1985) in Havana as well as at the Massachusetts College of Art, Painting and Media Arts in Boston (1988). In

1993–94 she was a fellow at the Mary Ingraham Bunting Institute, Radcliffe Research and Study Center in Cambridge, Massachusetts. As stated by the art critic and performance artist Coco Fusco, she "belongs to the generation that participated in the Cuban visual-arts renaissance of the 1980s," a generation that questioned the artistic tenets of Cuban art as defined exclusively by the artist's commitment to revolutionary ideals.

In oversized panels and installations that represent sexual organs as fruits and vegetables in the context of their popularized conception, Campos-Pons's art prior to 1990 establishes an ironic relationship between popular refrains and a mythological conception of sexuality. In her 1988 triptych *Sabor a Cuba* [A Taste of Cuba] and her 1988 installation *Jardín erótico o algunas notas sobre la hipocresía* [Erotic Garden or Some Notes on Hypocrisy], Campos-Pons questions sexist assumptions about feminine sexuality.[4] Her multimedia installations since leaving the island, (*Transfer/Transgression/Trouble/Tragedy* (1991) and *The Seven Powers Come by the Sea* (1993), concentrate on issues of border crossings and on the historical and current conditions of black people in the African diaspora (Fusco, "Magdalena Campos-Pons at Intar"). Her multipanel large-scale Polaroid photographs, installations, and performances often portray a mythic or ironic view of the self-portrait, using her own body as a canvas onto which she inscribes symbolic messages that define her individual artistic self in terms of religious and domestic rituals and her national identity in relation to mythic origins. Her works have been exhibited throughout Europe and the Americas since 1980.

As expressed by Campos-Pons in her 1990 essay, performance results from the interplay or dialogue between artistic and culturally determined languages. In her one-woman Boston show (September–October 1997 at the Mario Diacono Gallery), the artist's self-portrait as Eshu or Elegguá, the Yoruba trickster and keeper of the roads found in African and African-derived religions in Nigeria, Benin, Brazil, Cuba, and Haiti, is represented in ten Polaroid prints that are 29 x 22 inches and positioned in two rows of five so that they can be "read" from left to right—*Abridor de caminos*, 1997.[5] In trying to formulate a theoretical construct from which to analyze artistic expression of the African diaspora, the critic Henry Louis Gates Jr. turns to two trickster figures, Esu-Elegbara and the Signifying Monkey. I quote from his introduction to *The Signifying Monkey*: "These two separate but related trickster figures serve in their respective traditions as points of conscious articulation of language traditions aware of themselves as traditions, complete with a history, patterns of development and revision, and internal principles of patterning and organization. Theirs is a meta-discourse, a discourse about itself" (xxi). When Campos-Pons represents herself as Elegguá, she assumes the trickster's ability to refer to and revise the language tradition of Santería, the Cuban syncretic religion based on Yoruba and Catholic beliefs and rites. Likewise, the artist also utilizes Western artistic and literary conventions as she displays Polaroids with a visual narrative to be read from left to right. This performative dialogue between literature and art and between Western and non-Western traditions call attention to her enterprise as meta-discourse.

In *Abridor de caminos* the colors red and black predominate in all ten panels, symbolizing Elegguá, the Yoruba deity, as both old man and child, both facilitator in the encounter of roads and someone to be feared for his ability to trick you down the wrong path. All but two of the ten panels depict a close-up of the artist's fragmented body: her head as seen from different angles, her hands, her feet, her legs. Of the other two, one panel depicts Elegguá's stone at the center with four perpendicular lines (measuring tapes) coming together at the stone; the other panel pictures walking sticks with a V-shape at the top *(garabato)* used by the trickster to open the roads or by herb collectors to gather healing and incantatory materials from the forest. (The artist's father was an herbalist, a fact that infuses the piece with personal connotations). These *garabatos* are tied with red beads at the bottom of the panel as if gathering a bouquet of flowers. The beads form a tangled mass as if obstructing Elegguá's task of clearing paths. The gathering and tying of the *garabatos* translates an essentially male tradition of opening and clearing into a female tradition of gathering and binding together.

Abridor de caminos creates a narrative through the assembly of fragmented panels, body parts, and objects closely associated with Elegguá. Even though the photographs depict the artist, her fragmentation into body parts in large Polaroids create an effect of bright color rather than individualized image, suggesting a persona rather than a self-portrait. The body becomes a canvas on which to inscribe the ritualized gestures of the trickster, through the use of beads and body paint signifying scarification.[6] The photographs capture the solemnity of a body that becomes possessed by the spirit of Elegguá and thus devoid of its own personality.[7] The act of possession blurs boundaries so that a male deity finds a home in the female body, and his beads crown the head of his devotee. According to Miguel Barnet, possession "entails the will to represent an archetype" and to "assume an identity that links the possessed to the native culture"

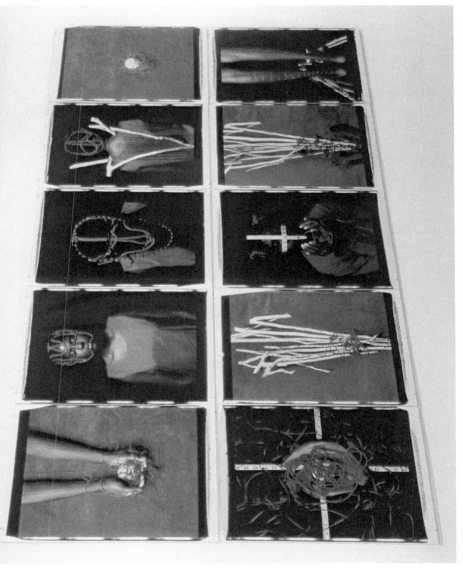

María Magdalena Campos-Pons, *Abridor de caminos* (detail), 1997. Polaroid photographs, 139.7 x 279.4 cm.

(86). By representing herself as someone possessed, the artist assumes the identity of Elegguá as cultural archetype and as artistic persona.

Also true to Elegguá, there is play and trickery in Campos-Pons's representation. Even though the body has been given over to the influence of the ritual in eight of the panels, the artist fails to relinquish her artistic power as exemplified in the other two, where in one the beads are used to tie the walking sticks, to empty them of their ability to open or close paths. In the other panel, where four roads meet at the central stone, there are ribbons that populate the spaces between the perpendicular lines. The red ribbons, signifying the flow of menstrual blood, contaminate the ordering and measurement of life forces by Elegguá with the fluidity of the feminine. In the panels where the artist is physically present, yet absent by virtue of her ritually possessed body, she tricks the trickster by invading his space and tying up his stone and *garabatos*.

In visual terms, the artist uses the bold contrast of black and red colors to give primacy to the photographic medium, emphasizing the geometric figures traced by the ribbons, beads, body paint, and walking sticks. The artist also uses crushed red velvet material as a backdrop to give tactile texture to the visual experience of the photograph while pointing to the color's ritualistic value as commemorative of Elegguá. This use of rich cloth as a backdrop ties the artist's endeavor to the practice of Santería altar-making, an aesthetically driven act to honor and celebrate a deity.[8] The ten panels as a whole allow for an interchange of mythical and artistic forces, ultimately having the effect of transforming the ritual act of possession into a mythical revision of the self-portrait. The artist is portrayed as an able manipulator of a multiplicity of languages, both religious and secular, both Western and non-Western. *Abridor de caminos* demonstrates the artist's ability to depict the process of self-representation as a solemn and playful performance.

The installations *Sustenance* and *Secret,* also displayed at the 1997 Boston show, establish a dialogue with *Abridor de caminos* and appeal to the value of feminine labor of washing, ironing, and embroidering sheets. In the panels of photographs, Campos-Pons positions herself in relation to the male tradition in her culture and family. In these other two installations, placed at the center of the gallery, she establishes the force of her female ancestors and the women in her family.

Sustenance consists of fifty cast-glass irons arranged in a circle in front of *Secret,* a low-set ironing board that holds neatly stacked linens elegantly embroidered in Spanish and English. Each stacked sheet resembles a book labeled on its spine with the beneficiaries of women's labor: for her father, for her son, for a stranger, and so forth. On top of the stacks is inscribed the reasons for the artist's labor—for necessity, for survival, for beauty—again in both languages. If *Abridor de caminos* mines the performative value of the archetypal figure of Elegguá as appropriated by the artist, *Sustenance* and *Secret* encode quotidian objects with the unrecorded history and value of women's work that sustained in secret ways the lives of emancipated slaves. The iron, a tool for survival, is cast in opaque glass to emphasize the fragility and the elegance of the material rather than the utility of its metal counterpart. The color white evokes the purity of Santería vestments. Their arrangement in a circle signifies a sense of containment and reunification of the self (Jung) resulting from the generational link of women who performed the labor of sustenance. The sheets become objects to be read within a feminine culture that engenders the backbreaking labor of ironing with artistic meaning through the domestic act of embroidering. When Campos-Pons appropriates domestic labor, she does so to transcend the ordinary, to link artistic process to personal and cultural history. The circle created by the irons faces the immaculate ironing board that holds the product of women's repetitive, unending labor.

Spoken Softly with Mama (1998) is the second in the series called *History of People Who Were Not Heroes*, the first of which is *A Town Portrait* (1994). In *A Town Portrait* Campos-Pons reproduces the sites of childhood and town congregations of "the eighteenth-century sugar cane plantation village and former (slave) barracks where the artist grew up in the rural province of Matanzas" (Berger, *History*). The sites include "The Door," "The Fountain," "The Tower," and "The Wall." In this installation, the artist combines the use of video, clay, glass, and graffiti to recall the people and events of her childhood. She also includes an epigraph to the piece that reads, "This piece has been made in collaboration with my mother, Estervina Pons, and my sisters Amparo Campos and Marta Campos, and other relatives" (Viso).

In a conversation between curator Sally Berger and the artist at the Museum of Modern Art on the occasion of the opening of *Spoken Softly with Mama* in March 1998, Campos-Pons emphasized the importance of the collaboration established between herself and her mother through letters in the production of *Spoken Softly with Mama*. The title itself alludes to this collaboration. In relation to *A Town Portrait*, the artist has said that "the wall, the tower and the fountain are rough and represent the outside history," while at the MoMA, "materials are ethereal to signify an interior history." *Spoken Softly with Mama* constitutes a coming-of-age piece for the artist as she looks back to reconstruct her personal history with the aid of her mother, "a stone in my life," according to Campos-Pons. This collaboration fulfills her mother's dream, which is for the daughter to achieve what the mother could only dream about. This desire echoes that of countless black artists and writers, who, like Alice Walker in her essay "In Search of Our Mothers' Gardens," lament the loss of creative energy in the lives of women who could only express themselves in domestic ways, as in a colorful garden or in beautifully pressed and embroidered sheets. It also makes those artists clearly indebted to their mothers' labor, which made possible their present artistic endeavors.

At the entrance to the video room housing *Spoken Softly with Mama*, there are three piles of carefully folded thick cotton sheets that recall the 1997 piece *Secret*. The top of each pile becomes a screen onto which are projected the following images: the artist embroidering with a large hoop; the artist dressed in white, shoulders lowered, folding sheets, while on the sheet as a screen there is the superimposition of the image of a young woman from the 1940s, most likely the artist's mother; hands covering scattered pearls, then pearls being blown softly as if by breath until they fall off the surface. These projected images anticipate motifs developed inside.

On the edge of each folded sheet one of the following dedications is embroidered. Left pile: para su novio, para su hijo, para su esposo, para su padre, para su primo, para su hijo, para un extraño, para el señor, para su abuelo, para su cuñado, para su hermano, para su amigo. Center pile: para su amante, para su hermano, to her son, to her husband, to an unknown, para su hijo, to her husband, to a friend, to an unknown, para su hijo, para su primo, para su sobrino. Right pile: para su marido, para su primo, para su amigo, to a friend, para que su, hija, siembra, lo que, ella, solo, pudo, sembrar [To her husband, to her cousin, to a friend, to her friend, so that her daughter may cultivate what she was only able to plant]. This anteroom acts as a dedication as in a book. The dedication refers to intimate as well as more formal relationships, such as with a master or a stranger. The inclusion of the words *master* and *unknown* in the dedication has the effect of addressing the viewer, but also of tying the present to a historical past when black women were enslaved by white masters. The dedication is written as if recorded by the artist about a piece that the mother produces: "so that her daughter [the artist] may cultivate what she [the mother] was only able to plant."[9]

The multimedia installation is housed in a room, about 15 x 20 feet with all walls painted black. Five white ironing boards, at least 8 feet tall, stand pointing toward the ceiling at the back of the room in a semicircle as if forming an altar. The middle and the outside ones become screens onto which video images are projected. The two ironing boards flanking the middle one each have embedded in them a full-length photograph of a woman—one older, seated, wearing a shawl; the other one younger, standing, holding a fan. By their dress they appear to be women of the early twentieth century. The boards are covered with layers of silk and organza to signify the layers of time and memory that are projected in the photographs and the video images.[10] At the foot of each screen a name is embroidered: Paulina, Telefora, Ñica, Amparo, Oneida.

At the center front of the space, triangular and round trivets made of white opaque glass, designed to appear like lace, form a circle shaped to suggest a flower or a pomegranate. From it radiate glass irons that seem to be aimed toward the various images on the screens. This use of the trivets and irons connects the sculptural aspect of the installation to the photographs and the video projections so that the static sculpture on the floor acquires kinetic value. Moreover, the ordering of the trivets to resemble the shape of a pomegranate finds cinematic elaboration in the middle screen. Individual glass trivets molded to look like embroidery repeat the motif of elegance of the elaborate organza material that covers the ironing boards.

Images are simultaneously projected onto the three ironing boards serving as screens. On each of the screens two sequences of images, each about seven minutes long, are projected and accompanied by sound.

First sequence of images on the left screen: View of the artist's legs, from mid-calf down, walking slowly and deliberately up to the camera. The artist walks back and forth; at the end of each trajectory, she stands on tiptoe, then knocks her heels together. At the end of this sequence, there is a close-up of the heels from the back; they look rosy and fleshy. One can even see tiny hairs on the ankle. The sound during this sequence is of an iron rubbing on starched sheets. This walking back and forth in connection with the tapping of the heels creates an incantatory atmosphere as if summoning a spiritual power. This fragmentation of the artist's body recalls that in *Abridor de caminos*. Here, the progressive close-ups enhance the intensity of the image and reinforce the ritualized nature of the action rather than comment on a postmodern sense of fragmentation in the life of contemporary humanity.

Second sequence of images on the left screen: Close-up of colorful scarves being aired out, shaken. These refer to Oyá, "mistress of lightning and of the wind, and gatekeeper of the cemetery. . . . Oyá is the

María Magdalena Campos-Pons, *History of People Who Were Not Heroes: Spoken Softly with Mama* (detail), 1997.

rainbow and is represented by its seven colors, seven being her symbolic number. . . . Her chants are grave, solemn, but of uncommon beauty; they almost always invoke justice or peace" (Barnet, 94). Then, the black-and-white photographic image of a group of girls flows on the screen as if the image were being processed photographically. This process of an image materializing before our eyes makes concrete the process of memory where images come into being, with water (in this case the photographic liquid) as the signifier of time. When this photograph comes into focus the image changes to that of the artist sitting next to a table with a white lace tablecloth onto which different photographic images of women are being projected: four women, then an older woman, then a child, then a woman sitting (the same as on the large photographic screen), then two children. This interest in the multiple projection of photographs on a cloth surface emphasizes the fluidity of the photographic process in time, rather than the static nature of the resulting frozen image. Yet, in the final projection of this sequence, the artist is quite static, sitting regally on a chair, wearing a white silk dress fitted close to her body, the skirt drapes from her knee down. Her hair is pulled back as if in a bun. She's wearing pearls (necklace and earrings). The style of the dress appears to be from the 1920s, perhaps as late as the 1940s. The fluidity of the photographic process, projected on the tablecloth placed alongside the artist's rigid pose, produces the impression that both occupy the same spatial and spiritual spheres.

As in the Polaroid close-up images of the artist in *Abridor de caminos*, here the full-length video portrait of the artist does not mean to project a self-portrait. Because she is quite static and dons the attire of an earlier generation of women, the image represents an act of possession; this time the artist means to embody the image of her mother, as if the mother's spirit possessed the artist's body. As Barnet has stated, the act of possession "attests to the determination to be something different, to assume an identity that links the possessed to the native culture" (86). In this particular case, because Campos-Pons's mother lives in Cuba and is absent from the artist's life in the United States, the video effects an act of summoning her presence so that the mother may be present in the artist's act of representation. Most importantly, however, the image of the mother appears as the nurturing source for the artist, with the mother's labor of ironing clothes as the sustenance that made the artist's success possible.

First sequence of images on the center screen: The screen is covered by foam, perhaps sea foam, perhaps soap suds. The ambivalent image ties the chore of washing sheets by hand to the power of Yemayá, the female deity of the sea who links the African and American shores with the constant movement of the waves reaching both extremes of the Atlantic with sea foam. This fades out. We see the artist's hand peeling a pomegranate, seed by seed, very slowly. The hands become progressively stained by the red juice of the fruit. The motion is of picking up the fruit, opening it, allowing the seeds to roll off the white flesh and then fall to the ground, where many seeds have accumulated. We hear the sound of the seeds falling. At the end of this sequence one seed is left. Fingers touch it tenderly, sensually; then fingers push the seed off the fruit. The shots are very close. On the ground we see all the fallen seeds; then from the top we see seeds as if it's raining seeds. The seeds disappear, and red ribbons take their place at the bottom of the screen. Fingers pull them up one by one, and they finally fill the screen as if being shaken from the top. The final shot is of red ribbons curled at the bottom of the screen.

This sequence is highly symbolic of the coming-of-age of a young woman, with the pomegranate perhaps representing the womb. The seeds fall off as the sloughing off of the uterine wall and their falling as the shedding of menstrual blood. The substitution of ribbons for seeds sets off a chain of meaning that connects blood with the sense of self-ornamentation that girls develop in their early years of sexual maturity. This sequence is highly charged with tenderness and sensuality with the reluctance to let go of the last seed, as if wanting to hold on to childhood just a bit longer. Because red ribbons were also present in *Abridor de caminos*, there is a grounding of the more generalized coming-of-age experience within the Afro-Cuban experience in which there is less of a necessity to divide the world into opposing spheres of the feminine and the masculine. In *Abridor de caminos* the color red signifies the color of the guardian of the roads, Elegguá, but it also signifies the menstrual flow of blood tied to menstruation. However, in *Spoken Softly with Mama*, pomegranate seeds and red ribbons acquire an almost exclusively feminine meaning given the entire context of the piece.

Second sequence of images on the center screen: The figure of the artist dressed in a white rough cotton dress, very simple, straight blouse, long skirt almost to the ankles. She is dancing and turning between two almost transparent cotton curtains, yet we don't see the face of the dancer. She is holding scarves, different colored scarves, starting with white, then red, green, purple, and so on, as if representing the colors of the rainbow closely linked with Oyá. The sound is very soft playing of drums. The drapes disappear, and we see the figure of the artist at the top of the screen, kneeling, only from the shoulders down; again, we don't see her face. She is carefully folding an ironed sheet that first covers the entire screen, is already folded as if a long rectangle, then gets folded toward the figure while "Arroz con leche" ["Rice Pudding," a children's rhyme] is being sung:

Arroz con leche	[Rice pudding
se quiere casar	wishes to marry
con una viudita	a little widow
de la capital.	from the capital.
Que sepa coser	Who knows how to sew
que sepa bordar	who also embroiders
que ponga la aguja	who places the needle
en su canevá.	in her burlap.
Rin, Ran.	Rin, Ran.
Aurora de mayo	Dawn of May
al campo salió	went out to the fields
en busca de flores	looking for flowers
de mar y de sol	of sea and sun
tan linda y tan bella	so pretty, so beautiful
me encuentro con quién	I'll meet with them all
elige a tu gusto	choose to your taste
que aquí tiene usted.	since here you have them.]
	(my translation)

In this second sequence, the singing of the children's rhyme suggests the gathering of flowers as if by maidens of marriageable age. It also announces the desire of "rice pudding," who wishes to marry a young widow from the capital who can sew and embroider well. The song refers to the domestic chores of women that are the subject of the installation.

Like the first panel, which utilizes the melting of one photographic image into another in order to produce the process of memory in concrete terms, this center panel starts with the powerful mythic image of Oyá, the keeper of the cemetery, the one who memorializes the lives of those who have departed, and ends with that of a faceless woman folding sheets. The long sheet, symbolizing the sequential passage of time, gets folded and compressed into smaller units, perhaps connoting the individual lives of women whose manual labor is immortalized by the process of folding while singing. One must recall the solemn nature of Oyá's chants that invoke both justice and peace. In this central panel the faceless woman who enacts the ritual process embodies all the unknown women who performed the same labor of remembrance back to time immemorial.

First sequence of images on the third screen: The artist from shoulders up, with hair in short tails all over her head. At the end of each tail is a white bead. On top of the head, there is a braided circle made of white cloth onto which are placed many folded white sheets, perfectly balanced on the head. The image of the head crowned with sheets recalls the long continuum of African women carrying the objects of their labor on their heads, down through the centuries, from the distant past before the Middle Passage to the present time. The movement is the same as with the feet on the left screen: very slow, very stately. The combined images of legs and head on the two screens connote a balancing act of remembrance done with ritual precision and with care.

Second sequence of images on the third screen: Pink petals falling from the top of the screen in bunches. Hands then sew petals, about five, very carefully with needle and thread. Then loose petals are seen at the bottom of the screen carefully moving around as if someone is handling them from underneath. This set of images recalls the singing connected to the images on the center screen. The sewing of petals harkens back to the video installation in *A Town Portrait,* in which the artist recalled her childhood games of stitching together petals to make garlands. Symbolically, it refers to the artist's painful and almost impossible task of stitching together the forgotten moments of her childhood. Moreover, it deals with the willful act of fashioning an artistic and spiritual self subsequent to the separation from family and country of origin experienced in 1991.

Third sequence of images on the third screen: Artist, as in the left screen, sitting next to the table, undoing the pearl necklace. Then, there is a projection of a colored picture of a young woman in a 1940s linen, very light yellow dress, almost ocher, projected on the screen—the artist's mother. Finally, a close-up of the artist's lips as if whispering. This last composite of images conjoins, on the one hand, the dispersal of the self as it is separated from the main strand of women in the family and, on the other hand, the connectedness between self and the mother figure through the act of whispering. This last video sequence constitutes an act of self-reflexivity in which Campos-Pons offers her multimedia installation to honor and exalt the women who came before her. She has described *Spoken Softly with Mama* thus: "A space can bear the imprint of its inhabitants even in their absence. An object can personify an individual even more than his or her portrait. This is the concept behind the selection of object-furniture for the installation; a portrait of a family narrated through the voices of objects that constitute their environment" (Campos-Pons, "Multimedia Artist").

Encountering the installation created by Campos-Pons, I was struck by the impression of crossing into a sacred space. The black walls, the absence of light other than that projected onto the screens, the preponderance of elegantly placed trivets, irons, and ironing boards to create an altar, and the soft sounds of a female voice singing, soft drums playing, and seeds and ribbons falling—all conjured an atmosphere of respect and beauty. After experiencing the multimedia installation for a while, I sensed the interconnected nature of the materials so that the objects, images, and sounds coalesced into the concrete manifestation of remembrance. Not one image, sound, or object stood out in isolation.

In *Spoken Softly with Mama*, Campos-Pons creates a performance by effectively making several artistic media enter into dialogue with one another. The photographs, videos, and sound design perform a voyage back in time to the artist's heritage through the appeal to the Yoruba figure of Oyá, the keeper of the cemeteries. As the artist impersonates her, or is possessed by her, her artistic persona is capable of turning personal and cultural absences into presence, while grounding the multimedia installation in the cultural and spiritual life of Santería.

By building an installation in the shape of an altar, Campos-Pons engages in an interpretive act vis-à-vis the Santería tradition of altar-making. In his article on altar-making and gift exchange, art historian David H. Brown points to "the relation of (systems of) art and aesthetics to ritual and cosmology in the Yoruba-Atlantic tradition" of constructing thrones to *orichas* (87). I contend that the Santería practice of altar-making consciously informs Campos-Pons's artistic process. Brown's articulation of the Santería practice is most helpful in understanding Campos-Pons' interpretive act:

> As special altars of *oricha*-celebration, *thrones* constitute a site for supplicants to approach, salute, praise, communicate with, and make offering *(ebó)* and tributes *(derechos)* to the *orichas*. Thrones are temporary installations, whose scale often requires reallocation of domestic space, and whose duration as an assemblage is coextensive with particular ritual periods and passages. These include events that have private and semi-public phases, in which the community is invited into the "sacred room" *(cuarto sagrado* or *igbodún)* to greet formally presented *orichas*. (88–89)

With *Spoken Softly with Mama*, Campos-Pons has created a temporary site to praise and communicate with female members of her family going back several generations. In order to do so, she has assumed the persona of her mother, to invoke her presence at a personal level. She has also portrayed herself as possessed by Oyá, to pay tribute to the Santería warrior figure of remembrance at the mythic level. In such a mythic site, the artist projects her own passage into womanhood as a symbolic moment that coincides with the same period of life as experienced by her mother and other women who came before. The video projections place the artist's figure in the spaces that her mother inhabits by reproducing a sitting room where the images of family members are projected. By portraying herself as possessed by her mother's image, Campos-Pons makes the mother present in the space of the installation. Likewise, by virtue of the fact that the artist is sitting in her mother's chair and wearing her dress and hairstyle, the artist places herself back in her family home in Cuba. Thus the relevance of the artist's words: "A space can bear the imprint of its inhabitants even in their absence." With this installation, Campos-Pons invites us, an artistic community, to share in the remembrance of her passage into womanhood and in her connectedness to a feminine tradition. Most importantly, however, she invites us to witness and understand the Yoruba performative traditions of possession and altar-making in their full ritualistic and aesthetic complexities.

True to her own interpretation of the Yoruba god Elegguá, Campos-Pons points to the "conscious articulation of language traditions aware of themselves as traditions, complete with a history, patterns of development and revision, and internal principles of patterning and organization" (Gates, *Signifying Monkey*, xxi). Placing herself within her own Afro-Cuban tradition as an artist, she reflects on the merits of her Cuban spiritual tradition but also transposes the spirituality of that tradition into the visually powerful language of the Western media. While describing the impact of Afro-Cuban artists since the 1980s on the art of the avant-garde, the Cuban critic Gerardo Mosquera gives us an apt description of Campos-Pons:

These young people constitute a fourth landmark in the expression of African origin in Cuban plastic arts. If Mendive works from within the Afro-Cuban focus, making use of myth and through "neoprimitivism," the younger artists give priority to the philosophical bases, the "cosmovisual," let us say, the Afro-Cuban thought in works of a conceptual type that attempt an interpretation of the world and the construction of an ethic from a nonwestern stance, with the aim of taking on contemporary problems. In some cases they modify the very character of art by bringing it close to a mystical-existential practice,

within personal liturgical processes. The descriptive, formal, and mythological aspects are minimized in order to work with the content itself, from the
interior of those world views, bringing a new spirituality to the art of the
avant-garde. ("Elegguá at the Post-Modern Crossroads," 244)

In *Spoken Softly with Mama* through the practices of spiritual possession and altar-making, the deceptively simple act of whispering in the
last sequence of *Spoken Softly with Mama* (third screen, third sequence)
transfers the personal into the realm of artistic performance.

The last section of this chapter defines how Campos-Pons represents
a feminine conception of memory through a childlike play between visibility and invisibility with the expressed purpose of rejecting a nostalgic
recollection of childhood. *Meanwhile, the Girls Were Playing* reinforces
the conception of the domestic realm as "a manifestly political space
where there is no comfort from the configurations of history or lived
experience" (Tawadros, 273). The installation displays three large, colorful, skirtlike circles laid on the floor of a mostly darkened black room.
Each skirt represents the childhood of either the artist or one of her two
sisters, Amparo and Marta Campos. In each circle that stands for the
waist of one girl, videos of playful scenes are projected, such as tops
gyrating, birds singing, hands reaching for colorful cotton candy. Against
the back wall of the room, a video projects the artist, dressed in a simple
white cotton dress, holding flowers and gyrating under a white canopy.
This figure represents the artist's grandmother who was a *santera* and
tried to protect the girls from the hardships and deprivations of living
in a former slave barracks in La Vega, Matanzas, between 1962 and
1974. My analysis shows how Campos-Pons, through a chain of gyrating
movements and seen and unseen associations in the piece, conflates the
seemingly innocent play of children's games with two layers of Cuban
history: slavery and Castro's repression of Afro-Cuban religious practices during the early years of the revolution.[11] At another level, the violence of sugar production and its sweetness—here represented by cotton
candy—is symbolic of the emotional violence of the artist's own displacement, transformed within the installation into snow falling on what at
first seems to be a Boston-area landscape but turns out to be the artist's
head. Throughout the piece, the vulnerability of childhood and inno-
cence go hand in hand with the strength displayed by the Afro-Cuban
culture that has survived in spite of multiple political and societal attacks.
In a conversation with Lynne Bell, Campos-Pons states that "from the
sea came slavery and tragedy, but seven powers came with them. Seven

powers stand for the Yoruba pantheon and the significance of Yoruba culture, which is one of the main components of Santería and one of the main cultural components of Cuba" (Bell, 36). Along with tragedy came strength through cultural memory and its representation.

Campos-Pons belonged to a group of artists stretching the limits of what was permitted culturally in Castro's Cuba of the 1980s.[12] In her case, she pushed the limits through conceptual art. The Cuban critic Gerardo Mosquera, describing artistic trends during that decade, states: "One important element is the weight of the conceptual. Even when a work is found at the opposite pole from conceptualism, it usually possesses discursive, analytical elements or a reflective dimension: it is an art of ideas, giving rise to the frequent use of texts" ("Infinite Island," 26). Okwui Enwezor gives us a more comprehensive definition of conceptualism that seems very apt when analyzing the work of Campos-Pons:

> Conceptual art, as commonly understood, attempted a fundamental restructuring of the viewer's relationship to the art object. First, its critique of systems of representation and presentation pitched art-making toward dematerialization of the object, thereby placing less value on the perceptual codes through which art is traditionally received. This strategy sought to challenge the autonomous value placed on objects, which value is, in turn, connected to cultural ways of looking. Second, conceptual art privileged linguistic, informational, and philosophical systems over materialist modes of production, making communication, performance, documentation, process, actions, and the world outside the studio part of the intensive phenomenology of process. (73)

As will be understood through my analysis, Campos-Pons makes us see objects conceptually. The girls' skirts, for example, are seen not only as beautiful, bright-colored objects but also as everyday pieces of clothing that capture a simulacrum of the childhood and of the girls who wore them. Moreover, the games projected on the screens inside the girls' waists lead us through a process of remembrance that unveils an intensely personal, yet also communal, history of the African diaspora.

One of the two most significant words in the title of the installation is "playing." The concept of play is clearly the most visually accessible in *Meanwhile, the Girls Were Playing*. Upon entering the dark room, the viewer does not associate the figure of the gyrating woman projected by video onto the back wall with a *santera*. One sees, instead, a woman, the artist, going around in circles while holding a bouquet of flowers. She seems much like a child gyrating in order to make herself dizzy. In her essay printed in the catalog for the installation, assistant curator Jennifer

L. Riddell suggests that "the blitheness of this childhood game and the impressionistic effects it generated offer a starting point from which to consider María Magdalena Campos-Pons' new installation" (3).[13] The motion of the gyrating game inscribes a center with a specific location and time; for the artist, it is Cuba at the time of her childhood in the 1960s and early 1970s. The concept of play gets reinforced by the artist's singing of a childhood song based on the repetition of a roundelay:

A la rueda rueda	[Round and round
dame un beso	give me a kiss
si no quieres ir	if you don't wish
a la escuela	to go to school
duérmete	fall asleep
en el campo	in a field
de perejil.	of parsley.]
	(my translation)

As the figure gyrates, she lets go of the bouquet of flowers, which is then returned by an outsider, presumably, another child in the game, or the viewer herself.[14] The flowers disappear to an unknown destination, yet return as if attracted by a magnet (much like the movement of the ocean waves, which approach and move away from the shores of Cuba). If interpreted strictly as an autobiographical installation, Campos-Pons uses the image of the flowers as a symbol for her own physical displacement from her childhood home in Matanzas, first to Havana to study art and then to Canada and the United States. The flowers, becoming a blur of color in the gyrating motion and in the act of being thrown, could very well signify the artist's ongoing reconstruction of memory from outside the circle of home. The flowers become brushstrokes on a video canvas (Campos-Pons, "Artist's Talk") as memory gets translated into color and sound.

The figure of the artist dressed in white, gyrating under a white canopy, also reproduces an Afro-Cuban cultural metaphor of the canopy as portable shelter, portable home. Under the canopy, Campos-Pons becomes the Iyalocha, the female priestess of Yoruba practices whose purpose, besides performing rituals as the mother of the saints (Yoruba deities), is that of creating community. Under the canopy, the artist becomes her grandmother, a respected Iyalocha, *santera* ("Artist's Talk"). At this level, Campos-Pons evokes the Santería practice of possession in which the spirit of a deity mounts the body of a practitioner—except here, the spirit of the absent grandmother possesses the body of the artist to make herself present through the artist's performance. Campos-Pons says that "performative and oral traditions are very important in Cuba. In Santería rituals the presence of the body is overwhelming, totally overwhelming" (Bell, 40). Through performative means in this installation, the artist represents her close relationship to her grandmother and, by extension, to her grandmother's ability to create a portable home. In this respect, critic Michael D. Harris compares Campos-Pons to Cuban artist Wifredo Lam, who introduced Africa in his painting in modernist Europe: "Like Lam, her (Campos-Pons') involvement in the religion is through artistic exploration rather than religious practice" (16).

Furthermore, in representing her relationship to her grandmother, Campos-Pons connects the mythical to the sense of play (the figure playing the dizzying game), as well as to the concept of an ancestral home. In Campos-Pons's video canvas, home is not limited to her home in Matanzas, but encompasses home within diasporic movement, in a constant displacement that took Campos-Pons's family from West Africa to Matanzas and then, in the case of the artist, to the United States. The gyrating game thus speaks of spatial and temporal displacements allowing the visual imprint of strokes of color to encompass the memory of the domestic, the mythical, and the historic.[15] Thus, the return of the flowers to the circle implies the artist's capacity to remember catastrophic displacement and recast it in the playful gesture of throwing and recovering a bouquet of flowers.[16]

Equally visible as the flowers are the three circles of bright fabric—yellow, blue, and green—signifying the girls' skirts, embroidered about the waist with appliqués of flowers. This design continues with richly colored translucent glass trivets that cover each of the skirts. There are about three hundred glass pieces in the installation. The richness of the colored skirts contrasts with the dark, unlit floor. The skirts are lit from above so that their color and glass flowers predominate as one enters the installation. As we have seen, this is not the first time that Campos-Pons has utilized glass. Michael D. Harris comments: "The glass elements in *Meanwhile, the Girls Were Playing* provide a layered signification in the work. For Campos-Pons they provide a sense of fragility, vulnerability, and a sense of the nature of experience and memory" (*Meanwhile,* 20). The use of glass, so vulnerable to breakage, also entails hard labor on the part of the artist, who participated in the casting of each of the objects. Behind apparent fragility stands strength in artistic labor.

Campos-Pons invests her use of glass with multiple conceptual meanings: "Transparency is about memory. Also, I think that transparency

María Magdalena Campos-Pons, *Meanwhile, the Girls Were Playing* (detail), 1999/2000.

[is] about displacement. When you are [an emigré] you are always in this space that is in-between, in-between physical and not seeing, but the [memories] are there" (Harris, 21; brackets are his). Through the physical glass object, particularly in the context of the video being projected on the wall, the artist and the viewer intuit the displacement inherent in Afro-Cuban personal and community history. On the occasion of the opening of *Spoken Softly with Mama,* as I have already noted, the artist stated that "a space can bear the imprint of its inhabitants even in their absence. An object can personify an individual even more than his or her portrait. This is the concept behind the selection of object-furniture for the installation; a portrait of a family narrated through the voices of objects that constitute their environment." This aspect of conceptualism in Campos-Pons derives from African artistic practices that became adopted by modernism in the West. Salah M. Hassam and Olu Oguibe state: "[T]hese cultures [African and Oceanic] integrated real life objects in art, contrary to the practice in the West where the artist was required to reproduce such objects, and not appropriate them. Second was the fact that the status of these objects as art was radically thrown into oscillation by their translocation from the cultures and contexts of their provenance" (14). If, in the previous installation, object-furniture was meant to narrate the story of a family through the generations and

in their displacement from Africa to the Caribbean, in *Meanwhile, the Girls Were Playing,* the skirts made of colored cloth and glass ornaments narrate the brightness of childhood in Cuba. The glass flowers also recall the video of the artist's hands making garlands of flowers to recollect her childhood in *A Town Portrait.* Moreover, glass speaks of the fragility of flowers and young girls themselves.

Most importantly, however, the glass flowers recall the labor of the mother who made beautiful skirts, replicated in the installation, for the girls to wear. In fact, as in other installations, Campos-Pons communicates closely with her family members as she designs her works. In her essay on *Meanwhile, the Girls Were Playing,* Lisa D. Freiman gives us the following information regarding the cast-glass flowers: "The idea for these forms stemmed from the original Cuban pattern books that Campos-Pons' mother used to sew her daughters' dresses. Still living in Cuba, she sent these books to Campos-Pons in Boston and the artist embroidered the designs into the installation material, eventually adapting the flat pattern into a glass mold for the florettes" (315). When Campos-Pons recovers the history of her family, she does it in collaboration, empowering her family members in her artistic enterprise. The glass florettes bear the imprint of the artist, but they also actualize the mother's domestic labor of sewing as art.

When Campos-Pons speaks of the artistic value of transparency, she also speaks of the "in-between physical and not seeing." When the viewers first walk into the installation room, they fail to see the projected scenes in the space where the girls' waists should be. One must approach each skirt to view the projections that present a variety of children's games, including "jacks, a spinning top, *quimbumba* (a game involving two pieces of wood, one of which is hit in the air), and a wheel being rolled with a stick" (Harris, 20). Another video shows sugar-making designs on a landscapelike surface that turns out to be the artist's braided head, then sugar cubes being mixed in a glass of water, then hands playing with cotton candy. The third video shows images of birds flying in and out of a bird feeder. The games depicted in the first video are all played with inexpensive, if not made-at-home, objects, reflecting the poverty of the family, which in no way diminishes the children's joy. The third video, rich with the color of birds and their sounds, adds to the atmosphere of beauty and play of the entire installation. The one projecting several contexts for the use of sugar, like the video on the back wall, can be interpreted at several levels. Sugar water, like the games the girls play, connotes the poverty of the family, who must resort to giving it to the girls both to quench their thirst and to appease their hunger. Cotton candy, a luxury for most children, who eat it only on special occasions, holds a much more difficult meaning for children of the African diaspora. Campos-Pons has stated: "Do you know of anything more innocent than cotton candy? But is anything more evil than how sugar came to be in Cuba? Or in any other place? Sugar was the blood of slavery. The blood of slavery was sugar" (*Meanwhile, the Girls Were Playing*, 19).

The production of sugar and its connotations for Africans in the Americas was already the subject of Campos-Pons's first installation, *A Town Portrait*. In that first work, the artist constructed a replica of the town where she grew up, a former slave barracks built under the shadow of the tower that was part of the sugar mill. The tower, represented by the artist with rough clay bricks, is described by her: "The tower was the place that let me know that home was near. How long had it been there, what was hidden between its red bricks? The lost ones and those who defied all, even time" (quoted in Herzberg, "Town Portrait," paragraph 6). The tower, like sugar, signals ambivalent meanings; it encloses the sacrifice of many lives, yet it represented home. Like the tower, sugar meant sustenance when mixed with water, yet that sustenance implied the lack of more nutritious food, the loss of lives, and the barbaric working conditions in the production of sugar in Cuba. Moreover, it was the production of sugar in the Caribbean that drove the slave trade, forcefully uprooting the artist's great-great-grandfather from Yoruba territory in West Africa (Harris, 24). Hidden behind the innocent image of children eating sugar candy is the history of a family whose men worked in the sugar-cane fields even after slavery was abolished, and whose women earned a living washing and sewing clothes.

Also not readily apparent when viewing the installation is the displacement that the artist suffered from Cuba to the United States. The viewer becomes quite perplexed at the image of a white powder falling on a surface that is not readily identifiable. The white powder, assumed to be sugar, implies at first that the girls are making designs with sugar on a dark surface as part of their games. Then the focus pulls back, and it becomes evident that the sugar is falling on a head of braided hair, the artist's hair. Seen in this context, the sugar implies an inherited burden that can only be surmounted through the artistic performance. The white powder interpreted as sugar at least brings the artist back home, sugar is in her head, in her state of mind. The use of her head as the recipient of sugar is also significant because in the Yoruba tradition, a person's head represents the place where the spirits or the force of the ancestors and deities reside. In this context, the sugar on the artist's head means that she wears her ancestor's victimized past as she does braided hair. Yet, given the artist's displacement from a place that produces sugar to a place that experiences snow falling in the winter, the white powder on her head also signifies a landscape covered in snow, marking yet another displacement. The diasporic movement is repeated from several generations back in history to the present. Given that the prevalent shape in the installation is that of the circle, history progresses, not linearly, but within a pattern of concentric repetitions, in which any one life in the circles refers back or forth to another, disclosing absence (that of her great-great-grandfather) and substituting presence (the artist's head). Against the Western conception of history as a linear progression, Campos-Pons offers the image of the circle, with the center, the head, as the site for intergenerational meetings and as the keeper of memories.

In *Meanwhile, the Girls Were Playing,* that which is evident, spectacularly seen, leads to more private, hidden, internal meanings that discover emotional and historical realities. In her study of the multiple meanings derived from black women's bodies in African American literature, Deborah E. McDowell talks about the dangers of over-interpreting the surface of black women's bodies and encourages us as critics to recover the body politic through a writer's or artist's discursive body. I quote at length her analysis of Sethe in Toni Morrison's *Beloved:*

> As Sethe's story suggests, "recovering" the body requires attending to its inside parts, its buried zones. Grief, affect, the logos of emotion, constitute one buried zone of black women's "body studies," largely because the boundaries of the body are typically drawn around the surface of the skin. But while the skin encases, compasses the body, it does not constitute the body's total compass, is not its beginning and its end. While recovering the emotions is an elusive prospect, in that emotions are difficult to materialize, the affective range is continuous with discourse on the body. (308–9)

For an artist like Maria Magdalena Campos-Pons, who repeatedly uses her body in most of her installations and large-scale Polaroid photographs, the body becomes a starting point, a surface on which to record emotions and discursive strategies that will enhance the understanding of a history of people whose deeds were not recorded in Western conceptions of significant memory. History is not interpreted as exclusive of human personal experience; rather, it begins with it and leads to the remembrance of significant events such as slavery, from the point of view of those who suffered it and continue to suffer its present consequences.

Given the interconnectedness of Campos-Pons's works, one must consider a reading of *Meanwhile, the Girls Were Playing* as an installation that serves to recover the bodies and the histories of women and men of the African diaspora who shared the Caribbean experience, an experience rooted in an economy based almost exclusively on the production of sugar.[17] Unlike *Spoken Softly with Mama,* in which women's bodies are represented in their full integrity and strength, there is an unprecedented absence in this installation of the bodies of the three sisters, even though in the video projected on the back screen of *Meanwhile* the grandmother appears as a source of vigilance and strength. What seems to be foregrounded, however, is the concept of the sisters' play. The absence of their bodies perhaps underscores the absence of childhood in the present of the installation. Play, then, serves to establish connections with a distant past, with a common history that the artist foregrounds with all its mythical connotations. But why have the bodies, or their symbolic representation, been elided in this installation?

I turn next to the essay on Lucille Clifton by Ajuan Maria Mance, who offers the term "myth-play" to describe the recovery of women's bodies that African American poets effect in defining their artistic identity:

> I have come to describe such literary acts of resistance and recreation as "myth-play," a term that connotes the joy and euphoria that accompany African American women poets' recuperation and exercise of the power of making identity. In this context, "myth" establishes identity as fabrication-in-progress; rather than a fixed position, identity as process. . . . "Play" implies the self-conscious exercise of agency, not merely in responsible service to the emancipation of the group (though that certainly is a significant part of black women poets' representation of the black female body and landscape) but in celebration of visibility, empowerment, and the return to voice. (135–36)

By substituting play for the girls' bodies, Campos-Pons makes their history visible. Furthermore, the three sisters who make up the present generation in the family history have been absented to foreground the "fabrication-in-progress" of the artist's identity.

But where is the artist's self-definition in her play of visibility and nonvisibility? Where is her voice? Always aware of the power of words in conceptual art, Campos-Pons has given great meaning to the words she engages in her installations. In *A Town Portrait,* for example, she inscribes words on the bricks of the buildings that represent the former slave barracks where she grew up, in order to appropriate buildings erected to enslave her ancestors. In *Spoken Softly with Mama,* words are embroidered on beautiful linen sheets that were presumably ironed by her mother and other female relatives in sustaining the family. The names of family relatives are inscribed on the sheets to connote the fact that each sheet ironed was done for those who benefited from women's labor of love. In the title of her last installation of this series, Campos-Pons emphasizes the word *Meanwhile*. All visible aspects of the work point to the idea of play; its mythical interpretations follow from what is not so easily seen. So what are the events or realities hidden behind the word "meanwhile," particularly as it concerns the artist?

At a surface level, it is evident that while the girls were playing, the grandmother was protecting them from the harsh reality of poverty. She was also protecting them from the fact that the practice of Santería was being discouraged at best and persecuted at worst, during the early years of the Castro revolution. In his analysis of *Meanwhile, the Girls Were Playing,* Michael Harris states: "Campos-Pons grew up immersed in Santería, even though it was suppressed in 1959. She says that it was "'a strange combination of practice and hiding in a way' and the *bembe* celebration of the saints was hidden . . . 'in an inner yard'" (16).

The suppression of Santería practices in her inner yard was extended in the 1970s and early 1980s to artists who desired to incorporate an Afro-Cuban context in their works. In my analysis, I could conjure all sorts of questions as to why the artist felt the necessity of displacing herself to the United States, repeating in her own life the circle of diasporic movement that her ancestors inscribed. The fact is that she came to the Massachusetts College of Art in 1988 with a fellowship, fell in love, and married Neil Leonard, a composer and musician working in the Boston area. He collaborates often with Campos-Pons, as she includes soundtracks in her installations. In her interview with Bell, Campos-Pons stated: "I didn't leave Cuba with the intention of staying out permanently. I am emotionally attached to Cuba. But at some point you need to take a radical decision in your life and I did. My decision was to stay with my husband and establish a family—he is from Boston" (37–38).

Her leaving must be placed within a wider context, however. During the 1980s Campos-Pons was also an integral part of a renaissance in the Cuban arts. In the interview with Bell she stated:

> I am a part of a generation that was intent on reshaping the Cuban cultural landscape: I wasn't only an artist, I was an activist too. There were things that I cared about, issues of social justice and the desire to make Cuba a modern country with a voice in the international scene. I thought people like me could

make a difference. I was the only black female in that group for a long time and I did feel a tremendous sense of responsibility. (38)

This artistic renaissance during the 1980s highlights a contradiction in Cuban cultural policy that during the 1970s undermined Afro-Cuban cultural practices yet ultimately allowed Cuban artists to explore cultural manifestations beyond the mandate to produce culture within the revolutionary context. During the 1980s, cultural tourism began to include the celebration of Cuba's African heritage as well. Campos-Pons joined a long list of Cuban artists who brought African culture to the forefront of their work, including Manuel Mendive, whose work began to be shown in the 1960s and was subsequently marginalized for a period in the 1970s (Mosquera, "Infinite Island," 24). The list also included contemporaries of Campos-Pons such as José Bedia, Marta María Pérez, the younger Belkis Ayón, and others. (See Mosquera's "Elegguá" for a presentation of their work.) The Cuban critic Antonio Eligio Fernández (Tonel), referring to artists working in the 1980s, many of whom left at the end of the decade, writes in "Tree of Many Beaches:" "We could also add to this list some of the most important artists of the moment, such as Carlos García, José Franco, José Bedia, María Magdalena Campos, Eduardo Ponjuán, René Francisco Rodríguez, and, in the field of theory, Orlando Tajonera, Madelín Izquierdo, Osvaldo Sánchez, Magaly Espinosa, and others. Undoubtedly, the influence of the migratory flux of leading artists and other crucial figures, almost over by 1990, could be seen in the ISA and the Bienal de la Habana" (41). At the end of the 1980s, official tolerance for exploration by young artists came to an end as the leadership decided not to join the transformative changes of the Soviet block. Mosquera writes in "Infinite Island":

> Various functionaries were removed, and a cultural closure was again imposed, and this time with more subtlety. Angel Delgado, who defecated during an opening as part of a performance, had to serve six months in prison with common criminals, giving a clear warning to intellectuals. This situation, together with the economic, moral, and social crisis brought about by the cessation of Soviet subsidies and the international interest in new Cuban art, provoked a diaspora of intellectuals that reached its climax at the beginning of the 1990s. (28)

Particularly in this context, hoping to make a difference internationally, Campos-Pons considers herself a Cuban artist in order to give voice to her Afro-Cuban experience in a contestatory manner. Based on her readings of Homi Bhabha's concept of "the interstitial space" ("Beyond the

Pale"), she states: "I place myself in a Third Space: a space between territory, between what is home, between languages, between media, between
performance versus ritual, between three- and two-dimensional, between
all these layers and what happens there 'in between.' As a black Cuban
female living outside of Cuba, I have something to say that is particular
and personal about this 'in-between' space" (Bell, 43). In her last installation about the African diaspora, the "in-between" coincides conceptually
with the "Meanwhile" of the title. Whether spatially or temporally, the
words place the artist outside, looking in as an insider. Campos-Pons also
speaks of her work as establishing a bridge between the United States and
Cuba. This statement can be taken almost literally when considering that
the artist works very closely with her sisters and mother in Cuba in the
production of her works. Ultimately, Campos-Pons has clearly stated her
position as a Cuban artist living in the United States. In the last decade of
the twentieth century, she participated in the IV Bienal in Havana (1991)
with her installation *Tra . . .*, which engages issues of transit, transculturation, and the slave trade (Ribeaux Diago). In praising her installation,
Ribeaux Diago acknowledged that only since the 1990s has the subject
of Afro-Cuban culture gained concerted attention across the disciplines
and wider cultural spaces in Cuba.[18]

In the introduction to the catalog to an extensive show of Cuban art
organized by Arizona State University in 1998 *(Contemporary Art from
Cuba),* Cuban critic Antonio Eligio Fernández (Tonel) speaks of the exo-
dus of many artists given the economic conditions of the country during
what came to be called by Castro "The Special Period of War in Time
of Peace": "The conditions were nothing short of impossible, with the
cultural space as depressed as the economy of the country. Suffering from
cuts in subsidies and reluctant to accept innovations, a community of
emigrating colleagues (ranging from indifferent to hostile) were taking
the dynamic stimulus for previous years with them in their suitcases"
("Tree of Many Beaches," 42). María Magdalena Campos-Pons's case
exemplifies those who left the country in order to be able to practice
their art on their own terms. For a multimedia artist like Campos-Pons,
the lack of resources on the island would mean that she would have
become a very different artist. Belkis Ayón, for example, a younger Afro-
Cuban artist who stayed, concentrated on the production of large-scale
collographs (prints made from collages). Marilyn A. Zeitlin comments:
"Ayón, like many of her colleagues, began to work with found materials
as much by necessity as by choice" (129). Another great consideration for
Cuban artists resides in whether to produce works that will be exhibited

successfully in Europe "rather than experimenting with a new work" (131). A privileged few travel abroad on fellowships and return to the island. Had Campos-Pons chosen to stay, personal considerations aside, she would certainly be included among the few who would continue to travel abroad and, consequently, would have access to dollars to buy materials and produce her work. Because she chose to live in the United States with her husband and new family, while still identifying herself as a Cuban artist, Campos-Pons feels the strain of uprootedness: "My work is as much about what is left behind as it is about what I encounter in the place I arrive in. I hope that something good will come of the hardship" (quoted in Bell, 38).

So far, even though Campos-Pons's work found a space in the 1991 Cuban Biennial (an engagement that might have been made prior to her leaving), most of the critical response to her work has appeared in the United States and worldwide, as her bibliography illustrates. When speaking about Cuban American artists who show their work in Cuba, Antonio Eligio Fernández (Tonel), in "Tree of Many Beaches," mentions Ana Mendieta, Ernesto Pujol, and Eduardo Aparicio, yet there is no mention of Campos-Pons (48). Perhaps he respects her own classification as a Cuban rather than as a Cuban American artist. However, in a round-table discussion about twentieth-century Cuban art ("¿Cómo nos sentamos en el malecón?" published in the Cuban journal *Revolución y Cultural*), Rufo Caballero addresses the ambivalence that critics have regarding the 1980s: "We know that these years are very controversial, a display case of great manipulation for people who have attempted to deny them for markedly ideological reasons, and for people who have attempted to overestimate them out of no less ideological interests, but if we make an attempt to lessen the tendentiousness, they turn out to be years of extraordinary richness for Cuban art" ("¿Cómo nos sentamos," 34, 39; my translation).

Because Campos-Pons insists on including herself among the 1980s generation, she assumes all the "tendentiousness" associated with any current discussions on the island. This results in an erasure of her name when Cuban art, particularly Afro-Cuban art of that period, becomes a topic. By calling herself Cuban, she positions herself outside the circle of Cuban American artists, even though her works have been exhibited in the Miami area (Miami Dade Community College, Gallery North, 1994; the Center for the Fine Arts in Miami, 1996; and the Ambrosino Gallery, Coral Gables, 1997). By defining herself in an in-between space, she inserts herself at the center of sociocultural debate in Cuban arts.[19]

Campos-Pons participated in the 49th Venice Biennial (2001), entitled *Authentic/Ex-Centric: Conceptualism in Contemporary African Art,* as one of seven accomplished artists who, according to African art critic Salah M. Hassan, "execute their work using their own images" and are "motivated by the quest for self-representation, interrogation of their own existential circumstances, or the negotiation of their identity." He goes on to state: "Because these artists also live and practice between two or more cultures, their works often investigate the intersections of autobiography, self and the other" (26). In the catalog for the Biennial, Campos-Pons is identified as being from Cuba/U.S.A.

In spite of how those from within Cuba and the Cuban American art community position Campos-Pons's work, I would rather concentrate on the fact that before coming to the United States, the art she produced focused on playful representations of Cuban sexual sayings from a feminist point of view *(Sabor a Cuba)* [A Taste of Cuba] (see Mosquera, "¿Feminismo en Cuba?" [Feminism in Cuba]). The Cuban poet Nancy Morejón, in the catalog to the 1989 exhibition at Düsseldorf, *Kuba o.k.,* describes Campos-Pons's 1989 work *Opciones para el mito: Leda piensa* [Options for the Myth: Leda Thinks] in the following manner: "This woman's work is interesting not only because of its artistic proposals, but because it nurtures itself, naturally, in certain symbols of sexuality that are nothing but a response to the secular sexual oppression that fundamentally women in our Caribbean and Latin American societies have endured" (my translation). It was only after having come to the United States that the artist began in earnest to explore her identity as a woman of the African diaspora. According to curator Sally Berger, that exploration is in part the result of not having been able to return to Cuba since leaving in 1990 (Berger, "María Magdalena Campos-Pons" in *Authentic/Ex-Centric,* 141). In this complexly beautiful trilogy of installations, *History of People Who Were Not Heroes,* Campos-Pons has left us her distinctive voice-in-progress. Prior to having finished the installation, the artist spoke of her third installation, which at the time she called *Sugar:* "The third piece, *Sugar,* has objects made of sugar: sugar is the reason the town was built as a plantation . . . , sugar is what my ancestors worked in, sugar was the main product of La Vega, sugar is Cuba. This third piece has a lot to do with home, place and territory" (quoted in Bell, 35). If the historical considerations of sugar appear explicit in the video shown on only one of the three projections in *Meanwhile, the Girls Were Playing,* the personal considerations of sugar remain more hidden behind the transformation of sugar into snow as it falls on the artist's braided hair. Here again, the artist represents herself as positioned in-between, between home in Matanzas where Africa was in her backyard (Bell, 35), and Boston, where her husband and son reside, and where white snow-flakes displace sugar in all its connotations. As an artist, she also occupies a third space: "It is interesting for me to listen to the discourse that is going on today in America about Africanism or Negritude. I sometimes feel torn apart because for me Africa is not a continent—Africa is my backyard in Cuba. Of course as an adult, as an intellectual, as an artist I have been looking at what constitutes Africa. How is it shaped? How has it affected me? What was brought to here? That is why I did *The Seven Powers Come by the Sea*" in 1992 (Bell, 35). For Campos-Pons, the in-between condition of having come to the United States has had a momentous consequence given the fact that the three installations that make up *History of People Who Were Not Heroes* concentrate almost exclusively on the question of "what constitutes Africa" at a personal, historical, and cultural level. Speaking from that place that is and is not home has allowed the artist/intellectual to conceptualize, as an outsider/insider, her positionality in a discussion with transnational dimensions.[20] When she states that "I hope something good will come of the hard-ship" (Bell, 38), María Magdalena Campos-Pons joins African American writers Toni Morrison and Lucille Clifton in their artistic acts of "re-sistance and recreation as 'myth-play.'" In *Meanwhile, the Girls Were Playing*, this Afro-Cuban artist recovers the meaning of the word "play-ing" in "celebration of visibility, empowerment, and the return to voice" (Mance, 136). With the multiple installations that constitute *History of People Who Were Not Heroes*, Campos-Pons brings to an international forum the powerful cultural practices of the African diaspora within the frame of performance art. By simultaneously drawing upon two aesthetic traditions, she is capable of enriching both.

Conclusion

IN THE AFTERMATH of the 1959 Revolution, Afro-Cuban women have transformed the island's culture by positioning themselves and their history at the center of the nation's cultural memory. Excilia Saldaña forcefully declares:

> Mi nombre
> en el nombre de los que recién deciden su nombre y
> sus recuerdos

> My name
> in the name of those who've recently decided their name and
> their memories
> *(In the Vortex of the Cyclone,* 110, 111)

Nancy Morejón equates her body with the islands of the Caribbean: "Mi cuerpo como islas" ["My Body like Islands"] ("El tambor," *Looking Within,* 156, 157). In "Mujer negra" "Black Woman," Morejón places the black woman at the center of the island's history, from the time of the Atlantic passage to the struggles of the most recent revolutionary period. The women whose works I have analyzed in these pages have invalidated the image of mulatta Cecilia Valdés, with her voiceless, invisible countenance, and have offered in its place the image of the black woman capable of participating in revolutions. They have even pushed the boundaries of the Castro revolution with its censorship of discussions of gender and race. The voices of Saldaña and Morejón and the visual images of Belkis Ayón, Gloria Rolando, and María Magdalena Campos-Pons have built on a historical struggle on the part of the Cuban intelligentsia to incorporate into the concept of Cubanness the strong heritage of the African diaspora. Their cultural contributions have given subjectivity to the previously objectified black woman.

In *Guarding Cultural Memory,* I have marked three moments in the intellectual history of Cuba that engaged the possibility of integrating fully its African diaspora cultural contributions. The first, during the first half of the nineteenth century, centered on the work of the del Monte circle with its abolitionist tendencies; the second, during the first half of the twentieth century, revolved around the involvement of the Cuban intelligentsia with modernism and the Afro-Cubanism movement; and the third, during the last four decades of the twentieth century, effected a reevaluation of issues of race, gender, and class in a new revolutionary society that claimed to redefine Cubanness according to José Martí's ideals of "a nation for all."

This study has explored how Cuban artists have succeeded at integrating their European and African heritages, through their writing, film, and the arts. Central to their artistic engagement is the concept of memory. Their acts of remembrance have counteracted the persistent undermining in the official historical record regarding cultural contributions by the descendants of African slaves brought to Cuba. Edward Mullen reminds us that "in one survey of the contents of a hundred anthologies of Spanish and Spanish-American poets published between 1940 and 1980, citations to only two black poets, Plácido and Nicolás Guillén, appear" (*Afro-Cuban Literature,* 167). Catherine Davies states that "African Cuban poetry written by women was unheard of before the 1959 Revolution" (*Place in the Sun?* 170). In particular, I analyzed the works of Cirilo Villaverde, Sergio Giral, and Lydia Cabrera as a backdrop against which to showcase the works of Afro-Cuban women performing their concepts of self and national culture: Nancy Morejón, Gloria Rolando, Belkis Ayón, Excilia Saldaña, and María Magdalena Campos-Pons. Throughout my study, I engaged the question of how Cuba's creative and intellectual minds remembered their Afro-Cuban legacy.

Given that throughout most of its history, Afro-Cuban culture has been undermined by the Euro-Cuban political elites (Helg; Mullen, *Afro-Cuban Literature;* Altunaga; and Morejón, "Grounding the Race Dialogue"), I engaged the theories of Franz Fanon regarding the fragmentation of the African diaspora subject as it responds to the hypervisibility of skin pigmentation at the same time that his or her subjectivity is made invisible by the colonial system. The character of Cecilia Valdés in Villaverde's novel exemplifies this best. Colonial subjects must constantly negotiate not only being objectified by a system that equates pigmentation with class position but also their desire to question the very system that denies their subjectivity. Ultimately, Fanon tied subjectivity to questioning in the present. In this study, I extended Fanon's ideas to include Paul Gilroy's notion that the subject must engage in the act of remembrance. Thus, Fanon's act of questioning can be rooted in a past that is both acknowledged for its power to victimize African subjects in the Americas and valorized for their practices of endurance and survival. Sergio Giral's film *María Antonia* stands as an example of the valorization of these practices. Following Gilroy, I am most interested in how "black expressive cultures practice remembrance" (212). To that effect, I have relied on the works of several social scientists, including, first, Lydia Cabrera, who recorded the testimonies of her Afro-Cuban informants illustrating the modes of signification that have allowed their cultures to survive, and second, the analytical work of Julia Cuervo Hewitt and Eugenio Matibag, who have performed the interdisciplinary work of elucidating a hermeneutics of Afro-Cuban practices as they inform the Cuban literary imagination.

Lydia Cabrera's *El Monte* illustrates how the performance of personal and national identities often coincide. Julia Cuervo Hewitt declares that Afro-Cuban narrative tries to capture the secret nature of an interior world, invisible and latent, in the idiosyncrasies of its people (250). Eugenio Matibag shows how the Ifá divination system, through its complex interaction of mythical narratives and personal history, achieves the paradoxical act of divining a person's life while allowing for the free exercise of one's subjectivity. The language of Ifá mediates "between individual desire and social context" ("Ifá and Interpretation," 151) and creates a complex relationship between text and author (Cuervo Hewitt, 285). It is precisely this mediation between the creation of the self as it interacts with the specificity of Afro-Cuban culture that has interested me most as I analyzed the works of Cuban women. For Lydia Cabrera, a white woman of independent means who presented the testimonies of Afro-Cubans in their acts of signification, *El Monte* represents the location where the author expressed her own autobiographical difference through her Afro-Cuban ethnographic work (Molloy). Cabrera exposed the sexist and racist practices of the Cuban intelligentsia as she wove autobiographical and national identity as a gender and racial difference that had been silenced in constructions of Cubanness.

Cabrera's inscription of a memory of exclusion, then, served as my model of interpretation as I both presented and analyzed the complex works of Afro-Cuban women, who, firmly grounded in their personal identity as black women, have chosen to use the languages of signification of the African diaspora and of European postmodern art, film, and literature. Nancy Morejón and Excilia Saldaña, both poets, offered their works during the early years of the 1959 Revolution, when the role of the Cuban intellectual was being redefined. By appealing to Nicolás Guillén's concept of *mestizaje*, Morejón, through her essays, and Saldaña, through her early *patakines* in *Kele Kele*, made strides in the nascent literary landscape by inscribing blackness on the canvas of Cuba's Hispanic poetic and literary traditions. They appealed as well to the concept of poetic language as *imago*, created by José Lezama Lima. Their mature poetry plays with the tension between idea (Guillén's *mestizaje*) and visual image (Lezama Lima's *imago*), thus accomplishing a mediation between individual desire and social context. Morejón and Saldaña enjoyed the recognition of their peers as winners of multiple national literary prizes— Morejón, at first, in the genre of the essay and Saldaña in that of children's literature. They went on to develop very different poetic idioms engaging the self. Morejón offered her forceful rendition of black women's role in the history of the African diaspora and of Cuba. Her landscapes of the city of Havana subsequently offered the reader some of her most intimate portraits. Saldaña, on the other hand, re-created the autobiographical genre through poetry in a bold gesture against the more prescribed genre of the personal as representative of a community, the *testimonio*. The figure of the grandmother and of the *madrina* (godmother) surfaced in the poetry of both to gain mythical dimension. In this respect, both Morejón and Saldaña reached out to give voice to the small, silenced histories of African diaspora women who were victimized but endured to perpetuate their ethnic traditions.

Like Morejón and Saldaña, who came before them, Gloria Rolando, Belkis Ayón, and María Magdalena Campos-Pons in the 1980s and 1990s addressed the silences regarding the participation of black women in Cuban history, concentrating as well on the role of black women as keepers of memory. Like Cabrera in *El Monte*, Rolando pointed to the diversity of ethnic cultures inherent in Afro-Cubanness, with origins dating back to before and after the Atlantic crossing. In all her documentaries, the filmmaker has engaged in visual terms, as in *Ifá*, the concepts of history and myth as they intersect with the lives of individual women. Given the commonality of the experience and survival of slavery, Rolando has placed the history of Afro-Cubans within a larger context of the Caribbean and of the African diaspora. Her entire oeuvre honors African deities by remembering and celebrating cultural practices through music, dance, and dress that make the past coincide with the present. Her images are meant to counter racism through the revelation of facts and the act of questioning. She presents cinematography as revisionist history.

The now internationally known artists Belkis Ayón and María Magdalena Campos-Pons have emphasized the act of mediation between the personal, the mythical, and the historical by inscribing on their own bodies Afro-Cuban memory. Ayón's large-scale collographs appropriate the symbology of the Abakuá, the most maligned of Afro-Cuban ethnic groups, with the intent of revalorizing their culture as well as giving power to the voiceless, victimized, female, Sikán. Through her mastery of symbolic transformations Ayón has given voice to that which had been silenced by European and African patriarchy. In Ayón's collographs, black women's subjectivity is expressed through dramatic bodily gestures. Her black, white, and gray prints endow the subject of the black female with a dramatic, forceful presence never before expressed in Cuban art.

While Ayón dramatized inherent racism and sexism in Cuban society, the multimedia artist María Magdalena Campos-Pons undertook no less than the *History of People Who Were Not Heroes*. Since she grounded *History of People* on the act of possession, through which the history of the African diaspora resides in the mythification of her own body, Campos-Pons has foregrounded memory as performance. In her three major installations, Campos-Pons articulated the concept of Africa for herself as a Caribbean woman living in the United States. Through the coincidence of the mythical with the representation of her own body, Campos-Pons, like Ayón, negotiated a self-representation that does not call attention to itself. Rather, she conceptualized identity as a fabrication in progress, as the artist represented the history of her own life and that of her family from the time she lived in the former slaves barracks in Matanzas to her present as an internationally known Cuban artist living in the United States. Her displacements, as inscribed in her multiple installations, have repeated the concentric movements of the African diaspora.

Acknowledging the initial trauma of the Atlantic passage, the artists whose works I have analyzed remember the violence perpetrated upon an entire people through the attempted erasure of their cultures and their subjectivity. Each of them, through the representation of their own lives as echoes of the lives of those who came before, have transcended their colonial status and created works like *History of People Who Were Not Heroes*, forcefully memorializing their African diaspora experience. Their achievements trace an indebtedness to Nicolás Guillén's concept of *mestizaje* and to Wifredo Lam's reinvention of "the African sense" (Mosquera, "Elegguá," 230). Most significantly, as women intellectuals, they have raised questions regarding issues of gender and race in Cuba that, if not already, will ultimately change the cultural landscape they inhabit.

Notes

Introduction

1. Ironically, at the end of the essay Alonso lists the works of twentieth-century writers and thinkers, such as Alejo Carpentier, Fernando Ortiz, Lydia Cabrera, Miguel Barnet, Reinaldo Arenas, and César Leante, who represent Afro-Cuban cultures in their works, but he fails to mention even one Afro-Cuban intellectual or writer who engages the issue of "the central role played by blacks in a comprehensive history of Cuban cultural production" (82). By failing even to mention such an outstanding figure as that of national poet Nicolás Guillén, a contemporary of Carpentier, Ortiz, and Cabrera, is Alonso not inadvertently participating in the erasure of contributions by Cuban blacks in the "comprehensive history of Cuban cultural production"? For an excellent article on how, historically, Cuban intellectuals have erased the Afro-Cuban difference in their intellectual and literary pursuits, see Williams, "Emergence of an Afro-Cuban Aesthetic."

2. Dilla Alfonso defines how the revolution has negotiated crises and political expediency in his essay "Cuba: The Changing Scenarios of Governability." Throughout the essay he engages "the contradictory relation between the exigencies of governability and the aspirations for a greater democratic opening" (60). Linda S. Howe's book *Transgression and Conformity* presents the most comprehensive analysis of such contradictions in Cuba's postrevolutionary cultural arena to date.

1. Constructions of the Cuban Mulatta

1. See Sollors, *Neither Black nor White Yet Both*, 224, and Kutzinski, *Sugar's Secrets*.

2. In Julien's documentary *Frantz Fanon: Black Skin, White Masks*, Vergès chastises Fanon for having misinterpreted Mayotte Capécia's memoir *Je suis martiniquaise* (1948). Novelist Maryse Condé also affirmed in the film that she found it difficult to identify with Fanon's theory of a split Martiniquean identity at a time in the 1950s when artists and intellectuals from the French protectorates

were at the height of their production in Paris. Fanon constructs his argument for the chapter "Woman of Color and the White Man" based on a memoir that depicts a woman of color's self-hatred and desire to be only with white men. For a critique of Julien's film and Vergès's objections, see Gordon, *Her Majesty's Other Children:* "Fanon never claimed that black women should not be romantically involved with white men. He argued that it was pathological to be romantically involved with whites on the sole basis of their being white, a position many of us share today. Capécia had declared that 'I should have liked to marry, but to a white man'" (251). Sharpley-Whiting agrees with Gordon in her analysis of Fanon's reading of Capécia and concludes: "Attempts to shame Fanon out of the category of a liberation theorist whose ideas are relevant to the lives of black women are, at best, disingenuous. Fanon's honesty in *Black Skin, White Masks* may be brutal, but it is not brutalizing" (161). More recently, Arnold has contested, with convincing textual proof, the authorship of the memoir. In an article published by *Revue de littérature comparée,* Arnold asserts that "*Je suis Martiniquaise* is a French novel, conceived by Frenchmen who have pillaged the memoirs of another Frenchman, and destined for the largest possible French audience" ("'Mayotte Capécia'"; my translation).

3. McGarrity and Cárdenas read Cuban history from an Afro-Cuban perspective.

4. Bhabha describes colonial discourse in *The Location of Culture,* 80.

5. In his comparative study of *Cecilia Valdés* and *Narrative of a Five Years Expedition Against the Revolted Negroes of Surinam* (John Gabriel Stedman, 1796), Phaf points to Villaverde's creation of a symbolic female character whose aspirations to marry a white man cannot be fulfilled owing to the country's fear of black insurrections in a prerevolutionary Cuba: "Anyway, the constant variable of a mulatto nation, whether it be named Joanna or Cecilia, in Surinam or Cuba, during the prenational times of a plantation economy, should fail given the fear of insurrections that threaten the productivity of a plantation system based on slave labor" (210; my translation).

6. See Christian in "The Rise and Fall of the Proper Mulatta" (in *Black Women Novelists*) for an analysis of the character of the mulatta in novels during the Harlem Renaissance.

7. All quotations from *Cecilia Valdés* are from the Porrúa edition. Translations are from the edition translated by Lorente. I translate some passages due to some discrepancies in the Lorente translation. Page numbers for Porrúa and Lorente will appear whenever I use the Lorente translation.

8. This fact becomes elucidated in fictional terms in the novel *Sab* (1841) by Gertrudis Gómez de Avellaneda when both Teresa, the cousin with no inheritance, and Sab, the mulatto slave, make it explicit that Enrique's interest in Carlota revolves around her inheritance. Because Gómez de Avellaneda is living in Spain when she writes the novel, and because she conflates the fate of the slave Sab, who loves a white woman, Carlota, with that of most women incapable of deter-

mining their futures, her novel stands as a much more radical analysis of Cuban society than *Cecilia Valdés*. Scott, in her introduction to her translation of *Sab* into English, addresses the radical nature of Gómez de Avellaneda's novel because it entertains crossing racial and social lines: "Nancy Morejón rightly urges the modern reader not to underestimate the radical nature of *Sab*'s plot: Avellaneda raised a slave, considered by most of her fellow Cubans to be not a person but a *thing*, to the status of protagonist; furthermore, the very idea that he could love a white woman was considered nothing short of heresy" (xxii).

9. See Barreda Tomás, who concludes that "space is the location and the physical expression of the internal war that divides society" (145; my translation).

10. In his article "El discurso jerárquico en *Cecilia Valdés*" [Hierarchical Discourse in *Cecilia Valdéz*], Gelpí points to the close relationship between the representation of space, the language uttered by the characters in those spaces, and the studied racist anatomy of the mulatto and black characters in relation to their utterances. In particular, he refers to the fear of open spaces because of the likelihood of encounters such as that between Isabel and Cecilia: "In *Cecilia Valdés* the streets of Havana figure as a fundamentally dangerous space: as a meeting place, of clashes and commotions, physical as well as verbal. They are also a space associated with uncontrollable passions" (49; my translation).

11. Gelpí points to Villaverde's propensity to inscribe his political beliefs on the body of his literary characters, a practice not uncommon in nineteenth-century narratives: "Physiognomies represent much more than the description of a face: they may also be seen as a way of inscribing the politics of power relations on the 'body' of literary characters" (55; my translation).

12. When she analyzes court cases involving the use of trains and steamships by upper-class African American women in the nineteenth century under Jim Crow laws, Higginbotham finds that race supersedes class when the Supreme Court rules that African American women of economic means may not ride the cars reserved for white "ladies." The prominent Afro-American critic concludes that under those laws, ladies' public spaces acquire the same value as private domestic spaces where African American servants are allowed but are invisible, but upper-class African Americans may not enter ("Racial Constructions of Citizenship").

13. In her study of what she terms the "metalanguage of race," Higginbotham contextualizes the conflation of class and race in historical terms: "Race came to life primarily as the signifier of the master/slave relation and thus emerged superimposed upon class and property relations" ("African-American Women's History," 6).

14. I owe this insight to my graduate assistant Katrina Olds at Harvard University.

15. In his "Excursus on the 'Tragic Mulatto,'" (220–45), Sollors describes the six elements of the "tragic mulatto" complex as defined by Sterling Brown. Brown's gender division in describing the mulatto stereotype seems to fit Villaverde's

characters well: "Brown notes a significant gender division in the type: the male 'mixed blood characters, merely because they were nearer white, were more intelligent and militant, and therefore more tragic in their enslavement' than their 'pure' black counterparts, whereas the women were, like Camille in John T. Trowbridge's *Neighbor Jackwood* (1856), 'jest dark enough to be ra'al purty,' exceptionally beautiful but often doomed" (*Neither Black nor White*, 224).

16. Sommer, in her brief analysis of the novel, emphasizes the tragic outcome of the events based on the secrecy that "obscures the slipperiness of racial categories" (*Foundational Fictions*, 129).

17. For an analysis of the syncretic nature of the figure of the Virgen de la Caridad del Cobre, see Benítez Rojo in his introduction to *The Repeating Island* and Portuondo Zúñiga in her study of the virgin as a symbol of Cubanness.

18. In her article "From Dusky Venus to Mater Dolorosa," Williams points to the mythical nature of Villaverde's plot and emphasizes that "Cecilia's ignorance of her own origin causes the Oedipus theme. . . . In a manner reminiscent of Sophocles' hero, Villaverde's protagonist fails to recognize a relative, and therefore she violates sacred familial bonds by engaging in sexual relations with a blood relative and bringing about his violent death" (131).

19. For an analysis of women and slavery in the Caribbean, see Reddock. She contends that throughout the Caribbean women worked in the fields just as men, and that often, because of their longer life expectancy, they were considered to be more profitable than men as slaves. For that reason, slave owners discouraged pregnancy in women, who, although they often worked through their ninth month of pregnancy, were then incapacitated for labor during the time of lactation. Their offspring were placed in nurseries and cared for by older women. In Cuba, during the mid-nineteenth century, with mechanization in sugar production, "Women were more and more relegated to the manual and agricultural tasks whereas some men moved into the more highly skilled operations" (136). It was also recorded that slave women either became sterile because of harsh work and living conditions or induced sterility and practiced infanticide so as not to bring children into slavery. Furthermore, for slave owners, the purchase of slaves was cheaper than bringing up children in the plantation economy. Reddock states: "Thus the practices of the ruling class during the sugar era, determined by its production needs and international market opportunities, led to the emergence of a dominant ideology in which both masters and slaves found the costs of bearing and rearing children greater than the benefits. This ideology led to a practice by slave women that served the interests of the ruling class even though it was derived from different considerations" (131).

20. See Luis in "*Cecilia Valdés*: El nacimiento de una novela antiesclavista" (*Cecilia Valdéz*: the birth of an antislavery novel) and Fusco in "Jineteras en Cuba" [Hustlers in Cuba].

21. See Williams in "The Representation of the Female Slave in Villaverde's *Cecilia Valdés*" and Méndez Rodenas in "Identity and Incest in *Cecilia Valdés*" for

a thorough analysis of María de Regla as bridging the gap between her maternal and erotic selves. Sommer, in "Cecilia no sabe, o los bloqueos que blanquean," and Méndez Rodenas, in "Identity and Incest in *Cecilia Valdéz,*" point to María de Regla as the source of information regarding incest in the novel precisely because she is a slave.

22. See Reddock, who maintains that "The nuclear family was actively discouraged by planters in all the Caribbean colonies" (131) and that "Regular sexual activity began very early in life, especially for girls, and both men and women maintained multiple associations" (132). Toward the end of the nineteenth century, the colonial governments sought to introduce laws aimed at humanizing slavery. But planters rejected these measures because "Although they recognized the necessity to increase the 'natural' reproduction of the local slave population, they resented any attempt to reduce their control over the life and labor of the slaves and their immediate profit" (133).

23. During the second half of the nineteenth century and the first half of the twentieth century, the landed elite subscribed to the racist discourse of works such as Gustavo Mustelier's 1912 *La extinción del negro* [The Extinction of the Negro], which sought to eliminate the Afro-Cuban existence as a race through *blanqueamiento*. See Morrison.

24. The character of Teresa in Gómez de Avellaneda's *Sab* shares many of the values of Isabel in Villaverde's work, and she also retires to a convent at the end of the novel. Gómez de Avellaneda's female characters, however, voice an antiracist agenda not present in Villaverde's work. In *Sab*, for example, Teresa, a white woman, falls in love with Sab, a slave. For a comprehensive analysis of *Sab*, see Netchinsky.

25. According to Higginbotham, "Race not only tends to subsume other sets of social relations, namely, gender and class, but it blurs and disguises, suppresses and negates its own complex interplay with the very social relations it envelops. It precludes unity within the same gender group but often appears to solidify people of opposing economic classes. Whether race is textually omitted or textually privileged, its totalizing effect in obscuring class and gender remains" ("African-American Women's History," 5).

26. Giral's film is based on the drama by Eugenio Hernández Espinosa, *María Antonia*, 1967. For an excellent analysis of the play, see Matibag, *Afro-Cuban Religious Experience*, 256–59, and Howe, *Transgression and Conformity*, 90–91.

27. See *Temas: Cultura, Ideología, Sociedad* [Themes: Culture, Ideology, Society], which includes eight articles focusing on ethnic and racial sociological studies about Cuban contemporary society. Of special interest is the article written by María del Carmen Caño Secade, 58–65. See also *La Gaceta de Cuba* 1 (enero–febrero 2005) for essays on race during Castro's revolutionary regime. The most direct statement regarding institutionalized silence on racism after the revolution is by Alejandro de la Fuente, 62–64. See also essays by Lázara Menéndez (18–21) and Gisela Arandia (59).

28. See Mulvey and her analysis of scopophilia in the conception of the language of cinema in "Visual Pleasure and Narrative Cinema."

29. Like his characters, Giral may have found that Cuba during the 1990s became too limited a society for his filmic enterprises. He left Cuba in the mid-1990s and now resides in Miami.

30. In this respect Giral's film fits neatly into a genre of Cuban films, such as *Portrait of Teresa* by Pastor Vega in 1979, which deal with women's concerns as articulated by male directors. See Benamou, 51–56.

31. With Julián's characterization, Giral alludes to an entire corpus of film genre that follows the fate of the ghetto or immigrant young man. He aspires to escape his class and race determination by succeeding either in the performing arts or sports. See Perry Henzel's *The Harder They Come*, Rouben Mamoulian's *The Golden Boy*, or Alan Crosland's *The Jazz Singer*. Gubar performs a masterful analysis of the last in her book *Racechanges*, 66–75. While in the Hollywood version of the genre piece tension arises between a promising future and the betrayal of a cultural heritage, in the Jamaican and Cuban films the theme of enslavement predominates as the subject reaches out to better himself in a capitalist world.

32. Piedra defines the Abakuá thus: "The Abakwa developed in the New World a strong tactic of defensive signification. The core of such a tactic was the assimilation of as many aspects as possible of the black and white codes surrounding it, to the point that the establishment considered the Abakwas as an esoteric appendage of Cuban culture. The composite cultural body emerges as hermetic code with a subtle hold over the hermeneutic values of Cuban signs" ("From Monkey Tales," 137). See Chanan, 286–92, and Benamou, 57–61 on *De cierta manera*.

33. For essays that reflect this debate, see the journals *Temas: Cultura, Ideología, Sociedad*, published in Havana, and *Encuentro de la cultura cubana* (Encounters of Cuban Culture), published in Madrid. Soon after the release of *María Antonia*, Giral left Cuba and arrived in the United States. One wonders whether the director's emigration was not already predetermined by the making of the film, and whether Julian's and María Antonia's frustrations were not also Sergio Giral's.

34. A movie review in the *Miami Herald* reporting on the Miami Film Festival in 1993 classifies the film as all sex and no politics. See Cosford.

35. Taylor has published an excellent study of paternalistic images of Argentine women in theatrical and national cultural representations. See *Disappearing Acts*. Her analyses of Argentine literature and theater have been influential in my work here. See also Rodríguez in *House/Garden/Nation*.

2. El Monte

1. A first version of *El Monte* was published as "Eggüe o Vichichi Nfinda" in 1947 in the *Revista Bimestre Cubana* [Bimonthly Cuban Journal] 60.2: 47–120. When I later quote from this first version, I will do so from its subsequent

publication as found in Cabrera, *Páginas sueltas* [Loose Pages]. Editions of *El Monte* were published in 1954 (Cuba) and in 1968, 1971, 1983, 1986, and 1992 (Miami). I quote from the 1992 edition. All translations of Cabrera are mine.

2. In his book *Afro-Cuban Religious Experience,* Matibag deals with the generic classification of *El Monte:* "Cabrera's classic *El Monte* presents us with related special problems of generic classification. Reading it, we pause to ask: what is it?" (35). The work of Cuervo Hewitt also explores the same question: "Her book *El Monte* became since then the Bible of Afro-Cubanisms for many blacks. 'Ortiz did not know what I was doing,' Cabrera told me, 'and when I gave him a copy of the book tears flowed from his eyes'" (7; my translation).

3. Most of the biographical information in this essay has been synthesized from the introduction to Cabrera's *Páginas sueltas,* edited by Isabel Castellanos, and from Hiriart's *Lydia Cabrera: Vida hecha arte* [Lydia Cabrera: Life Made Art].

4. For an analysis of Lam's legacy, see Herzberg, "Rereading Lam."

5. On Lam, see Mosquera, "Elegguá at the Post-Modern Crossroads"; on Guillén, see Morejón, *Nación y mestizaje en Nicolás Guillén* and "Prólogo" to *Recopilación de textos sobre Nicolás Guillén,* and Kutzinski, *Against the American Grain* and "Poetry and Politics"; on Ortiz, Coronil and Santí, and Carpentier, see González Echevarría, *Alejo Carpentier,* and Piedra, "Afro-Cuban Esthetics."

6. In *Afro-Cuban Religious Experience,* Matibag states: "Lydia Cabrera anticipates Miguel Barnet and carries on the work of Ortiz before her in collecting and transcribing the testimonies of many participants in a set of related events" (35).

7. Cabrera's relationship to Carpentier must be seen in the context of Carpentier's participation in the Grupo Minorista during the 1930s, which turned to Afro-Cuban religion "as social structure, doctrine, slave ideology, mythic archive, transcendence" to redefine Cuban national culture "by reopening the question of identity with a notion of difference" (Matibag, *Afro-Cuban Religious Experience,* 94).

8. It is quite telling that when the Cuban novelist Guillermo Cabrera Infante, in *Tres tristes tigres* [Three Trapped Tigers], parodies various writers and their literary styles, he chooses to include Cabrera alongside Carpentier, Novás Calvo, and others (see Matibag in *Afro-Cuban Religious Experience,* 166). Matibag states: "Cabrera's language is displayed as a tour de force of multilingual musicality, an amalgam of magic and rationalism, of syntactic rhythms and lexical color. Cabrera Infante's parody is also a tribute to Cabrera" (167).

9. Afro-Cubans have historically developed strategies against repression. See Piedra, "From Monkey Tales."

10. For an analysis of the Abakuá dances during the Feast of the Three Kings, see Méndez Rodenas, *Cuba en su imagen.* For a more comprehensive study of Cuban religious national holidays see González Echevarría's "Fiestas cubanas" [Cuban Holidays].

11. In his dissertation, Piedra studies Carpentier's "utilization of ritual as literary performance, highlighting the cooperation between literature and choreographic interpretation" as one of the several strategies that reveal the Cuban writer's interest in "multi-ethnic esthetics central to modernity" (8). Méndez Rodenas also points to the works of Ortiz and Benítez Rojo, which underline the performative nature of Afro-Cuban dance and theater; see *Cuba en su imagen*.

12. See Cuervo Hewitt, *Aché, presencia africana*, and Matibag, *Afro-Cuban Religious Experience*. See also Lindsay, *Santería Aesthetics*.

3. Cuban National Identity in Morejón, Rolando, and Ayón

1. Mullen wrote the introduction to the 1996 issue of the *Afro-Hispanic Review* dedicated to Morejón.

2. For a clarification of the role of the Cuban intellectual in the public sphere, see Navarro.

3. See DeCosta-Willis, *Singular Like a Bird*; and the Spring 1996 issue of *Afro-Hispanic Review*.

4. For "Palabras por el Premio Nacional de Literatura," February 12, 2002, turn to http://www.afrocubaweb.com/nancymorejon.htm. All translations of Nancy Morejón are mine unless otherwise noted.

5. See the bibliography for these essays.

6. Luis ("Race, Poetry and Revolution") and Howe ("Nancy Morejón's *Womanism*") describe these intellectual periods.

7. For analyses of these poems see essays by McKenzie, Williams, Hampton, Gutiérrez, Martin-Ogunsola, DeCosta-Willis, and RoseGreen-Williams in DeCosta-Willis, *Singular Like a Bird*. RoseGreen-Williams cautions that in "Mujer Negra," "the title of the poem may even be seen as ironic, since the racial specificity which it anticipates is undercut by the raceless nationalism which the poem espouses" (197). James reads "Obrera del tabaco" [Woman in a Tobacco Factory] and sees it as a failure on Morejón's part to construct a liberated female subject: "I prefer to read the poem, however, as an example of the truncation of female experience in an attempt to uphold socialist values and maintain a harmonious national rhetoric" (53). James reads the poem against the background of policies in socialist Cuba that discourage the production of autobiography as a revolutionary genre. As we all know, the *testimonio* was the favored genre starting in the 1960s.

8. In other essays found in *Fundación de la imagen* [Foundation of the Image], Morejón speaks of the same commitment to popular language and service to the people on the part of other writers such as Langston Hughes (267–70), Edward Brathwaite (234–44), Jacques Stephen Alexis (222–33), and Jacques Roumain (203–21). Excerpts from the essay on Hughes were translated and published in the *Langston Hughes Review*.

9. In his book on race and inequality in twentieth-century Cuba, *A Nation*

for All, de la Fuente states that Guillén desires to transform society, and not the level of education of blacks, in order to solve "the black problem" (34).

10. For another way of considering terminology that refers to the African diasporic experience, see Smart, *Amazing Connections* (169–72).

11. I owe this observation and the suggestion to consult *La visualidad infinita* to an avid reader of Lezama Lima, Raysa Mederos.

12. Note that in one of her early essays published in *Fundación de la imagen,* Morejón writes in defense of Lezama Lima's hermetic style (135–49). For a presentation of the Cuban avant-garde painters, see Martínez.

13. For the best analysis of the film, see Chanan in his book on Cuban cinema. See also Davies ("Modernity, Masculinity") and López.

14. See also de la Fuente's book, *A Nation for All,* which qualifies Helg's book as falling within a thesis of Cuban history that he designates as "the dominance of racism." The alternative thesis, proposed by Castellanos and Castellanos, becomes classified as "the possibility of integration" (6). Here I focus on Helg's account mostly because it was one of the main sources in the production of Rolando's film.

15. All translations of Gloria Rolando's works are mine.

16. For a discussion of black hair in U.S. society and its connotations for African American women, see Rooks.

17. All translations of Belkis Ayón are mine.

18. All translations of Cabrera are mine.

19. See also the development of Cuban rap, which addresses issues of gender and race. For an example of rap lyrics, see Rodríguez Mola and López Cabrera for a response to black female stereotypes, particularly in publications for tourists: "My intention is not to come out like / a pretty black girl on posters" (207; my translation).

4. The Autobiographical Poetry of Excilia Saldaña

1. All translations from *In the Vortex of the Cyclone* are a collaboration between myself and Rosamond Rosenmeier. The three paragraphs that follow were first published as my introduction to *In the Vortex,* 4–5. Translations of "Vieja trova sobre soporte CD ROM" are mine.

2. See Reddock, who states: "The nuclear family was actively discouraged by planters in all the Caribbean colonies. Where such families did develop, they could be easily destroyed through sale of members to creditors and/or to other plantations. In Jamaica, children were taken from their mothers after weaning and placed with a driveress first in the grass gang and then in other gangs as they grew older. Similarly, in Cuba slave mothers returned to work about six weeks after childbirth, at which time the child was turned over to the plantation nursery" (131).

3. In *Cecilia Valdés,* María de Regla insinuates that Cecilia, the bastard mulatta, and Adela are half sisters, both Gamboa's daughters. The secret that

needs to be divulged, by extension, is that Leonardo and Cecilia are half siblings. María de Regla, who speaks Spanish well and is gifted in spinning a tale, becomes a spokesperson for other slaves who do not have entry into the white family's quarters. In her article "The Representation of the Female Slave in Villaverde's *Cecilia Valdés*," Williams states: "María de Regla is evidently positioned to speak on behalf of the silent slaves on the surrounding plantations that are reportedly similar to *La Tinaja*" (82).

4. For the form of signification that resists disclosure in Afro-Cuban culture, see Piedra, "From Monkey Tales."

5. For an analysis of how poets engage autobiography as a "sexual/textual site," see Schenck, who states: "Poetry as autobiography constitutes a potential space in which a subject may be repeatedly and repeat*ably* present to herself during the act of utterance" (292), a statement that I find quite apt in relationship to Saldaña's poetic subjectivity.

6. For a discussion of how "Afro-Cuban tradition" intersects with "Western tradition," see Palmié, *Wizards and Scientists,* 1–38.

7. Gilmore's statement on the subject: "Self-representational speech about trauma seems to require the subject to work herself into the symbolic" (67). In "Monólogo de la esposa" the subject becomes the wife; in *Mi nombre,* an "I" is stated in third person and later encapsuled in the name.

8. All quotations from Saldaña's "Vieja trova" come from *La Isla Infinita* [The Infinite Island]. Translations are mine.

9. The opening image of the swan also refers to the poetry of Rubén Darío, "Por un momento" [For Just a Moment]; in particular, it utilizes the swan Jupiter as a metaphor for the speaking subject in his moment of seduction of Leda during the poet's mature years. In Darío's poem, the image of the swan refers only to masculine desire: "For just a moment, O Swan, I will link my longings / to those of your two wings, which embraced Leda" *(Selected Poems of Rubén Darío,* 176, 177).

10. This progression toward emotional release on the part of the Afro-Cuban woman finds paradigmatic expression in Nancy Morejón's poem "Amo a mi amo" [I Love My Master] found in *Where the Island Sleeps Like a Wing,* 74–77.

11. For a masterly analysis of the poem's intertextuality with Shakespeare's *Macbeth* and Aeschylus's *Oresteia,* see Catherine Davies, "Hybrid Texts." In this essay, Davies establishes the literary relationships between the wife and Lady Macbeth and Clytemnestra: "The poem is subversive in that it inscribes publicly two social taboos: incest and parricide" (210).

12. In her study of this poem, Davies concludes that "Monólogo de la esposa" is about both incest and parricide. See my note 11.

13. In conversations with the author in Cambridge, Mass., in May 1998, Saldaña stated that after being raped by her father she ran to her grandmother, who expelled the father from the home. From then on, only Saldaña's grandfather communicated with his son, and only outside the family house. The grandmother

refused to leave the house herself and, as is recorded in the poem, prefers to turn it into a haven where the poet may find refuge (*In the Vortex of the Cyclone,* 104–5).

14. The Cuban critic Virgilio López Remus has stated that "Excilia Saldaña is a living classic of literature written for children and young adults" (*In the Vortex of the Cyclone,* 3). Although this essay does not concentrate on Saldaña's poetry for children, it is my belief that in her writing for children, Saldaña healed the child in herself. This may be best analyzed in her most famous of books in Cuba, *La noche.* Both *La noche* [Night] and *Cantos para un Mayito y una paloma* [Songs for Mayito and a Dove] have both been adopted by the Cuban school system as reading material at the elementary and secondary levels.

15. See James, "Women, Life Writing and National Identity," and Davies, "Cross-Cultural Homebodies in Cuba," 197–98.

16. All quotations from "Vieja trova" [Old Ballad] come from *La Isla Infinita.* Translations are mine.

17. My article "Borges y 'El Aleph'" appears in *Revista de la Universidad de México.*

18. For my analysis of "Las tres suspirantes" [The Three Sighing Girls], see "El afán de nombrarse en la obra poética de Excilia Saldaña" [The Insistence of Naming Herself in the Poetic Works of Excilia Saldaña].

19. These images constitute an ironic rendering of Georgia O'Keeffe's representations of female genitalia as flowers. They also reflect the reality of phallus-shaped tropical flowers.

20. See James in his analysis of the role of Afro-Cuban music in *Mi nombre.*

5. Possession and Altar-Making

I wish to express my appreciation to Ms. Campos-Pons for her generosity in inviting me to the opening of *Spoken Softly with Mama* at the MoMA in March of 1998. I also thank the Academic Affairs Office and the Graduate Studies Office at Emerson College, which sponsored a visit of the artist so that she could show slides of her work. The editorial comments of my colleague Maria Koundoura have been invaluable in the preparation of this chapter.

1. Campos-Pons's first two works are posted on the Internet at http://ca80 .lehman.cuny.edu/gallery/web/AG/campospons/Portrait.html (accessed May 31, 2005) for *A Town Portrait,* and http://www.universes-in-universe.de/car/venezia/ bien49/auth-exc/e-campos.htm for *Spoken Softly with Mama.* Essays on these two installations were written by curators Julia P. Herzberg and Sally Berger. For an essay on several works by Campos-Pons, including *Spoken Softly with Mama,* see González, "Possession and Altar-Making." Excellent photographs of *Meanwhile, the Girls Were Playing* have been published by the MIT Visual Arts Center. For color illustrations of several of Campos-Pons's works see Sally Berger, "María Magdalena Campos-Pons."

2. The critical anthology *Santería Aesthetics,* edited by Lindsay, stresses the

centrality of Santería aesthetics in the current postmodern/postcolonial artistic and critical dialogue. Mosquera's essay "Elegguá at the Post-Modern Crossroads" is of particular interest to the area of Cuban Studies.

3. This self-reflexive act inherent in the film's narrative derives directly from the Afro-Cuban practice of Ifá divination defined thus: "In Ifá, one performs a discursive, intertextual act in which myth and personal history are meant to interact through the medium of language" (Matibag, "Ifá and Interpretation," 151). For an analysis of Giral's film, see González, "De lo invisible a lo espectacular."

4. For a review of these works, see Mosquera in "¿Feminismo en Cuba?" [Feminism in Cuba?].

5. Gates defines Esu-Elegbara thus: "Each version of Esu is the sole messenger of the gods in Yoruba *iranse,* he who interprets the will of the gods to man; he who carries the desires of man to the gods. Esu is the guardian of the crossroads, master of style and of stylus, the phallic god of generation and fecundity, master of that elusive, mystical barrier that separates the divine world from the profane. Frequently characterized as an inveterate copulator possessed by his enormous penis, linguistically Esu is the ultimate copula, connecting truth with understanding, the sacred with the profane, text with interpretation, the word as a form of the verb *to be* that links subject with its predicate. He connects the grammar of divination with its rhetorical structures" (*Signifying Monkey,* 6).

6. In his *Afro-Cuban Religious Experience,* Matibag speaks of the initiation rites for the Regla de Palo, the Cuban religious practices originating in the West African Bantu nations, which include "*rayamiento en palo,* the 'marking' central to the regla's rite of passage" (169).

7. Barnet describes a possessed person: "A possessed is a person who receives a god; the god mounts his 'horse'—that is, the person's body—and forces him into contortions and gestures that characterize the deity. . . . Previous awareness is critical for any type of possession to occur. Those who are entitled to be possessed by a santo and who succeed in faithfully interpreting the santo's gestures and character immediately attain a higher level of power within the social milieu where these cults [sic] are practiced. Possession thus plays as much a social and representational as a religious function because it entails the will to represent an archetype. This archetype is profoundly bound to the identity of the person who deliberately chooses to assume the traits and attributes of the deity. I believe, also, that in many cases possession attests to the determination to be something different, to assume an identity that links the possessed to the native culture" ("La regla de ocha," 86).

8. Brown describes the basic form of Santería thrones: "Thrones employ a basic dominant form: an installation of colorful cloth creating a canopy overhead, a curtain backdrop behind, and symmetrically parted and tied back curtains in front. The enclosure, hung, draped, and stapled in plain swatches, is constructed of relatively more or less expensive cloth, depending on the means of the house" (105–6).

9. Strangely, Campos-Pons's use of only the Spanish masculine gender of the nouns seemingly dedicates an installation inspired primarily by women only to men.

10. This use of layering of fabric to produce connotations at an abstract or mythical level is rooted in Santería practices of decorating altars to venerate deities. The elegant lining of rich fabrics using the appropriate textures and color combinations has the effect of conjuring up specific qualities attributed to the deity for whom the altar is being built (See Brown, "Toward an Ethnoasthetics").

11. For an important film by the Afro-Cuban filmmaker Sara Gómez, with the topic of transforming Afro-Cuban practitioners by asking them to reject their community practices in favor of revolutionary values, see *De cierta manera*.

12. Fernández (Tonel), in "70, 80, 90," places the beginning of the 1980s generation with the foundation of the Ministry of Culture and the creation of the Instituto Superior de Arte (ISA) in 1976. More formally, the generation of artists came into being with the exposition *Volumen I* at the Centro de Arte Internacional in 1981. The decade ends with the closing of project *Castillo de la Fuerza,* where new artists showed their works on a yearly basis. Campos-Pons had several entries in that last show. See *Cuba Siglo 20,* 417–18. According to Camnitzer, the cultural opening in the 1980s was due in part to the influence of Minister of Culture Armando Hart, who, in a speech before the UNEAC in 1977, stated: "When government officials with responsibilities in the cultural area misunderstand their mission and feel justified in interfering with the artists' creative work, they lose prestige and influence and become unable to fulfill their duties" (Camnitzer, 128). In "¿Cómo nos sentamos en el Malecón?" [How Do We Sit on the Malecon?] (the Malecon is the Havana sea wall), Espinosa describes three fundamental forms of expression for this generation: "That coincidence defines three fundamental lines, one line of social criticism, another line of the kitsch/vernacular, and another of the religious/anthropological" (my translation). At different times in her career so far, Campos-Pons has explored all three.

13. For other essays on African conceptualism, see Hassan, "'<Insertions>,'" 26–49; and Hassan and Oguibe, *Authentic/Ex-Centric,"* 10–23. See also Temin's review in the *Boston Globe,* which emphasizes spinning as the soul of the piece.

14. During the artist's talk at the opening, Campos-Pons expressed the fact that she did not want to produce work to be hung on the wall; rather, she wanted the audience to walk around and participate in her installations ("Artist's Talk").

15. In her analysis of three black women artists in Britain, Tawadros concludes: "Like patchwork and collage, the use of pastels by these artists forges links with the history of women's creativity. Furthermore, it sustains the idea of an ambivalent femininity which defies simplistic categorization as inherently passive and apolitical. And finally, it corroborates the historical and cultural conjuncture of the personal and political and the private and public in the diasporan experience. It is in this context that the home and the domestic environment can be seen

to define the space of black women's creativity. It is a space, first of all, in which the past and the present become fused together, where the discontinuous histories of black peoples and the history of Western civilizations are locked together inextricably" (272).

16. In her excellent article on the African American poet Lucille Clifton, Mance paraphrases bell hooks in her essay "Eating the Other": "Hooks explains that members of nondominant identity groups can use their histories against Euro-dominance to reconstruct themselves so that tragic losses and defeats are recast in ways that encourage celebration" (137).

17. For an analysis of a shared culture of all Caribbean peoples based on the model of the sugar economy, see Benítez Rojo.

18. The journal *Temas* dedicated an entire issue to the discussion of race in Cuba in 1996. See particularly the article by Caño Secade. See also *La Gaceta de Cuba* 1 (2005).

19. Caballero defines the 1980s generation as a group of artists for whom the creative act becomes a sociocultural gesture (39). The other members of the round-table discussion published in *Revolución y Cultura* are Luisa Campuzano, Eduardo Morales, Magali Espinosa, Arturo Montoto, Pedro de Oraá, and Rafael Acosta. Magali Espinosa, current president of the section on art criticism at UNEAC, collaborated with Campos-Pons in an essay on performance art in the late 1980s.

20. In his essay on globalization and cultural difference, the Cuban critic Mosquera talks about the installation artist as "a global nomad who roams from one international exhibit to another, his or her suitcase packed with the elements for a future work of art or the tools to produce it *in situ*" ("Alien-Own/Own-Alien," 164.

Bibliography

Acosta de Arriba, Rafael. "Un homenaje para Belkis." In *Imágenes desde el Silencio: Colografías y Matrices de Belkis Ayón, 3*. Havana: Exposición Transitoria Museo Nacional de Bellas Artes, 2001.

Alonso, Carlos. *The Burden of Modernity: The Rhetoric of Cultural Discourse in Spanish America*. New York: Oxford Univ. Press, 1998.

Altunaga, Eliseo. "*The Dead Come at Midnight*: Scripting the White Aesthetic/Black Ethic." In *Afro-Cuban Voices: On Race and Identity in Contemporary Cuba*, ed. Pedro Pérez Sarduy and Jean Stubbs, 87–96. Gainesville: Univ. Press of Florida, 2000.

Andreu, Alicia G. *El testimonio peruano oral y las ciencias sociales: Una problemática postmoderna*. Ann Arbor: Latinoamericana Editores, 2000.

Arandia, Gisela. "Somos o no somos." *La Gaceta de Cuba* 1 (enero–febrero 2005): 59.

Arnold, A. James. "*Créolité*: Power, Mimicry, and Dependence." *Review: Literature of the Americas* 68, 37.1 (2004): 19–26.

———. "Frantz Fanon: Lafcadio Hearn et la Supercherie de 'Mayotte Capécia.'" *Revue de la Littérature Comparée* 2 (avril–juin 2002): 148–166.

———. "'Mayotte Capécia': De la parabole bilique à Je suis Martiniquaise." *Revue de la Littérature Comparée* 1 (janvier–mars 2003): 35–48.

Ayón, Belkis. *Dossier 1986–1999*. CD Rom. Katia Ayón, Estate Belkis Ayón, belkat@cubarte.cult.cu. 2003. (Includes *Acoso*, 1998; *¡¡Déjame salir!!* 1998; *Resurrección*, 1998; and *Untitled* Woman in Fetal Position, 1996.)

———. *Imágenes desde el Silencio: Colografías y matrices de Belkis Ayón*. Exposición Transitoria, Museo Nacional de Bellas Artes, julio 2001: 3.

———. *Siempre vuelvo: Colografías de Belkis Ayón*. Exposición Homenaje. VII Bienal de La Habana. Curated by David Mateo. Galería Habana. 15 de noviembre–18 de diciembre, 2000. Tokyo: Galería Tan, 2000.

Babcock, Barbara A. "'Not in the Absolute Singular': Rereading Ruth Benedict." In *Women Writing Culture*, ed. Ruth Behar and Deborah A. Gordon, 104–130. Berkeley: Univ. of California Press, 1995.

Barnet, Miguel. "La Regla de Ocha: The Religious System of Santería." In *Sacred Possessions: Vodou, Santería, Obeah, and the Caribbean,* ed. Margarite Fernández Olmos and Lizabeth Paravisini-Gebert, 79–100. New Brunswick, N.J.: Rutgers Univ. Press, 1997.

Barradas, Efraín. "Nancy Morejón o un nuevo canto para una vieja culebra." *Afro-Hispanic Review* 15.1 (Spring 1996): 22–28.

Barreda Tomás, Pedro. "La visión conflictiva de la sociedad cubana: Tema y estructura de *Cecilia Valdés.*" *Anales de Literatura Hispanoamericana* 5 (1976): 131–153.

Behar, Ruth. "Introduction: Out of Exile." In *Women Writing Culture,* ed. Ruth Behar and Deborah A. Gordon, 1–29. Berkeley: Univ. of California Press, 1995.

Behar, Ruth, and Deborah A. Gordon, eds. *Women Writing Culture.* Berkeley: Univ. of California Press, 1995.

Bell, Lynne. "History of People Who Were Not Heroes: A Conversation with Maria Magdalena Campos-Pons." *Third Text* 43 (Summer 1998): 33–42.

Benamou, Catherine. "Cuban Cinema: On the Threshold of Gender." *Frontiers* 15.1 (Winter 1994): 51–75.

Benítez Rojo, Antonio. *The Repeating Island: The Caribbean and the Postmodern Perspective.* Trans. James Maraniss. Durham: Duke Univ. Press, 1992.

Bennett, Michael, and Vanessa D. Dickerson. Introduction to *Recovering the Black Female Body: Self-Representations by African American Women,* ed. Michael Bennett and Vanessa D. Dickerson, 1–15. New Brunswick, N.J.: Rutgers Univ. Press, 2001.

Berger, Sally. *History of a People Who Were Not Heroes, Part II.* Curated by Sally Berger, March 5–May 26, 1998. New York: Museum of Modern Art. http://ca80.lehman.cuny.edu/gallery/web/AG/campospons/SpokenText.html.

———. "María Magdalena Campos-Pons, 1990–2001." In *Authentic/Ex-Centric: Conceptualism in Contemporary African Art,* ed. Salah M. Hassan and Olu Oguibe, March 5–May 26, 1998, 122–142. Ithaca, N.Y.: Forum for African Arts, 2001.

———. "Maria Magdalena Campos-Pons: Spoken Softly with Mama." Review by the assistant curator to the Department of Film and Video. New York: Museum of Modern Art, 1998. N. pag.

Bhabha, Homi K. "Beyond the Pale: Art in the Age of Multicultural Translation." In *1993 Biennial Exhibition,* ed. Elisabeth Sussman, Thelma Golden, John G. Hanhardt, and Lisa Phillips, 62–73. New York: Whitney Museum of American Art & Harry N. Abrams, 1993.

———. *The Location of Culture.* London: Routledge, 1994.

Brown, David H. "Toward an Ethnoasthetics of Santería Ritual Arts: The Practice of Altar-Making and Gift Exchange." In *Santería Aesthetics in Contemporary Latin American Art,* ed. Arturo Lindsay, 77–146. Washington, D.C.: Smithsonian Institution Press, 1996.

Bunzel, Ruth. Introduction to *Anthropology and Modern Life*, by Franz Boas, 4–10. New York: Dover, 1962.

Burton, Julianne. *Memories of Underdevelopment and Inconsolable Memories.* New Brunswick, N.J.: Rutgers Univ. Press, 1990.

Cabrera, Lydia. *Anaforuana: Ritual y símbolos de la iniciación en la sociedad secreta Abakuá.* Madrid: Ediciones R., 1975.

———. *Cuentos negros de Cuba.* Barcelona: Icaria Literaria, 1989.

———. *La laguna sagrada de San Joaquín.* Fotografías de Josefina Tarafa. Madrid: Ediciones R., 1973.

———. *La lengua sagrada de los ñáñigos.* Miami: Colección del Chicherekú en el exilio, 1988.

———. *El Monte, Igbo Finda, Ewe Orisha, Vitti Nfinda, Notas sobre las religiones, la magia, las supersticiones y el folklore de los negros criollos y el pueblo de Cuba.* 7th ed. Miami: Ediciones Universal, 1992.

———. *Páginas sueltas.* Intro., ed., and notes by Isabel Castellanos. Miami: Ediciones Universal, 1994.

———. *La sociedad secreta Abakuá: Narrada por viejos adeptos.* Miami: Colección del Chicherekú, 1970.

———. *Yemayá y Ochún: Kariocha, Yalorichas y Olorichas.* New York: CR, 1980.

Camnitzer, Luis. *New Art of Cuba.* Austin: Univ. of Texas Press, 1994.

Campos-Pons, María Magdalena. *Meanwhile, the Girls Were Playing.* Cambridge, Mass.: MIT List Visual Arts Center, 1999.

———. "Artist's Talk." MIT List Visual Arts Center, October 9, 1998.

———. "Multimedia Artist María Magdalena Campos-Pons to Premiere Installation at the Museum of Modern Art." MoMA Press Release. http://www.afrocubaweb.com/magdalenacampos.htm (accessed 17 June 2002).

"Campos-Pons, María Magdalena." Artist-Info, contemporary art database. http://www.artist-info.com (accessed 17 June 2002).

Campos-Pons, María Magdalena, and Espinosa, Magali. "El performance, una revolución en la morfología del arte." *Revolución y cultura,* 6 Junio 1990, 66–68.

Caño Secade, María del Carmen. "Relaciones raciales, proceso de ajuste y política social." *Temas: Cultura, Ideología, Sociedad* (nueva época) 7 (septiembre 1996): 58–65.

Capote, Leonel. Introduction to *La visualidad infinita*, by José Lezama Lima. Havana: Letras cubanas, 1994.

Carpentier, Alejo. *Tientos y diferencias.* Montevideo: Arca Editorial, 1967.

Castellanos, Isabel. "From Ulkumí to Lucumí: A Historical Overview of Religious Acculturation in Cuba." In *Santería Aesthetics in Contemporary Latin American Art,* ed. Arturo Lindsay, 39–50. Washington, D.C.: Smithsonian Institution Press, 1996.

———. Introduction to *Páginas sueltas,* by Lydia Cabrera, 13–16. Miami: Ediciones Universal, 1994.

Castellanos, Jorge, and Isabel Castellanos. *Cultura afrocubana 2: El negro en Cuba, 1845–1959.* Miami: Ediciones Universal, 1990.

———. *Cultura afrocubana 3: Las religiones y las lenguas.* Miami: Ediciones Universal, 1992.

Chanan, Michael. *The Cuban Image: Cinema and Cultural Politics in Cuba.* London: BFI Publishing; Bloomington: Indiana Univ. Press, 1985.

Christian, Barbara. *Black Women Novelists: The Development of a Tradition, 1892–1976.* Westport, Conn.: Greenwood Press, 1980.

Chomsky, Aviva. "'Barbados or Canada?' Race, Immigration, and Nation in Early Twentieth-Century Cuba." Paper delivered at the Latin American History Workshop, Harvard University, 7 April 1998.

Cirlot, Juan Eduardo. *A Dictionary of Symbols.* Trans. Jack Sage. New York: Philosophical Library, 1971.

Clifford, James. "On Ethnographic Allegory." In *Writing Culture: The Poetics and Politics of Ethnography,* ed. James Clifford and George E. Marcus. Berkeley: Univ. of California Press, 1986.

Clifford, James, and George E. Marcus, eds. *Writing Culture: The Poetics and Politics of Ethnography.* Berkeley: Univ. of California Press, 1986.

Cole, Sally. "Ruth Landes and the Early Ethnography of Race and Gender." In *Women Writing Culture,* ed. Ruth Behar and Deborah A. Gordon, 166–185. Berkeley: Univ. of California Press, 1995.

"¿Cómo nos sentamos en el Malecón? Seis voces replantean cien años de arte en Cuba." *Revolución y Cultura* 3 (mayo–junio 2001): 32–43.

Cordones-Cook, Juanamaría. "Voz y poesía de Nancy Morejón." *Afro-Hispanic Review* 15.1 (Spring 1996): 60–71.

Coronil, Fernando. Introduction to *Cuban Counterpoint: Tobacco and Sugar,* by Fernando Ortiz, ix–lvi. Durham, N.C.: Duke Univ. Press, 1995.

Cosford, Bill. "*María Antonia* Full of Steam, Not Politics." Movie review. *Miami Herald,* 8 February 1993, 5C.

Cuervo Hewitt, Julia. *Aché, presencia africana: Tradiciones yoruba-lucumí en la narrativa cubana.* New York: Peter Lang, 1988.

Darío, Rubén. *Selected Poems of Rubén Darío: A Bilingual Anthology.* Trans., ed., and intro. by Alberto Acereda and Will Derusha. Lewisburg, Penn.: Bucknell Univ. Press, 2001.

Davies, Catherine. "Cross-Cultural Homebodies in Cuba: The Poetry of Excilia Saldaña." In *Latin American Women's Writing: Feminist Readings in Theory and Crisis,* ed. A. Brooksbank Jones and C. Davies, 179–200. Oxford: Oxford Univ. Press, 1996.

———. *A Place in the Sun? Women Writers in Twentieth-Century Cuba.* London: Zed Books, 1997.

———. "Hybrid Texts: Family, State and Empire in a Poem by Black Cuban Poet Excilia Saldaña." In *Comparing Postcolonial Literatures: Dislocations,* ed. Ashok Bery and Patricia Murray, 205–215. New York: St. Martin's Press, 2000.

————. "Modernity, Masculinity and Imperfect Cinema in Cuba." *Screen* 38.4 (Winter 1997): 345–359.

DeCosta-Willis, Miriam, ed. *Singular Like a Bird: The Art of Nancy Morejón,* Washington, D.C.: Howard Univ. Press, 2001.

de la Fuente, Alejandro. "Un debate necesario: Raza y cubanidad." *La Gaceta de Cuba* 1 (enero–febrero 2005): 62–64.

————. *A Nation for All: Race, Inequality, and Politics in Twentieth-Century Cuba.* Chapel Hill: Univ. of North Carolina Press, 2001.

————. "La 'raza' y los silencios de la cubanidad." *Revista Encuentro de la Cultura Cubana* 20 (2001): 107–118.

Dilla Alfonso, Haroldo. "Cuba: The Changing Scenarios of Governability." *boundary 2* 29.3 (Fall 2002): 55–75.

Díaz, Rolando. *Si me comprendieras.* Canarias, Spain: Luna Llena Producciones, 1999.

Enwezor, Okwui. "Where, What, Who, When: A Few Notes on 'African' Conceptualism." In *Authentic/Ex-Centric: Conceptualism in Contemporary African Art,* ed. Salah M. Hassan and Olu Oguibe, 72–82. Ithaca, N.Y.: Forum for African Arts, 2001.

Fanon, Frantz. *Black Skin, White Masks.* Trans. Charles Lam Markmann. New York: Grove Press, 1967.

Feal, Rosemary Geisdorfer. "Feminist Interventions in the Race for Theory: Neither Black nor White." *Afro-Hispanic Review* 10.3 (September 1991): 11–20.

Felman, Shoshana. *What Does a Woman Want? Reading and Sexual Difference.* Baltimore: Johns Hopkins Univ. Press, 1993.

Fernández, Antonio Eligio (Tonel). "Arbol de muchas playas: del arte cubano en movimiento, 1980–1999." In *Cuba: Contemporary Art from Cuba/Arte Contemporáneo de Cuba,* 53–66. New York: Arizona State University Art Museum and Delano Greenidge Editions, 1999.

————. "Tree of Many Beaches: Cuban Art in Motion, 1989–1990." In *Contemporary Art from Cuba: Irony and Survival on the Utopian Island,* 39–52. New York: Delano Greenidge Editions and Arizona State University, 1999.

————. "70, 80, 90 . . . Tal vez 100 impresiones sobre el arte en Cuba." *Cuba Siglo 20: Modernidad y Sincretismo,* 281–301, 413–422. Las Palmas, Gran Canaria: Centro Atlántico de Arte Moderno, 1996.

Fischer, Michael M. "Ethnicity and the Post-Modern Arts of Memory." In *Writing Culture: The Poetics and Politics of Ethnography,* ed. James Clifford and George E. Marcus, 194–232. Berkeley: Univ. of California Press, 1986.

Fowler Calzada, Víctor. *Conversaciones con un cineasta incómodo: Julio García Espinosa.* Lincoln, R.I.: Pukara-Fortitude Art and Cultural Organization, 1997.

Freiman, Lisa D. "Circling Campos-Pons." In *Unpacking Europe: Towards a Critical Reading,* ed. Salah Hassan and Iftikhar Dadi, 314–319. Rotterdam, Netherlands: NAI, 2001.

Fusco, Coco. "Jineteras en Cuba." *Encuentro de la Cultura Cubana* 4/5 (1997): 53–64.

———. "Magdalena Campos-Pons at Intar." *Art in America* 82.2 (February 1994): 106–107.

La Gaceta de Cuba 1 (enero–febrero 2005).

Gates, Henry Louis, Jr. "Critical Fanonism." *Critical Inquiry* 17.3 (1997): 457–470.

———. *The Signifying Monkey: A Theory of Afro-American Literary Criticism.* New York: Oxford Univ. Press, 1987.

Geertz, Clifford. *Works and Lives: The Anthropologist as Author.* Stanford, Calif.: Stanford Univ. Press, 1988.

Gelpí, Juan G. "El discurso jerárquico en 'Cecilia Valdés.'" *Revista de Crítica Literaria Latinoamericana* 17.34 (1991): 47–61.

Gendzier, Irene L. *Frantz Fanon: A Critical Study.* New York: Pantheon Books, 1973.

Gilmore, Leigh. *The Limits of Autobiography: Trauma and Testimony.* Ithaca, N.Y.: Cornell Univ. Press, 2001.

Gilroy, Paul. *The Black Atlantic: Modernity and Double Consciousness.* Cambridge, Mass.: Harvard Univ. Press, 1993.

Giral, Sergio. *María Antonia.* Havana: ICAIC, 1990.

Glissant, Edouard. *Caribbean Discourse: Selected Essays.* Trans. J. Michael Dash. Charlottesville: Univ. Press of Virginia, 1989.

Gómez, Sara. *De cierta manera.* Havana: ICAIC, 1975.

González, Aníbal. "Literary Criticism in Spanish America." In *The Cambridge History of Latin American Literature,* vol. 2: *The Twentieth Century,* ed. Roberto González Echevarría and Enrique Pupo Walker, 425–457. New York: Cambridge Univ. Press, 1996.

González, Flora M. "El afán de nombrarse en la obra poética de Excilia Saldaña." *Afro-Hispanic Review* 16.2 (Fall 1997): 34–42.

———. "Borges y 'El Aleph': De lo imposible a lo inefable." *Revista de la Universidad de México,* nueva epoca, 40.38 (junio 1984): 19–23.

———. "De lo invisible a lo espectacular en la creación de la mulata en la cultura cubana: *Cecilia Valdés y María Antonia.*" In *Revista Iberoamericana: 1898–1998: Balance de un siglo,* ed. Aníbal González, 184–185 (Julio–Diciembre 1998): 543–557.

———. "Possession and Altar-Making: Reconstruction of Memory as Artistic Performance in the Multimedia Installations of María Magdalena Campos-Pons." *Cuban Studies* 31 (2000): 102–117.

González Echevarría, Roberto. *Alejo Carpentier: The Pilgrim at Home.* Ithaca, N.Y.: Cornell Univ. Press, 1977.

———. "Fiestas cubanas: Villaverde, Ortiz, Carpentier." *Revista Encuentro de la Cultura Cubana* 20 (2001): 57–74.

Gordon, Lewis R. *Her Majesty's Other Children: Sketches of Racism from a Neocolonial Age.* Oxford: Rowman & Littlefield, 1997.

Gubar, Susan. *Racechanges: White Skin, Black Face in American Culture.* New York: Oxford Univ. Press, 1997.

Hall, Stuart. "Cultural Identity and Diaspora." In *Contemporary Postcolonial Theory: A Reader,* ed. Padmini Mongia, 110–121. London: Arnold, 1996.

Harris, Michael D. "Meanwhile, the Girls Were Playing." In María Magdalena Campos-Pons, *Meanwhile, the Girls Were Playing,* 10–26. Cambridge, Mass.: MIT List Visual Arts Center, 1999.

Hassan, Salah M. "'<Insertions>': Self and Other in Contemporary African Art." In *Authentic/Ex-Centric: Conceptualism in Contemporary African Art,* ed. Salah M. Hassan and Olu Oguibe, 26–49. Ithaca, N.Y.: Forum for African Arts, 2001.

Hassan, Salah M., and Olu Oguibe. "Authentic/Ex-Centric: Conceptualism in Contemporary African Art." In *Authentic/Ex-Centric: Conceptualism in Contemporary African Art,* ed. Salah M. Hassan and Olu Oguibe, 10–23. Ithaca, N.Y.: Forum for African Arts, 2001.

Helg, Aline. *Our Rightful Share: The Afro-Cuban Struggle for Equality, 1886–1992.* Chapel Hill: Univ. of North Carolina Press, 1995.

Hernández Espinosa, Eugenio. *María Antonia.* Havana: Letras Cubanas, 1979.

Hernández, Graciela. "Multiple Subjectivities and Strategic Positionality: Zora Neale Hurston's Experimental Ethnographies." In *Women Writing Culture,* ed. Ruth Behar and Deborah A. Gordon, 148–165. Berkeley: Univ. of California Press, 1995.

Herzberg, Julia P. "Rereading Lam." In *Santería Aesthetics in Contemporary Latin American Art,* ed. Arturo Lindsay, 149–169. Washington, D.C.: Smithsonian Institution Press, 1996.

———. "A Town Portrait: Memory Streams." *History of a People Who Were Not Heroes, Part I.* Curated by Julia P. Herzberg, 4 February–16 May 1998, Lehman College Art Gallery, New York. http://ca80.lehman.cuny.edu/gallery/web/AG/campospons/TextTower.html.

Higginbotham, Evelyn Brooks. "African-American Women's History and the Metalanguage of Race." In *"We Specialize in the Wholly Impossible": A Reader in Black Women's History,* ed. Darlene Clark Hine, Wilma King, and Linda Reed, 3–23. Brooklyn, New York: Carlson, 1995.

———. "Racial Constructions of Citizenship." Lecture delivered at W. E. B. Du Bois Institute of Afro-American Research, Harvard University, Cambridge, Mass., 5 November 1997.

Hiriart, Rosario. *Lydia Cabrera: Vida hecha arte.* New York: Eliseo Torres and Sons, 1978.

Howe, Linda S. "Nancy Morejón's *Womanism*," In *Singular Like a Bird: The Art of Nancy Morejón,* ed. Miriam DeCosta Willis, 153–168. Washington, D.C.: Howard Univ. Press, 2001.

———. "The Fluid Iconography of the Cuban Spirit in Nancy Morejón's Poetry." *Afro-Hispanic Review* 15.1 (Spring 1996): 29–34.

————. *Transgression and Conformity: Cuban Writers and Artists after the Revolution.* Madison: Univ. of Wisconsin Press, 2004.

James, Conrad. "Women, Life Writing and National Identity in Cuba: Excilia Saldaña's *Mi nombre: Anti-elegía familiar.*" In *The Cultures of the Hispanic Caribbean,* ed. Conrad James and John Perivolaris, 50–71. Gainesville: Univ. Press of Florida, 2000.

Jones, Ann. "Belkis Ayón: The Illusory Rectification of a Myth." In *Trabajando p'al Inglé,* 28–29. London: Barbican Centre, 14 May–27 June, 1999.

Julien, Isaac. *Frantz Fanon: Black Skin, White Masks.* Great Britain, 1996.

Kutzinski, Vera. *Against the American Grain: Myth and History in William Carlos Williams, Jay Wright, and Nicolás Guillén.* Baltimore: Johns Hopkins Univ. Press, 1987.

————. "Poetry and Politics: Two Books on Nicolás Guillén." *MLN* 98.2 (March 1983): 275–284.

————. *Sugar's Secrets: Race and the Erotics of Cuban Nationalism.* Charlottesville: Univ. Press of Virginia, 1993.

Lamphere, Louise. "Feminist Anthropology: The Legacy of Elsie Clews Parsons." In *Women Writing Culture,* ed. Ruth Behar and Deborah A. Gordon, 85–103. Berkeley: Univ. of California Press, 1995.

Leante, César. "Cecilia Valdés, espejo de la esclavitud." *El espacio real,* 29–42. Havana: Contemporáneo, UNEAC, 1975.

Lezama Lima, José. *La visualidad infinita.* Intro. Leonel Capote. Havana: Letras cubanas, 1994.

————. *Poesía completa.* Ed. César López. Madrid: Alianza Editorial, 1999.

Lindsay, Arturo, ed. *Santería Aesthetics in Contemporary Latin American Art.* Washington, D.C.: Smithsonian Institution Press, 1996.

López, Ana. "Parody, Underdevelopment, and the New Latin American Cinema." *Quarterly Review of Film and Video* 12 (1990): 63–71.

Luis, William. "*Cecilia Valdés:* El nacimiento de una novela antiesclavista." *Cuadernos hispanoamericanos* no. 451–452 (1988): 187–193.

————. *Literary Bondage: Slavery in Cuban Narrative.* Austin: Univ. of Texas Press, 1990.

————. "The Politics of Aesthetics in the Poetry of Nancy Morejón." *Afro-Hispanic Review* 15.1 (1996): 35–43.

————. "Race, Poetry and Revolution in the Works of Nancy Morejón." In *Singular Like a Bird: The Art of Nancy Morejón,* 45–67. Washington, D.C.: Howard Univ. Press, 2001.

Lutkehaus, Nancy C. "Margaret Mead and the 'Rustling-of-the-Wind-in-the-Palm-Trees School' of Ethnographic Writing." In *Women Writing Culture,* ed. Ruth Behar and Deborah A. Gordon, 186–206. Berkeley: Univ. of California Press, 1995.

Mance, Ajuan Maria. "Re-locating the Black Female Subject: The Landscape of the Body in the Poems of Lucille Clifton." In *Recovering the Black Female Body: Self-Representations by African American Women,* ed. Michael Bennett and Vanessa D. Dickerson, 123–140. New Brunswick, N.J.: Rutgers Univ. Press, 2001.

Marcus, George E. "Contemporary Problems of Ethnography in the Modern World System." In *Writing Culture: The Poetics and Politics of Ethnography,* ed. James Clifford and George E. Marcus, 165–193. Berkeley: Univ. of California Press, 1986.

Marks, Morton. "Exploring *El Monte:* Ethnobotany and the Afro-Cuban Science of the Concrete." In *En torno a Lydia Cabrera cincuentenario de "Cuentos negros de Cuba": 1936–1986,* ed. Isabel Castellanos and Josefina Inclán. Miami: Ediciones Universal, 1987.

Martí, José. "Nené traviesa." In *La edad de oro,* 73–76. Havana: Editorial Gente Nueva, 1979.

———. *Ismaelillo.* Santa Fe, N.M.: Editorial Huemul, 1963.

Martínez, Juan A. *Cuban Art and National Identity: The Vanguardia Painters, 1927–1950.* Gainesville: Univ. Press of Florida, 1994.

Mateo, David. "I Always Come Back: Irregular Conversation with Belkis Ayón." Interview made available by the Phyllis Kind Gallery, New York, November 1993.

Matibag, Eugenio. "Ifá and Interpretation: An Afro-Caribbean Literary Practice." In *Sacred Possessions: Vodou, Santería, Obeah, and the Caribbean,* ed. Margarite Fernández Olmos and Lizabeth Paravisini-Gebert, 151–170. New Brunswick, N.J.: Rutgers Univ. Press, 1997.

———. *Afro-Cuban Religious Experience: Cultural Reflections in Narrative.* Gainesville: Univ. Press of Florida, 2001.

McDowell, Deborah E. "Recovery Missions: Imaging the Body Ideals." In *Recovering the Black Female Body: Self-Representations by African American Women,* ed. Michael Bennett and Vanessa D, Dickerson, 296–317. New Brunswick, N.J.: Rutgers Univ. Press, 2001.

McGarrity, Gayle, and Osvaldo Cárdenas. "Cuba." In *No Longer Invisible: Afro-Latin Americans Today,* 77–107. London: Minority Rights Group, 1995.

Méndez Rodenas, Adriana. *Cuba en su imagen: Historia e identidad en la literatura cubana.* Madrid: Verbum, 2002.

———. *Gender and Nationalism in Colonial Cuba: The Travels of Santa Cruz y Montalvo, Condesa de Merlín.* Nashville, Tenn.: Vanderbilt Univ. Press, 1998.

———. "Identity and Incest in *Cecilia Valdés:* Villaverde and the Origins of the Text." *Cuban Studies/Estudios Cubanos* 24 (1994): 83–104.

Menéndez, Lázara. "Por los *peoples* del barrio." *La Gaceta de Cuba* 1 (enero–febrero 2005): 18–21.

Molloy, Sylvia. "Disappearing Acts: Reading Lesbian in Teresa de la Parra." In

¿Entiendes?: Queer Readings, Hispanic Writings, ed. Emilie L. Bergmann and Paul Julian Smith, 230–256. Durham, N.C.: Duke Univ. Press, 1995.

Morejón, Nancy. "Arco iris con esperanza." *Casa de las Américas* 37.207 (abril–junio 1997): 140–142.

———. "El arco iris de Martha Jean Claude." *Casa de las Américas* 27.157 (julio–agosto 1986): 132.

———. "Arte Joven en Cuba." *Kuba o.k.,* 27–31. Städtische Kunsthalle Düsseldorf and Centro de Desarrollo de las Artes Visuales, Cuba, 1990.

———. "La Casa de las Américas y el Caribe en su porvenir." *Casa de las Américas* 36.202 (enero–marzo 1996): 128–130.

———. "César López y su quiebra de la perfección." *La Nueva Gaceta* 3 (1984): 9.

———. "A Cuban Perspective: The America of Langston Hughes." Trans. Victor Carrabino. *Langston Hughes Review* 6.1 (Spring 1987): 1–3.

———. "Elogio de Manuel Mendive." *Casa de las Américas* 226 (enero–marzo 2002): 146–148.

———. "La experiencia de Black Scholar." *La Nueva Gaceta* 1 (1985): 18.

———. *Fundación de la imagen.* Havana: Editorial Letras Cubanas, 1988.

———. "Grounding the Race Dialogue: Diaspora and Nation." In *Afro-Cuban Voices: On Race and Identity in Contemporary Cuba,* ed. Pedro Pérez Sarduy and Jean Stubbs, 162–169. Gainesville: Univ. Press of Florida, 2000.

———. *Looking Within / Mirar Adentro: Selected Poems, 1954–2000.* Ed. and intro. Juanamaría Cordones-Cook. Detroit: Wayne State Univ. Press, 2002.

———. "Las poéticas de Nancy Morejón." *Afro-Hispanic Review* 15.1 (1996): 6–9.

———. "Melvin Edwards: El mundo de un artista maravilloso." *Revista Proposiciones, Fundación Pablo Milanés* 1.2 (1994): 52–55.

———. "'Un modo de ser': El cine más reciente de Rigoberto López." *La Gaceta de Cuba* (Marzo 1990), 18.

———. *Nación y mestizaje en Nicolás Guillén.* Havana: Ediciones Unión, 1982.

———. "Pablo Armando: 'España siempre es una revelación.'" *La Nueva Gaceta* 9–10 (1983): 10–11.

———. *Paisaje célebre: Poemas 1987–1992.* Caracas: Fundarte, 1993.

———. "Palabras por el Premio Nacional de Literatura," 12 February 2002, http://www.afrocubaweb.com/nancymorejon.htm.

———. "Para presentar canción negra sin color." *La Nueva Gaceta* 7–8 (1983): 20.

———. "El pintor Lawrence Zúñiga." *La Nueva Gaceta* 5 (1984): 10–11.

———. "Prólogo." In *Recopilación de textos sobre Nicolás Guillén,* 7–29. Havana: Casa de las Américas, 1974.

———. "Prólogo." In *In the Vortex of the Cyclone: Selected Poems by Excilia Saldaña,* ed. and trans. Flora González Mandri and Rosamond Rosenmeier, vii–xiii. Gainesville: Univ. Press of Florida, 2002.

————. "Un ritual para Bola de Nieve." *La Gaceta de Cuba* 3 (mayo–junio 1999): 59–60.

————. "Rostgaard: La rosa recobrada." *Casa de las Américas* 38.209 (octubre–diciembre 1997): 140–143.

————. "Teatro de pantomima cubana para sordos." *La Nueva Gaceta* 1 (1981): 20–21.

————. "Tres notas sobre obras presentadas en el Festival de Teatro de La Habana." *La Nueva Gaceta* 4 (1984): 17–18.

————. "El venezolano Oscar de León." *La Nueva Gaceta* 2 (1984): 12–15.

————. "Viaje a Suráfrica." *Casa de las Américas* 36.200 (julio–septiembre 1995): 126–135.

————. *Where the Island Sleeps Like a Wing: Selected Poetry by Nancy Morejón.* Trans. Kathleen Weaver. San Francisco: Black Scholar Press, 1985.

Mosquera, Gerardo. "Alien-Own/Own-Alien: Globalization and Cultural Difference." *boundary 2* 29.3 (2002): 163–173.

————. "Elegguá at the Post-Modern Crossroads: The Presence of Africa in the Visual Art of Cuba." In *Santería Aesthetics in Contemporary Latin American Art,* ed. Arturo Lindsay, 225–258. Washington, D.C.: Smithsonian Institution Press, 1996.

————. "¿Feminismo en Cuba?" *Revolución y Cultura* 6 (junio 1990): 52–57.

————. "The Infinite Island: Introduction to New Cuban Art." In *Contemporary Art from Cuba: Irony and Survival on the Utopian Island,* curated by Marilyn A. Zeitlin, 23–29. New York: Delano Greenidge Editions and Arizona State University Art Museum, 1999.

————. "Strokes of Magical Realism in Manuel Mendive." In *Afro-Cuba: An Anthology of Cuban Writing on Race, Politics and Culture,* ed. Pedro Pérez Sarduy and Jean Stubbs, 146–153. Melbourne: Ocean Press, 1993.

Morrison, Karen Y. "Civilization and Citizenship through the Eyes of Afro-Cuban Intellectuals during the First Constitutional Era." *Cuban Studies* 30 (2000): 76–99.

Moyers, Bill D. "Derek Walcott." In *A World of Ideas: Conversations with Thoughtful Men and Women about American Life Today and the Ideas Shaping Our Future,* ed. Betty Sue Flowers, 426–434. New York: Doubleday, 1984.

Muguercia, Magaly. "The Body and Its Politics in Cuba of the Nineties." *boundary 2* 29.3 (Fall 2002): 175–185.

Mullen, Edward J. *Afro-Cuban Literature: Critical Junctures.* Westport, Conn.: Greenwood Press, 1998.

————. "Introducing Nancy Morejón to the Reader." *Afro-Hispanic Review* 15.1 (Spring 1996): 4.

Mulvey, Laura. "Visual Pleasure and Narrative Cinema." In *Feminism and Film Theory,* ed. Constance Penley, 57–58. New York: Routledge, 1988.

Navarro, Desiderio. "In Medias Res Publicas: On Intellectuals and Social Criticism in the Cuban Public Sphere." *boundary 2* 29.3 (Fall 2002): 187–203.

Netchinsky, Jill A. "Engendering a Cuban Literature: Nineteenth-Century Anti-slavery Narrative: Manzano, Suárez y Romero, Gómez de Avellaneda, A. Zambrana." Ph.D. diss., Yale University, 1985, 175–216.

O'Keeffe, Georgia. *One Hundred Flowers*. Ed. Nicholas Callaway. New York: Barnes and Noble Books, 1998.

Olavarria, Margot. "Rap and Revolution: Hip-Hop Comes to Cuba." *NACLA Report on the Americas* 35.6 (May/June 2002): 28–30.

Ortiz, Fernando. *Los negros brujos: Apuntes para un estudio de Etnología Criminal*. Miami: Ediciones Universal, 1973.

————. *Los bailes y el teatro de los negros en el folklore de Cuba*. Havana: Letras Cubanas, 1981.

Ovid. *Ovid's Metamorphoses: The Arthur Golding Translation 1567*. Ed. and intro. John Frederick Nims. New York: Macmillan, 1965.

Palmié, Stephan. *Wizards and Scientists: Explorations of Afro-Cuban Modernity and Tradition*. Durham, N.C.: Duke Univ. Press, 2002.

Phaf, Ineke. "La introducción emblemática de la nación mulata: El contrapunteo híbrido en las culturas de Suriname y Cuba." *Revista de Crítica Literaria Latinoamericana* 19.38 (1993): 195–215.

Phyllis Kind Gallery. *Belkis Ayón: Biography, Exhibitions and Awards*. New York, 1998. N. pag.

Piedra, José. "The Afro-Cuban Esthetics of Alejo Carpentier." Ph.D. diss., Yale University, 1985.

————. "From Monkey Tales to Cuban Songs: On Signification." In *Sacred Possessions: Vodou, Santería, Obeah, and the Caribbean*, ed. Margarite Fernández Olmos and Lizabeth Paravisini-Gebert, 122–150. New Brunswick, N.J.: Rutgers Univ. Press, 1997.

Pogolotti, Graziella. "Marcelo Pogolotti, todavía desconocido." *Revolución y Cultura* 3 (marzo 1990): 32–39.

Portuondo Zúñiga, Olga. *La Virgen de la Caridad del Cobre: Símbolo de Cubanía*. Santiago de Cuba: Editorial Oriente, 1995.

Pratt, Mary Louise. "Fieldwork in Common Places." In *Writing Culture: The Poetics and Politics of Ethnography*, ed. James Clifford and George E. Marcus, 27–50. Berkeley: Univ. of California Press, 1986.

Quiroga, José. *Tropics of Desire: Interventions from Queer Latino America*. New York: New York Univ. Press, 2000.

Reddock, Rhoda E. "Women and Slavery in the Caribbean: A Feminist Perspective." In *"We Specialize in the Wholly Impossible": A Reader in Black Women's History*, ed. Darlene Clark Hine, Wilma King, and Linda Reed, 127–141. Brooklyn, New York: Carlson, 1995.

Ribeaux Diago, Ariel. "1998 Exhibit at the Museum of Modern Art," 1998. http://www.afrocubaweb.com/magdalenacampos.htm.

Riddell, Jennifer L. "Centrifugal Force." In *María Magdalena Campos-Pons,*

Meanwhile, the Girls Were Playing, 3–9. Cambridge, Mass.: MIT List Visual Arts Center, 1999.

Rodríguez, Ileana. *House/Garden/Nation: Space, Gender, and Ethnicity in Postcolonial Literature by Women.* Durham, N.C.: Duke Univ. Press, 1994.

Rodríguez Mola, Alexey, and Magia López Cabrera. "Obsesión/Mambí Rap." *boundary 2* 29.3 (Fall 2002): 205–210.

Rolando, Gloria. *The Eyes of the Rainbow.* Havana: Imágines del Caribe, 1997.

———. *Forever Present: Oggún.* Havana: Imágines del Caribe, 1991.

———. "Gloria Rolando's Biography." http://www.afrocubaweb.com/Rolbio.htm.

———. "Gloria Rolando: 'Searching in My Dreams'—The 1912 Genocide." 1997, updated 1999. http://www.afrocubaweb.com/searchinginmydreams.htm.

———. "Gloria Rolando: Speech at Black Women Writers and the Future Conference, Oct. '97, New York." 17 October 1997. http://www.afrocubaweb.com/rolandospeech.htm.

———. "Interview de Gloria Rolando, productrice et réalisatrice cubaine." Interview with Mathilde Mansoz and Barbara Aranda. http://www.cinema.presse.fr/racine/interview_de_gloria_rolando.htm (accessed 14 February 1999).

———. "Interview in *Mujeres*" [Women]. Havana, 1996. http://www.afrocubaweb.com/gloriarolando.htm (accessed 26 October 1997).

———. *My Footsteps in Baraguá.* Havana: Imágines del Caribe, 1996.

———. *Las raíces de mi corazón.* Havana: Imágines del Caribe, 2001.

Rooks, Noliwe. "Wearing Your Race Wrong: Hair, Drama, and a Politics of Representation for African American Women at Play on a Battlefield." In *Recovering the Black Female Body: Self-Representations by African American Women,* ed. Michael Bennett and Vanessa D. Dickerson, 279–295. New Brunswick, N.J.: Rutgers Univ. Press, 2001.

Rosario-Sievert, Heather. "Nancy Morejón's Eye/I: Social and Aesthetic Perception in the Work of Nancy Morejón." *Afro-Hispanic Review* 15.1 (1996): 44–49.

RoseGreen-Williams, C. "Re-writing the History of the Afro-Cuban Woman: Nancy Morejón's 'Mujer negra.'" In *Singular Like a Bird: The Art of Nancy Morejón,* ed. Miriam DeCosta-Willis, 187–200. Washington D.C.: Howard Univ. Press, 1999.

Saldaña, Excilia. "Excilia Saldaña" and "Autobiografía." In *Breaking the Silences: An Anthology of 20th-Century Poetry by Cuban Women,* ed. and trans. Margaret Randall, 196–214. Vancouver, B.C.: Pulp Press, 1982.

———. *In the Vortex of the Cyclone: Selected Poems by Excilia Saldaña.* Ed. and trans. Flora González Mandri and Rosamond Rosenmeier. Gainesville: Univ. Press of Florida, 2002.

———. *Mi nombre: Antielegía familiar.* Havana: Ediciones Unión, 2003.

———. "Las tres suspirantes," *Kele Kele,* 19–41. Havana: Editorial Letras Cubanas, 1987.

————. "Vieja trova sobre soporte CD ROM." *La Isla Infinita* 1.2 (1999): 22–33.

Santí, Enrico Mario. "Towards a Reading of Fernando Ortiz's *Cuban Counterpoint.*" *Review: Literature and Arts of the Americas* 37.1 (2004): 6–18.

Schenck, Celeste. "All of a Piece: Women's Poetry and Autobiography." In *Life/Lines: Theorizing Women's Autobiography,* ed. Bella Brodzki and Celeste Schenck, 281–305. Ithaca, N.Y.: Cornell Univ. Press, 1988.

Scott, Nina M. Introduction to *Sab and Autobiography* by Gertrudis Gómez de Avellaneda y Arteaga, trans. and ed. Nina M. Scott, xi–xxvii. Austin: Univ. of Texas Press, 1993.

Shakespeare, William. *The Tempest.* Ed. Robert Langbaum. New York: Signet Classic, 1998.

Sharpley-Whiting, T. Denean. "Anti-black Femininity and Mixed-Race Identity: Engaging Fanon to Reread Capécia." In *Fanon: A Critical Reader,* ed. Lewis R. Gordon, T. Denean Sharpley-Whiting, and Renée T. White, 155–162. Oxford: Blackwell, 1996.

Smart, Ian Isidore. *Amazing Connections: Kemet to Hispanophone Africana Literature.* Washington, D.C.: Original World Press, 1996.

Smith, Sidonie, and Julia Watson. "Introduction: De/Colonization and the Politics of Discourse in Women's Autobiographical Practices." In *De/Colonizing the Subject: The Politics of Gender in Women's Autobiography,* ed. Sidonie Smith and Julia Watson, xiii–xxxi. Minneapolis: Univ. of Minnesota Press, 1992.

Sollors, Werner. *Neither Black nor White Yet Both: Thematic Explorations of Interracial Literature.* New York: Oxford Univ. Press, 1997.

Sommer, Doris. *Foundational Fictions: The National Romances of Latin America.* Berkeley: Univ. of California Press, 1991.

————. "Cecilia no sabe, o los bloqueos que blanquean." *Revista de Crítica Literaria Latinoamericana* 19.38 (1993): 239–248.

Stolcke, Verena. *Marriage, Class and Colour in Nineteenth-Century Cuba: A Study of Racial Attitudes and Sexual Values in a Slave Society.* 2nd ed. Ann Arbor: Univ. of Michigan Press, 1989.

Tawadros, Gilane. "Beyond the Boundary: The Work of Three Black Women Artists in Britain." In *Black British Cultural Studies: A Reader,* ed. Houston A. Baker, Diawara Baker, and Ruth Lindeborg, 240–277. Chicago: Univ. of Chicago Press, 1996.

Taylor, Diana. *Disappearing Acts: Spectacles of Gender and Nationalism in Argentina's "Dirty War."* Durham, N.C.: Duke Univ. Press, 1997.

Temin, Christine. "A Delicate Spin on a Life in Cuba." *Boston Globe,* 17 Nov. 1999, F1, F5.

Vergès, Françoise. "Creole Skin, Black Mask: Fanon and Disavowal." *Critical Inquiry* 23.3 (Spring 1997): 578–595.

Villaverde, Cirilo. *Cecilia Valdés: Novela de costumbres cubanas.* México: Editorial Porrúa, 1986.

————. *The Quadroon or Cecilia Valdés: A Romance of Old Havana.* Trans. Mariano J. Lorente. Boston: L. C. Page, 1935.

Viso, Olga. "María Magdalena Campos-Pons: Transcending the Borders of Memory." Essay by the curator, West Palm Beach, Fla.: Norton Gallery of Art, 1994, N. pag.

Vitier, Cintio. "Resistance and Freedom." *boundary 2* 29.3 (Fall 2002): 245–252.

Walker, Alice. *In Search of Our Mothers' Gardens: Womanist Prose.* New York: Harcourt Brace Jovanovich, 1983.

Williams, Lorna V. "The Emergence of an Afro-Cuban Aesthetic." *Afro-Hispanic Review* 14.1 (Spring 1995): 48–57.

————. "From Dusky Venus to Mater Dolorosa: The Female Protagonist in the Cuban Antislavery Novel." In *Woman as Myth and Metaphor in Latin American Literature,* ed. Carmelo Virgilio and Naomi Lindstrom, 121–135. Columbia: Univ. of Missouri Press, 1985.

————. "The Representation of the Female Slave in Villaverde's *Cecilia Valdés.*" *Hispanic Journal* 14.1 (1993): 73–89.

————. *The Representation of Slavery in Cuban Fiction.* Columbia: Univ. of Missouri Press, 1994.

Zeitlin, Marilyn A. "Luz Brillante." In *Contemporary Art from Cuba: Irony and Survival on the Utopian Island,* ed. Marilyn A. Zeitlin, 125–137. New York: Arizona State University Art Museum and Delano Greenidge Editions, 1999.

Index

Vera M. Kutzinski, *Sugar's Secrets: Race and the Erotics of Cuban Nationalism*

Richard D. E. Burton and Fred Reno, editors, *French and West Indian: Martinique, Guadeloupe, and French Guiana Today*

A. James Arnold, editor, *Monsters, Tricksters, and Sacred Cows: Animal Tales and American Identities*

J. Michael Dash, *The Other America: Caribbean Literature in a New World Context*

Isabel Alvarez Borland, *Cuban-American Literature of Exile: From Person to Persona*

Belinda J. Edmondson, editor, *Caribbean Romances: The Politics of Regional Representation*

Steven V. Hunsaker, *Autobiography and National Identity in the Americas*

Celia M. Britton, *Edouard Glissant and Postcolonial Theory: Strategies of Language and Resistance*

Mary Peabody Mann, *Juanita: A Romance of Real Life in Cuba Fifty Years Ago*, Edited and with an introduction by Patricia M. Ard

George B. Handley, *Postslavery Literatures in the Americas: Family Portraits in Black and White*

Faith Smith, *Creole Recitations: John Jacob Thomas and Colonial Formation in the Late Nineteenth-Century Caribbean*

Ian Gregory Strachan, *Paradise and Plantation: Tourism and Culture in the Anglophone Caribbean*

Nick Nesbitt, *Voicing Memory: History and Subjectivity in French Caribbean Literature*

Charles W. Pollard, *New World Modernisms: T. S. Eliot, Derek Walcott, and Kamau Brathwaite*

Carine M. Mardorossian, *Reclaiming Difference: Caribbean Women Rewrite Postcolonialism*

Luís Madureira, *Cannibal Modernities: Postcoloniality and the Avant-garde in Caribbean and Brazilian Literature*

Elizabeth M. DeLoughrey, Renée K. Gosson, and George B. Handley, editors, *Caribbean Literature and the Environment: Between Nature and Culture*

Flora González Mandri, *Guarding Cultural Memory: Afro-Cuban Women in Literature and the Arts*